ANIMATION

BEHIND
THE SILVER
SCREEN

BEHIND THE SILVER SCREEN

When we take a larger view of a film's "life" from development through exhibition, we find a variety of artists, technicians, and craftspeople in front of and behind the camera. Writers write. Actors, who are costumed and made-up, speak the words and perform the actions described in the script. Art directors and set designers develop the look of the film. The cinematographer decides upon a lighting scheme. Dialogue, sound effects, and music are recorded, mixed, and edited by sound engineers. The images, final sound mix, and special visual effects are assembled by editors to form a final cut. Moviemaking is the product of the efforts of these men and women, yet few film histories focus much on their labor.

Behind the Silver Screen calls attention to the work of filmmaking. When complete, the series will comprise ten volumes, one each on ten significant tasks in front of or behind the camera, on the set or in the postproduction studio. The goal is to examine closely the various collaborative aspects of film production, one at a time and one per volume, and then to offer a chronology that allows the editors and contributors to explore the changes in each of these endeavors during six eras in film history: the silent screen (1895–1927), classical Hollywood (1928–1946), postwar Hollywood (1947–1967), the Auteur Renaissance (1968–1980), the New Hollywood (1981–1999), and the Modern Entertainment Marketplace

(2000–present). *Behind the Silver Screen* promises a look at who does what in the making of a movie; it promises a history of filmmaking, not just a history of films.

Jon Lewis, Series Editor

$1000 [to each] of... for the later... commission approve... is to down when it th...
real... more to... bottom... Displaying outline... the type class

1. SCREEN...
2. DIRECTION... [in] screen
3. AND DIRECTION AND... DIRECTION DIR...
4. CINEMATOGRAPHY...
5. COSTUME, MAKEUP, AND HAIR LAYO...
6. DIRECTING...
7. EDITING AND... VISUAL EFFECTS...
8. PRODUCING...
9. SCRIPT/WRITING...
10. SOUND, DIALOGUE, MUSIC, AND EFFECTS...

ANIMATION

Edited by Scott Curtis

RUTGERS
UNIVERSITY PRESS

New Brunswick, Camden, and Newark, New Jersey, and London

For Ava; Gabby, Declan and Alex; Maggie, Annika, Bridget, and
Dominique; Julian; Nina and Flora; and Zachary and Trevor

Library of Congress Cataloging-in-Publication Data
Names: Curtis, Scott, editor.
Title: Animation / Scott Curtis, ed.
Description: New Brunswick, New Jersey : Rutgers University Press, [2019] | Series:
Behind the silver screen ; 2 | Includes bibliographical references and index.
Identifiers: LCCN 2018008988 | ISBN 9780813570266 (cloth) | ISBN 9780813570259 (pbk.)
Subjects: LCSH: Animation (Cinematography)—United States—History—20th century. |
Animation (Cinematography)—United States—History—21st century. |
Animation (Cinematography)
Classification: LCC TR897.5 .A55 2019 | DDC 776/.6—dc23
LC record available at https://lccn.loc.gov/2018008988

A British Cataloging-in-Publication record for this book is available
from the British Library.

♾ The paper used in this publication meets the requirements of the American National
Standard for Information Sciences—Permanence of Paper for Printed Library Materials,
ANSI Z39.48-1992.
www.rutgersuniversitypress.org
Manufactured in the United States of America

CONTENTS

ACKNOWLEDGMENTS

The editor would like to thank Dan Bashara for research assistance and help with the glossary and Academy Awards list; Don Crafton for his help with photograph selection and permissions; Maureen Furniss for being a part of the project all too briefly; Jocelyn Sage Mitchell for her keen editorial eye; Kirsten Pike for her constant encouragement; Dean Everette Dennis for resources that allowed the authors to meet for an initial planning session; Jon Lewis and Leslie Mitchner for their finite patience; and all the authors for their excellent work and perseverance.

ANIMATION

INTRODUCTION   Scott Curtis

However we might perceive American animation—as a magic act, an industrial process, an artistic endeavor, a scientific experiment, or a mass entertainment—we have always been fascinated with how it is made. Even more insistently than **live-action** fiction cinema, animation has consistently depicted and discussed its **mode of production**.[1] Its films and the literature around them often represent and describe how animation works; in the 1910s and 1920s, for example, barely an article about animation made it to press without some description of the process by which animated cartoons are constructed. Cartoons themselves, especially in the studio era from the 1920s to the 1950s, obliquely depicted the often-tedious process of making one image after another by making assembly lines a favorite topic or trope. The process itself is not difficult to grasp immediately: drawings or objects are exposed **frame** by frame, with subtle changes made to the drawing or object between exposures so that, when projected, those changes appear as fluid movement or transformation. But the results—drawings or objects that seem to move of their own accord—are so surprising that they pique curiosity and demand constant explanation. This collection of essays examines the history of American commercial and independent animation through the lens of its modes of production: its tools, its techniques, the organization of its labor, the relationship between them, and how they have changed over the decades.

Animation is a labor-intensive process: there are 24 frames per second, 1,440 per minute, over 10,000 frames in a seven-minute film at standard projection speed. Creating a film frame by frame requires an incredible amount of work for even a short production. So the organization of labor on any given project is central to understanding how it is made, and how it is made affects what we see on screen. The organization of labor is the first piece of the puzzle for understanding its mode of production. From the early twentieth century to today, animation has seen three major modes of production: **artisanal**, **collaborative**, and **industrial**. These three modes differ in two fundamental ways: hierarchy and scale.

The artisanal mode relies primarily on an individual, crafts-centered approach to the product; one person, usually, makes the entire film from beginning to end. To do this, this individual must master all aspects of the production, including the tools and techniques for achieving various effects. This is different from the other modes, which divide the labor. The artisan might have assistants helping with various tasks, but the organization of labor is hierarchical—the assistants do what they are assigned and have no creative input.

When the organization of labor is not hierarchical but more democratic, with two or more individuals sharing labor, technical knowledge, and creative vision more or less equally, this is the collaborative mode. Here, the salient feature is that the labor is not strictly defined; each member of the team can do any job required, so the work can be (but is often not) divided into specialties.

A hierarchical division of labor into strictly defined specialties characterizes the industrial mode. Here, one person, often the director, oversees many workers, each doing only the job he or she is assigned. The difference between this and the artisanal mode is scale, of course: the industrial mode implies many, many workers turning out products at a relatively rapid pace.

In the history of American animation, the studio era (chapters 2 and 3) exemplifies the industrial mode, while the early years of the silent era (chapter 1) and the independent animators of the postwar years and beyond (chapter 4) exemplify the artisanal mode. Independent animators might also collaborate on projects, while the early years of **computer-generated imagery (CGI)** (chapter 5) were often collaborative almost by definition, given the need for disciplinary skill in both computer programming and filmmaking. Today, with the renaissance of studio animation (industrial) alongside the renewed popularity of **stop-motion animation** (often collaborative) or homemade **machinima** on YouTube (artisanal), all three modes are in plain view, as we will see in chapter 6.

Mapping the history of animation in terms of its modes of production therefore produces overlapping time lines, as it would for live-action film history as well. Any given mode obtains at any given moment in animation or film history. But for Hollywood or independent live-action films made for the mainstream marketplace—consistently recognized by the Academy of Motion Picture Arts and Sciences, for example—the division of labor (industrial, in this case) has not changed significantly over the decades. Of course, live-action film has other modes, but home movies have yet to win Oscars. That is not the case for animation. The complete list of Academy Award–winning animated films (see the appendix) reflects the different modes of production and animation's changing trends over the twentieth century, from Disney's dominance during the studio era to the rise of UPA (United Productions of America) and other representatives of **limited animation** in the 1950s, to the recognition of artisanal and collaborative ventures in the 1960s and especially the 1970s, to the 1980s when the emergence of digital technologies corresponded with the renaissance of studio animation. Yet even in the twenty-first century, artisanal creations like *Harvie Krumpet* (2003) or collaborative projects like *Ryan* (2004) sit alongside industrial blockbusters like *Finding Nemo* (2003) or *The Incredibles* (2004). In other words, the mainstream marketplace for animation has always included films in a variety of modes. To catch the canonical films, any history of American animation must look beyond the studio.

This collection, then, weaves between these overlapping time lines to provide a history of American animation and its modes of production; the historiographical difference between live-action film and animation also explains why the table of contents for this volume diverges from those in other volumes in the series. A thumbnail sketch of this history could, for example, trace its trends by following the careers of certain key representatives of the different modes, such as Walt Disney (industrial), Mary Ellen Bute or Oskar Fischinger (artisanal), or John and Faith Hubley (collaborative). Let's begin, however, before Disney.

In the early period, "animated cartoons" were not known as such; as occasional examples of frame-by-frame animation, they were recognized as types of **trick film** and were not a regular feature of the theatrical program. The great examples from that era, such as Emile Cohl's *Fantasmagorie* (1908) or Winsor McCay's *Gertie* (1914), were made in the artisanal mode, necessarily, as these pioneers worked out solutions to the mysteries of animation on their own, and their films made their way into the theaters only now and again. McCay, for example, used his films as part of his vaudeville act, and the *Gertie* we know today was made only after he stopped using it in his stage appearances. Other aspiring cartoonists/animators took notice of these early examples, and soon, by the mid-1910s, animated films appeared more regularly on American movie screens, especially as distributors gave these animators contracts that called for cartoons to be delivered for inclusion in the theatrical program. These deadlines meant that the artisanal approach was no longer viable. John Randolph Bray, especially, helped to develop new technologies (such as **cels**) and new divisions of labor that allowed cartoons to be made on an industrial scale. By the late 1910s, a number of small studios had emerged to take advantage of this market with this new mode of production, and "animated cartoons" entered the popular lexicon.

Almost all of these small studios in the 1920s were located in New York City. With only eight, twelve, or maybe sixteen animators and staff employed at any given studio, it was a small community, and as they circulated among the companies, leaving one job for another, being poached and moving on, tricks of the trade disseminated throughout the fledgling industry. Bray Studios, the Fleischer brothers' Out of the Inkwell studio, Pat Sullivan's studio, Paul Terry's Terrytoons studio, and Disney's small atelier comprised the best-known group of animation companies during this period. Together they created some of the most memorable cartoon characters of the silent period: Bobby Bumps (Bray), Koko the Clown (Fleischer), Felix the Cat (Sullivan), Farmer Al Falfa (Terry), Alice in Cartoonland, and Oswald the Lucky Rabbit (both Disney). Felix the Cat, for example, was a hit in theaters, as well as toy stores, as Sullivan learned that merchandising could be even more lucrative than the box office, a lesson that Disney took to heart. These cartoons borrowed **gags** and sensibility from comic strips and vaudeville, but as the decade progressed, animators, especially Disney, adapted not just gags but editing and narrative techniques from live-action cinema. Disney and others created more immersive, appealing cartoons through the effective use of editing and by simulating live-action cinematographic techniques. But they also capitalized on the difference between live-action film and animation: 1920s animation conventions such as the **rubber-hose** style—a drawing style in which character extremities look and move like rubber hoses—kept silent-era animation firmly in the realm of fantasy, despite the adaptation of live-action editing and cinematography.

Disney left an even more obvious mark on the industry with *Steamboat Willie* (1928), the first cartoon with synchronized sound and dialogue and the world's introduction to Mickey Mouse. New technologies had always been tools of product differentiation in Hollywood, and in their adoption and successful implementation, Disney was unrivaled in the animation industry.[2] The studio's Silly Symphony series was an explicit testing ground for new ideas and technologies, including **three-strip Technicolor** (*The Flowers and the Trees*, 1932) and the **multiplane camera** (*The Old Mill*, 1937). At the same time, Disney pioneered new approaches to drawing and character by conducting art-instruction classes at the studio and insisting on the relationship between lifelike movement and personality. Disney's dual emphasis on technological and representational innovation culminated in the studio's first feature film, *Snow White and the Seven Dwarfs* (1937), which used the multiplane camera and Technicolor but also combined these new animation principles with older approaches to figure movement, such as the **rotoscope**, which was used to animate Snow White herself.

Disney's lead animator in the 1920s, Ub Iwerks, was a master of rubber-hose animation. This style offered a fantastical, elastic vision of how animated characters move, but because the style tended to isolate the movements of extremities (only one part of the body moving at any given time, such as an arm stretching to

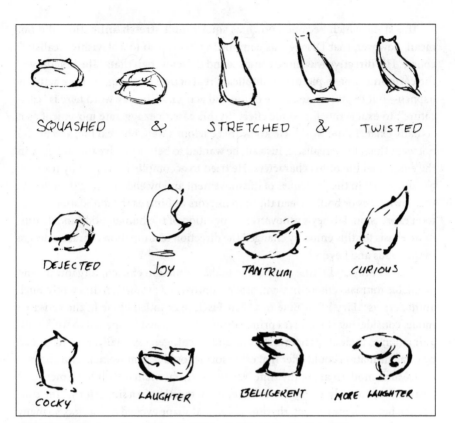

SQUASHED & STRETCHED & TWISTED

DEJECTED   JOY   TANTRUM   CURIOUS

COCKY   LAUGHTER   BELLIGERENT   MORE LAUGHTER

FIGURE I.1: The famous flour sack exercise, from Frank Thomas and Ollie Johnston, *The Illusion of Life: Disney Animation* (1981).

grab something), the effect was lashed to the comic, and the range of emotions the characters expressed tended to be limited. Disney realized that our ability to identify with characters stems from our shared understanding of how we physically express emotion. The "flour sack" exercise in animation illustrates this principle (fig. I.1), which teaches us that emotion can be expressed through the *whole* body; indeed, if the object expressing the emotion happens to be a flour sack (or some other typical cartoon character or object), animators need to use the shape in its entirety to convey the emotion. In the 1930s, Disney moved away from the rubber-hose style toward a style that emphasized the importance of the interrelatedness of different parts of the body to express personality. The studio insisted that animation should be based on principles of lifelike movement and physics—that the body is fluid, that it can change shape but not volume (another lesson of the flour sack). These principles formed the basis of cartoon characters who were still elastic—they stretched and squashed—but within these parameters of shape and volume.

This style, which became known as **squash-and-stretch animation**, did not mean, however, that Disney was committing his studio to a slavishly "realistic" course. His directive was more complex and difficult than that: "The first duty of the cartoon is not to picture or duplicate real action or things as they actually happen—but to give a caricature of life and action."[3] The key word here is "caricature": to exaggerate for comic effect, in this case to exaggerate movement as it actually exists in the world. He knew that cartoons were not real life, and he did not want them to be realistic; instead, he wanted to better involve the audience in the emotional life of his characters. He tried to accomplish this goal by training his animators in the principles of life movement and by encouraging them to use their own faces or bodies (seen through mirrors or film) as the foundation of cartoon expression. Disney's innovative recognition of the human body and its limits as a basis for this empathy changed the direction of animation character design in the 1930s and beyond.

Even as Bray and Disney worked to make animation efficient, organized, and profitable for mass entertainment, others approached animation differently. Such animators as Mary Ellen Bute or Oskar Fischinger toiled alone in the artisanal mode, considering themselves primarily artists who just happened to work with animation as their chosen format. Bute and Fischinger, especially, were intrigued by what animation could offer that other forms could not: movement and abstraction. Much modern art of the time was similarly fascinated with movement and abstraction, but only animation brought them together in a single form. The connection between movement, rhythm, color, and shape evoked music, too, so many artist-animators of the day experimented with the relationship between the visual expression of rhythm and its musical counterpart. Indeed, the idea of **visual music** caught the imagination of Bute, Fischinger, and others who worked from the 1920s onward. Bute, one of very few female animators at the time, was also one of the few artists in the United States working on this aesthetic issue; her eleven abstract films from 1934 to 1959 all concern the problem of visual music and how it can be expressed through movement, light, color, and sound. *Tarantella* (1940), for example, combines a piano score with matching, rhythmic images of basic forms, such as rectangles, polygons, circles, spirals, and squiggly lines (in collaboration with famed animator Norman McLaren). McLaren animated an earlier Bute film, *Spook Sport* (1939), with the same goals—"Color, music and movement combine," the opening credits read, "to present a new type of Film-Ballet"—but its lines and shapes are much more anthropomorphized than in the later film. Set to a well-known classical piece, Camille Saint-Saëns's *Danse Macabre, Spook Sport* anticipates Disney's famous entry in visual music, *Fantasia* (1940), which was a feature-length exploration of visual music by way of a series of pieces set to classical music. Fascinated by abstract animation since the mid-1930s, Disney hired Fischinger for *Fantasia* after Fischinger's escape from Nazi Germany, but the collaboration between the two did not succeed, given Fischinger's solitary approach and Disney's keen sense for mass tastes. Still, *Fantasia* contains moments indebted to the artisanal, abstract animation of the prewar period.

Parallel to its functions as art or entertainment, animation also functioned as a pedagogical or propagandistic tool. World War I had already proven animation's worth as a training tool; the U.S. government hired Bray Studios to animate training films during the conflict—or, more precisely, drafted Bray's animators—and Bray himself eventually turned his attention in the 1920s from entertainment to education. But World War II offered even more opportunities for animation to prove its mettle. Most of the output of the various studio animation units during the war consisted not of cartoons for the domestic audience but war-related training for the armed forces or propaganda films for foreign audiences. Disney Studio is a good case study here, too, having produced such films as *Saludos Amigos* (1942), aimed at cultivating the hearts and minds of Latin American audiences; educational films for the same audience in its Health for the Americas series; and armed forces training films, from *Four Methods of Flush Riveting* (1942) to *Know Your Enemy: Japan* (1945). The boost provided by the U.S. government during the war propelled the use of animation for educational purposes in the decades after, especially as Sputnik and the Cold War prompted government and institutions to funnel more funds into classroom education.

This new educational-film market opened at a fortuitous time for many animators who began to lose work as the studio animation units shut down. The immediate postwar period saw record box office receipts, but this boom turned into a bust by the end of the 1940s. Along with the **Paramount Decision of 1948**, which forced **vertically integrated** motion-picture studios to divest themselves of their theaters, the economic crunch was too much for the theatrical cartoon, the cost of which had already exceeded its receipts by many times. Once-strong studio animation units at Warner Bros. and MGM shuttered, and Disney cut back on its **theatrical shorts** program as well, focusing on features and cheaper live-action offerings. The theatrical market had collapsed, but new markets opened up, including television, advertising, and educational-film production houses, drawing newly unemployed studio animators to them. But these new venues did not have the resources of fully vested Hollywood studios, so they modified the industrial mode of production to make animated films more cheaply: they did not make as many drawings, so movement was less smooth and continuous than before; they often outsourced some of their labor to foreign houses in Mexico or South Korea, for example; and they found ways to cut back on visuals by emphasizing dialogue, especially in television animation. All these modifications and more came to be known as "limited animation," which had both economic and aesthetic or political motivations as some studios, such as UPA, adopted a more limited style as a way of distinguishing their work from the model exemplified by Disney and the other major studios. Limited animation had perhaps an even broader impact on animation than Disney, given that we can see its mark in television programming from *The Flintstones* to *The Simpsons*, in Japanese **anime**, in animated advertising, and even Adobe Flash animation on the web.

John Hubley is a good representative of the new approach to animation after the war. A former Disney animator who left the studio after the strike of 1941, Hubley joined UPA and had great success there; he was one of its founding creative directors, guiding its vision with such box office winners as the Mr. Magoo character, such Oscar winners as *Gerald McBoing Boing* (1950), and such critical favorites as *Rooty Toot Toot* (1951). Hubley and UPA were enormously influential in their expression of the country's changing design sensibility at mid-century: moving away from "pigs and bunnies" in animation, they articulated a more adult approach to animation that was not just thematic but also visual in their adoption of modernist design principles and goals.[4] But after running into trouble during the McCarthy era, he and his wife and artistic partner, Faith Hubley, established their own studio, Storyboard Studios. Initially the company focused on producing commercials, such as the famous "I Want My Maypo" (1956) campaign for Maypo cereal. These animated advertisements used an innovative approach, recording unrehearsed actors, such as Hubley's own four-year-old son, and basing the animation on their conversation. The ad was wildly successful, but the Hubleys capitalized on their interesting approach to sound and image with a series of independent films, such as the Oscar winners *Moonbird* (1959) and *The Hole* (1962). The mode of production at Storyboard Studios was a combination of collaborative and industrial: collaboration between John and Faith and between them and their head animators, but they also hired an animation staff to help to execute their vision. Fusing an inventive approach to the soundtrack, a modern-art-inspired visual design, and an emphasis on intimacy and empathy over action and comedy, the Hubleys received six Academy Award nominations and three Oscars from the 1950s through the 1970s. The socially conscious messages of such films as *The Hole* (1962) and *The Hat* (1963) made them especially popular in the classroom, where the Hubleys found a welcome market.

Disney continued to make features, and educational companies continued to make instructional animations, but artisanal or collaborative short animations seemed to best express the mood of the 1960s and 1970s. The classroom was not the only venue for these films; animators found audiences through newly founded film festivals and exhibition programs as well. Some festivals, such as the Festival International du Film Expérimental and Poétique, established in 1949 in Brussels, focused on animation and experimental films, while other festivals, such as the International Film Festival Rotterdam, founded in 1972, included animation in its programming. Associations dedicated to promoting animation included the International Animated Film Association (Association International du Film D'Animation, or **ASIFA**), founded in 1960, which now has thirty chapters all over the world and was instrumental in establishing or sponsoring the four largest ongoing international festivals of animation: the Annecy International Animated Film Festival (roughly coinciding with the emergence of ASIFA in 1960), the World Festival of Animated Film in Zagreb (established by ASIFA in 1972), the Ottawa International Animation Festival (established by the Canadian Film Institute in 1976 and sponsored by ASIFA), and the Hiroshima International Animation Festival (founded by ASIFA in 1985). In addition to these new audiences abroad, American independent animators found growing interest in their work on college campuses and through community-run film associations; new distributors specializing in independent film supplied these exhibition venues, which proliferated in the postwar era, with discoveries from festivals. Art institutions, such as the Museum of Modern Art and the Guggenheim Foundation, took interest in animation's new links to modern painting. Experimental film exhibitions in New York and elsewhere helped place independent and experimental animation in rental catalogs and then in film society screenings in communities across the United States. In the 1970s, the Oscar wins of such films as *Frank Film* (1973) and *The Sand Castle* (1977) seemed to express the current taste for artisanal or collaborative projects.

Meanwhile, another type of collaboration was taking place between artists and computer engineers and programmers as such corporations as IBM encouraged experimentation by giving these teams time on their huge **mainframe computers**. In the 1960s and 1970s, experiments resulted in abstract animations similar in goal to the visual music of the 1920s and beyond. By the late 1970s, however, experiments with digital animation turned toward solving problems in realistic representation, especially as they applied to special effects in Hollywood feature films, such as *Star Wars* (1977) and *Star Trek II: The Wrath of Khan* (1982). Soon the line between animation and special effects became blurry as computer-generated imagery (CGI) became incorporated into Hollywood spectacles and workflows. The Academy Award for Pixar's *Tin Toy* in 1988 and the huge success of *Toy Story* (1995) signaled the renaissance of studio-based industrial animation, accelerated not only by ever faster microprocessors over the next twenty years but also by the availability of formerly proprietary software, such as RenderMan and Maya, which standardized the production workflow and allowed labor specialization in the same way that cel technology had done in the 1910s. Digital animation transformed from a collaborative mode to an industrial mode as soon as the technologies could be disseminated, standardized, taught, and the labor divided.

But even as all-digital studio blockbusters seemed to dominate the animation market and imagination, other approaches competed well. Stop-motion animation, as in Nick Park's plasticine *The Wrong Trousers* (1993) or Laika Entertainment's puppet film *Coraline* (2009), stubbornly resists industrialization. It is almost impossible to create stop-motion films on an assembly line, so they retain an artisanal, crafts-oriented ethic in this era of slick digital studio product. Indeed, such Oscar winners as *Peter and the Wolf* (2007) and *Wallace & Gromit: The Curse of the Were-Rabbit* (2009) and such nominees as *Madame Tutli-Putli* (2007), *Fantastic Mr. Fox* (2009), and *Anomalisa* (2015) have kept the artisanal mode in our view.

We could imagine the history of modes of production in American animation as a set of overlapping layers cycling forward and back in our attention, all visible in the picture simultaneously if we look closely, but at different points in time, one layer captures our imagination or matches our tastes better than another. There is another related but slightly different historiographical approach to American animation production: animation history as a series of problems and solutions. In this approach, any given organization of labor emerges as a response to particular problems or historical circumstances. Artisanal production arises as a trade begins, while collaborative production proceeds as more craftspeople gain skill, and industrial organization, in turn, as economies of scale demand more and more labor. Commercial animation has had a recurring and central problem that has demanded an industrial organization if the product were to be mass produced: how to generate that many images in a limited amount of time? The choices of tools, techniques, and division of labor have always responded to specific problems; animators have found different solutions for these problems over time as historical circumstances changed. The specific problems have changed with time, too, but an aerial view of the history of **drawn animation** reveals at least three persistent problems that have prompted a variety of solutions over time:

1. Image generation: how to create so many images in a timely and efficient manner?

2. Image stabilization: how to ensure that the images are consistent from frame to frame, thereby creating fluid and continuous movement?

3. Image storage: how to create a library of images, thereby reducing labor and ensuring consistency from film to film?

Each of these problems is related to the other, in that many techniques address more than one problem at a time. But each also applies to separate but related phases of production: drawing the images and photographing the images. For example, animators learned quickly that when depicting a rhythmic movement, such as walking, they did not need to redraw every part of the cycle each time; rather, they could rephotograph the complete cycle so that, when projected, the movement appears rhythmic. **Cycling**, as this technique is known, took advantage of the photographic process to reduce the number of drawings required by creating a mini library of images that could be reused.

Some solutions even reappear in different forms over the course of animation history. For example, in the 1910s, Bray came upon the idea of printing the cartoon's background on paper, allowing him to reduce the number of lines drawn and keep the background stable as he drew foreground images. This technique soon faded as cel technology gained prominence, but mechanically reproducing some part of the image came back in style in the 1950s and 1960s with **xerography**, which Disney used to print and reproduce images on celluloid for *101 Dalmatians* (1961). Similarly, Bray and other animators of the time would often reduce their workload by animating only the part of a character that moved, keeping the rest of the body frozen. This gave animation a stiffness that eventually fell out of fashion at the height of the studio era, especially at Disney, which prized plausible character movement. But after the studio era, as animators were forced to work very cheaply, they adopted this solution again, which characterized the limited animation of the postwar era.

Likewise, keeping the image stable frame to frame required a **registration** technique, such as marks precisely measured on the paper or, more commonly, punching holes in the paper and threading it through pegs in the **animation table** or desk. This technique kept the image stable and the movement fluid as long as the animator could see the previous image, which was often accomplished through translucent paper or transparent celluloid. So both a registration technique and a special tool (paper or celluloid) were required to solve this particular problem, but as animators came upon new tools and techniques, such as computers, they had to solve this issue in other ways. In another example, animation studios used **model sheets** to train their staff to draw a particular character. These sheets usually depicted a series of poses with specific directions about gesture, wardrobe, or body details. In the early days, assistant animators would trace the characters from these model sheets, but when that became too restrictive, they learned how to draw in the style that the model sheet depicted. Model sheets were therefore a form of image storage; they were used to convey institutional or managerial memory about a character that reduced the need to redesign or reimagine it. In the digital age, such storage often takes the form of an object library, as in the Autodesk Maya software, where animators can keep computer-generated items, such as furniture or character shapes, on file for reuse.

This collection will focus on these problems and solutions as it outlines this history, but it will also describe how these choices and history affect what we see on the screen. Other themes emerge as well, especially regarding the complex and varied relationship between animation and live-action cinema. This relationship has always been both complementary and oppositional. On one hand, animation has always been complementary to live-action film. Animation appeared in the United States at a moment when the novelty of early cinema had grown stale, gradually being replaced by the narrative immersion afforded by feature films. Animation and the intense interest in its process served the industry's need for "perpetual novelty," as Kristin Thompson argues.[5] That is, as movement for movement's sake lost its appeal, animation promised to restore some of that faded magic; animation provided what the industry needed. Hybrid films, which combine live-action and animation, are another complementary aspect of this relationship. In the 1920s, combining animation and live-action was especially popular. Cartoon characters, such as the Fleischers' Koko the Clown, moved easily between animated and live-action environments—a trope explored continuously since then, from *Anchors Aweigh* (1945) to *Who Framed Roger Rabbit* (1988) to *Alvin and the Chipmunks* (2007). Even instructional films often combine live-action and animated sequences, each helping to frame the information in its particular way. At a less obvious level, American commercial cartoons often adopted live-action conventions in terms of narratives, characters, and even editing or cinematography. As we have seen, Disney and others used **crosscutting**, **analytical editing**, and simulated **pans** and **tilts** to make their cartoons more appealing and involving. And perhaps it goes without saying that the emphasis on short, complete narratives with recurring characters in American commercial animation since the 1920s borrows from classical Hollywood narrative conventions.

On the other hand, animation has always also been somewhat oppositional to live-action cinema. In educational film, animation has often been charged with (even limited to) doing what live-action cannot, such as depicting that which is invisible or conceptual. Independent animators often worked against—or even ignored—live-action conventions and dominance in their creative and innovative productions. But commercial animation, too, follows its own rules in depicting a fantastic and elastic world of animal characters and cartoon physics. If Koko the Clown entered the live-action world, it was often to torment his creator or to escape similar torment, demonstrating a playful yet fraught relationship filled with resentment and one-upmanship. Koko was created using a rotoscope (described in detail in chapter 1), which projected live-action footage of a man in a clown suit onto an animation table; then, the live-action image was traced onto paper, and the drawn images, photographed and projected to give an eerily lifelike yet wholly animated depiction of movement. In some ways, this process is a metaphor for the relationship between animation and live-action: tracing functions as mimicry, as a means of hewing closely to live-action, but it also results in something that is emphatically not live-action, which comes alive to bedevil it, causing as much satirical damage as possible.

As a form, American commercial animation was often marginal to the live-action feature in terms of the evening program and also in terms of relative cultural and economic importance to the industry. Its association with fantasy, imagination, and comedy was always only a step away from an association with childhood, a step taken with Disney but firmly and forever solidified with the rise of Saturday-morning television animation.[6] Animation was for kids, not just in terms of audience but also in terms of industrial priority and scholarly attention. Today, the connotations may remain, but the marginality is gone, replaced by a cultural ubiquity and dominance that has been wholly surprising to anyone who considered animation merely kids' stuff. Animation may have adapted live-action conventions, but today live-action struggles to keep up with (and even co-opts) what animation can do. Animation is perhaps the model to which many live-action features today aspire.

The present collection traces this development over the course of the last hundred years or more. Each chapter can be read on its own, but the collection as a whole also aims to provide an introductory survey of the history of American animation.

Scott Curtis, in his chapter on the silent era, focuses on the various solutions that emerged during the transition from an artisanal to an industrial mode of production. He breaks the era into three periods. In the first period, from roughly 1908 to 1914, animation production was sporadic (or, at least, irregular), owing to the amount of labor required for the crafts-like approach taken up by only a few hearty souls, such as Cohl and McCay. In the second period, from 1914 to 1921, Bray and others developed technological innovations (such as celluloid transparencies) and managerial practices (such as a division of labor) that allowed animators to generate images more quickly and efficiently. This allowed them to produce films more regularly, meet distributor demand, and thereby put commercial animation on solid footing. World War I also established animation's use as a useful technology for instruction and training. In the third period, from 1921 to 1928, animation studios spread in New York and Hollywood to meet the growing demand and competition for cartoons. This was the era of recurring characters, such as Felix the Cat and Koko the Clown, that were to be the engine behind animation's lasting run in the American motion-picture industry. Each period also had a dominant trope or convention in the animations of the period: (1) the **"hand of the artist"** device that showed the animator drawing his (often impish) creation; (2) the animated diagram or technical drawing, which showed not only "how things work" but also how animation works; and (3) the "assembly-line" motif, representing not just the rage for efficiency and productivity in American capitalism of the day but also the sometimes tedious routine of image generation in the studio era. Along the way, Curtis introduces key technologies and techniques that eventually became standard in the American animation industry and beyond; he describes such techniques as "pose-to-pose animation," puts them in their historical context, and demonstrates, with examples from *Gertie* (McCay, 1914) to *Sky Scrappers* (Disney, 1928), how they influenced the way animation looked on-screen. He also discusses how knowledge of animation spread through the industry and public sphere via the circulation of people and texts, such as patents, trade journals, fan magazines, and manuals. Curtis argues that this discursive support for animation was just as important as technological innovations for the transition to an industrial mode.

Susan Ohmer's chapter places animation in the context of classical Hollywood after the coming of sound, focusing on the industrial, social, economic, and aesthetic factors that shaped this culture and animation's place within it. To produce cartoons for their theatrical programs after the coming of sound, major studios (such as Warner Bros. and MGM) created their own animation units or signed distribution deals with independent animation houses (as RKO did with Disney). Even before this boom in production, during the 1920s, cross-fertilization was common among animators at different studios as they circulated from job to job; Ohmer argues that this circulation was vital for stylistic and technological innovation in the industry. This chapter also describes in detail the methods studios used to create cartoons on an industrial scale, using Paul Terry's studio as an example of the typical yet varied solutions to common problems in animation production. In the 1930s and 1940s, the market was tight and profits even tighter; Ohmer argues for the importance of innovation as a means of product differentiation during the age of the double bill, when cartoons had a difficult time finding space on a program that included double features. World War II—just like World War I—had a definite impact on animation production and style, including innovations to speed up production and to reach out to foreign markets. But the goodwill animation earned during wartime did not secure it a place at the table after the war, when trust-busting decrees and a decline in attendance sent studios scrambling for revenue. Cartoons were definite loss leaders—their production costs going up but their rental prices remaining the same—so the writing was on the wall in the postwar era: cartoons would soon play a sharply diminished role in theatrical programming.

Kevin Sandler's chapter on limited animation tells the history of the animation studios after the studio era. The history of animation diverges from the history of live-action at this moment because commercial animation was forced to leave movie theaters and find a home on television screens. Due to the loss of markets in the theatrical sector, animators were pressed to find new solutions to common problems, specifically how to produce animation more cheaply and quickly for the emerging television market. **Full animation**, so called because it creates and exposes up to twenty-four drawings per second to depict movement as fully and fluidly as possible, gave way to limited animation, a set of strategies that reduced character movement drastically, often by reducing the number of sequential drawings and exposing any given drawing for four, six, or even eight frames at a time, unlike the one or two frames exposed at a time in full animation. These production strategies were usually economically motivated, but some studios, such as UPA, saw limited animation as an aesthetic and even political strategy that differentiated and distanced their cartoons, such as *Gerald McBoing Boing*

(1950), from Disney's aesthetic approach. Other production houses, such as Hanna-Barbera, had no such pretensions yet adapted especially well to new market realities and media; after winning Oscars for their fully animated *Tom and Jerry* series (1940–1958), they went on to break new ground in television with *The Flintstones* (1960–1966) and other series that relied more on dialogue and sound effects than character movement to tell stories. This chapter describes the various production methods associated with limited animation, as well as the different aesthetic goals of UPA, Hanna-Barbera, Filmation, and Jay Ward (*Rocky and Bullwinkle*, 1959–1964). As animation virtually disappeared from movie theater screens from the 1960s to the 1980s, studios such as these kept the craft of commercial animation alive, albeit in a much different form than was practiced in the heyday of Hollywood. Saturday-morning television became the garden—some would say the graveyard—where American commercial animation changed and developed into the dialogue-driven success stories of *The Simpsons* (1989–present) and *South Park* (1997–present).

Full and limited animation were different approaches to the industrial mode of production. But it would be a mistake to assume that American animation left the artisanal mode behind after the early period. If limited animation became the industrial style of commercial animation after the studio heyday, then the artisanal approach of independent animators produced some of the most innovative work in animation of the postwar era. In her chapter, Alla Gadassik describes why the artisanal mode flourished during this period and how it shaped the visual techniques and tropes of the films. She divides the field into three broad areas: (1) filmmakers who saw themselves as fine artists rather than cartoonists; (2) studio animators who left to pursue independent animation; and (3) a younger generation of animators, coming of age in the 1960s and 1970s, who drew inspiration from both of these groups and took advantage of new distribution outlets of that period. But the challenges of the artisanal mode had not changed since the silent era; animation still required an inordinate amount of labor. Gadassik argues that independent animators adopted two strategies to cope with the demands of artisanal animation: they embraced the visible roughness of fast-paced work, incorporating it into their style, and they found new techniques and tools for generating large numbers of images. This chapter examines the philosophies, motivations, and strategies of artists who created animation on their own, including Oskar Fischinger, Len Lye, John and Faith Hubley, Robert Breer, Douglass Crockwell, and Caroline Leaf, while describing the variety of animation styles and objects beyond drawn animation. In many cases, the adoption of a technique (such as xerography) or animation material (such as **clay**) was not simply artistic exploration but also an attempt to negotiate the demands of animation while simultaneously resisting models that came before.

The development of information-processing machines in the 1960s and 1970s also promised a new strategy for generating animated images. What if a computer could do the work for you? This was an exciting prospect, but the excitement was immediately tempered—as always in the history of animation—by the limitations of the technology. But as Andrew Johnston argues in his chapter on the rise of computer-generated imagery, it was not just this potential that led researchers to CGI; the specific aesthetic features of these images also intrigued early experimenters. Filmmakers, artists, programmers, and engineers worked together in labs to test this new technology and to explore the aesthetic impact of computerized shapes in motion. Working collaboratively across disciplinary lines—often combining analog and digital technologies to accomplish their goals—experimenters created animations that held potential for both the avant-garde and commercial sectors. Some of the early work found its way into special-effects sequences of feature films; John Whitney's credit sequence of *Vertigo* (1958) or Douglas Trumbull's "Stargate" sequence of *2001: A Space Odyssey* (1968) are two well-known examples. Whitney and others struggled to find new solutions to old problems, such as how to generate the images consistently and how to store them for future manipulation and use. Johnston describes in detail the experiments, problems, and solutions that resulted in exceptional examples of the artistic avant-garde, such as Lillian Schwartz's *Olympiad* (1971) and Larry Cuba's *Arabesque* (1975). Hollywood took notice, and this work eventually led to the dominance of CGI in the commercial film industry, starting with *Star Wars* (1977), *Tron* (1982), and *Star Trek II: The Wrath of Khan* (1982). The material and historiographical difficulty of this work is that it consists of a series of discrete experiments on platforms and in languages or algorithms that do not necessarily relate to each other; a wire-framing program may have nothing in common with a coloring program, so they cannot speak to each other. Pixar's RenderMan interface solved this problem and allowed the digital animation workflow to be efficient and commercialized, which laid the foundation for animation to once again be an important part of the motion-picture industry.

As microprocessors became faster and memory storage greater, and as software became widely available, the tools of American commercial animation changed from ink, paint, and cels to mouse, keyboard, and monitor. Indeed, the development of digital hardware, the standardization of and access to formerly proprietary software, and the accommodation of these tools to an industrial mode of production allowed animation to flourish in feature filmmaking. Bob Rehak's chapter describes how animation became ubiquitous in the industry and in our daily lives. Covering the years from around 1990 to the present, this chapter explores the push and pull of analog and digital technologies during the transitional years, when Disney's **ink-and-paint** approach adopted new workflow technologies, such as the **animation photo transfer (APT)** process and the **Computer Animation Production System (CAPS)**, which incorporated both analog and digital elements, while Pixar rendered all of their images fully digitally. As we now know, Pixar eventually led the way as Disney closed its traditional animation units.

New software options, such as Autodesk Maya, replaced some of the older solutions to common animation problems; the emergence of these new solutions coincided with the rise of new studios to capitalize on them, such as DreamWorks and Nickelodeon. Conversely, as the digital aesthetic became omnipresent, filmmakers at the turn of the twenty-first century turned to **object animation** and streamlined an artisanal approach to give their films a handcrafted feel. These films, such as *Coraline* (2009), nevertheless incorporated both analog and digital techniques to achieve this aesthetic. Given that a hybrid approach is vital for films that combine **motion capture** and digital animation, such as *The Polar Express* (2004) or *Avatar* (2009), this chapter shows that, despite the popularity of Pixar's all-digital approach, the line between analog and digital has never been stark, even as animation blurs with cinematic special effects and spreads across media platforms, from YouTube to video games to smartphones.

In sum, this collection of essays flips us through the historical movement of staff and styles in American animation, while also keeping us focused on the labor and techniques used to keep that history moving. Animation does not move on its own. This volume insists that we need to look behind the screen to explain what we see on the screen.

1

THE SILENT SCREEN, 1895-1928 Scott Curtis

Within twenty years, from around 1908 to 1928, American animation grew from an intermittent series of experiments and curiosities to a full-fledged arm of the motion-picture industry. As countless articles and interviews proclaimed, animation involved a lot of work; it was precisely this hard labor that shaped the raw idea of animation into a viable commercial product. Key to this transformation was a shift in animation's mode of production. Animators, such as Winsor McCay and Emile Cohl, were prodigious draftsmen, capable of creating an animated film almost entirely on their own, sometimes within weeks. They worked essentially as individual craftsmen in an artisanal mode of production: they produced animations on their own, mastering themselves (or with minimal help) all the different tasks required. But during and after World War I, such animators as J. R. Bray adopted technological innovations (e.g., reusable celluloid sheets) and new managerial methods (e.g., a division of labor among many animators) to create an industrial mode of production: animation produced on an "assembly line" of sorts with discrete tasks divided among a team of specialists. This shift allowed animated films to be made in a timely way to meet distributors' quotas and to be shown in theaters on a regular basis; animation became a standardized and reliable commodity. It also changed the way animation looked; the graphic and cinematographic style of animation changed over the course of two decades and would continue to change. But the standard approaches to commercial animation—mostly drawn animation, as opposed to object or other sorts of animation—were established during this era. The solutions to the problems that animators faced in making films were set during this crucial period. This chapter will provide an overview of these problems and solutions and of the technological, managerial, and stylistic changes to American commercial animation before the coming of sound to the motion-picture industry.

American commercial animation in the silent era emerged from a variety of cultural practices, forms, and genres. Before the mid-1910s, animation as we know it was not a regular feature of the popular entertainment landscape. Indeed, what we understand to be an "animated cartoon" was not recognized as such by either the industry or its audiences at this time. This was due partially to the relative scarcity of such films before 1914. But it was also due to the prominence of another, related genre that audiences did recognize: the trick film. Trick films featured a surprising substitution through a cinematographic or editing sleight of hand: as the action before the camera played out, the actors and the camera could be stopped; a substitution (such as a female for a male) could be made, and the action and camera resumed; it would then appear on-screen as an instantaneous, even magical transformation. France's George Méliès was the acknowledged master of the trick film genre, also often known at the time as a "stop film," because the camera literally stopped before the substitution and resumed again. Animation is built on the principle of the stop film, except that it continues to stop in serial fashion, rather than for a single isolated substitution; that is, it stops and resumes frame by frame. So for pre-1914 producers and audiences, the few films that employed frame-by-frame animation were clearly "trick films."[1] The first films that contained true frame-by-frame animation featured a limited application of the stop-motion technique to make objects move on their own, as in such films as James Stuart Blackton's *The Haunted Hotel* (Vitagraph, 1907) or Edwin S. Porter's *The "Teddy" Bears* (Edison, 1907).[2] (Indeed, even today any animation that uses objects or puppets is known as "stop-motion" animation.) But as animated films became more elaborate, their extreme novelty and flamboyant technical expertise surpassing most trick films, and as they became more common, they became recognized as something else: "animated cartoons." We might even speculate that the preference for drawn animation over object animation in post-1914 animation also facilitated this new recognition; trick films before had been almost entirely associated with object movement and substitution, whereas drawn animation was clearly something different. This change in recognition accompanied a shift in the mode of production as well: by 1920, drawn animated cartoons were often made according to an industrial model, at a larger scale, so they occupied more and more of the theatrical program, meaning that they were produced, packaged, and sold as a category unto themselves. "Cartoons" became a genre of motion picture in the American industry.

"Cartoons" as a term brings up the thorny question of the exact relationship between animated films and drawn cartoons, the kind published in magazines and newspapers. This is not the place to rehash the debate, only to say that the relationship is not as straightforward as it might initially appear.[3] It is not entirely clear, for example, that the temporal sequence or relationship between panels that we find in drawn cartoons had a direct influence on the formation of editing conventions in animated cartoons. We can say with confidence, however, that early animation and live-action films in general owed quite a lot to the ready-made storehouse of gags, characters, and story material in cartoon strips of the day.[4] But there was not even an attempt to translate a cartoon strip into an animated film until Winsor McCay adapted his own strip *Little Nemo* for a one-reeler in 1911. It took another two years for an adaptation of a comic strip—George McManus's *The Newlyweds*, released by Éclair in March 1913—to appear in theaters. The success of *The Newlyweds* emboldened print cartoonists to lend their signatures to this new format, and comic strip–based series of animated cartoons were much more common. Again, this may have been due to the change in mode of production that allowed more efficient production of drawn animation. But it is also true that the pioneers of drawn animation—and hence, in many ways, the animation industry—virtually unanimously had experience in cartooning, editorial illustration, or other forms of graphic arts.[5] This meant that these draftsmen (and they were almost universally men) came from a tradition that not only provided handy fodder for gags and characters, which they could adapt for a new medium, but also trained them to draw quickly and efficiently, which would be absolutely vital to their success as they attempted to generate the thousands of images necessary for a single animated film.

However, in terms of the conventions or iconography of animation during its early period (1908–1913), the vaudeville **lightning sketch** is perhaps the most important influence. This popular act on the vaudeville stage featured a quick-draw artist who, with a few careful and choreographed strokes of his crayon on a white board, could effect the most startling and amusing transformations of objects and caricatures. A drawing might start out as a sunset, then become a house on a lake, and with a few extra quick strokes turn into a young boy on a bicycle (fig. 1.1). What would this stage act have in common with early animation? First, in a purely practical sense, the quick and sure drawing skills necessary for this act would translate well to the requirements for making an animated cartoon—and two of the most adept lightning sketchers, James Stuart Blackton and Winsor McCay, would become the pioneers of American animation. Second, the convention of instant transformation of objects into something else would become a standard convention in animation as well. **Metamorphosis** is perhaps

FIGURE 1.1: Edwin G. Lutz, *The Lightning Sketcher*, *Life* (April 15, 1897).

the single most important convention of drawn animation; it starts with this practice in lightning sketches. Third, the stage presence of the lightning sketcher
translated into early animation as the convention of **self-figuration**: over and over
again in animation, we find "the hand of the artist," as Donald Crafton calls this
familiar iconography.[6] That is, in early animation, it is common to see the animator begin to draw the figures before the figures come to life. The lightning sketch,
Crafton claims, was "the mechanism by which self-figuration first occurred."[7]
Fourth, early animators often adopted the conventions of the stage in other ways,

especially in choosing to present animation as an illusion or magic. Film could indeed bring objects and drawings to life, it seemed, and the urge to present oneself as a conjurer was irresistible. Animator as magician was one of the major tropes of the early period, at least partially owing to the stage practices of lightning sketchers.[8] A film such as Blackton's *Humorous Phases of Funny Faces* (1906) exemplifies these practices in the way it presents its animation as a stage illusion, its sudden transformation of the faces, and its presentation of the artist as the creative force behind this startling metamorphosis. So the conventions, iconography, and practices of trick films, comic strips, vaudeville, and lightning sketches all contributed to the shape of early animation, which we will explore further in the next section.

The Artisanal Mode, 1908–1914

If trick films, comic strips, vaudeville, and lightning sketches all shaped early animation, a good deal of our understanding of animation's integration of these forms comes from our acquaintance with Emile Cohl and Winsor McCay, two animators who perhaps best exemplified the merger of these various cultural practices. Cohl enjoyed fame as a caricaturist in France before he made *Fantasmagorie* (1908), which is arguably the first drawn animated film. After *Fantasmagorie*, Cohl worked for Gaumont in Paris for many years, producing many animated and trick films, before coming to the United States in 1912 to make an enormously influential animated series, *The Newlyweds* (1913–1914).[9] Indeed, Cohl's inventiveness and prodigious output makes him most responsible for transforming the early trick film into the animated art form we recognize today.[10] McCay, too, was one of the most famous cartoonists of his era; he worked as an editorial cartoonist for New York newspapers and also created several successful comic strips, including *Dream of the Rarebit Fiend* (1904–1911) and *Little Nemo in Slumberland* (1905–1911). In addition to drawing cartoons, he also appeared frequently on the vaudeville stage, first as a lightning sketcher around 1906 and then as a multimedia act combining his drawing and filmmaking talents. Cohl and McCay employed much different methods, but they also faced common problems as artisanal animators: how to generate images in a timely and efficient manner; how to ensure smooth continuity of movement from frame to frame as they drew; and how to ensure that the images remained stable from frame to frame without jumps or gaps as they photographed them. These problems were related to each other in the drawing and photographing processes, and they were not the only problems they faced, but the solutions they developed would be significant and useful for all animators for decades afterward. This section, then, will describe the artisanal approach to animation, the problems McCay and Cohl faced, the solutions they decided upon, and how these problems and solutions affected their animation style.

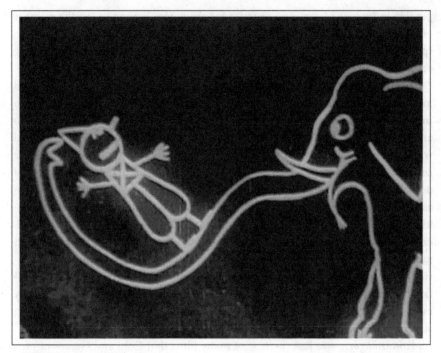

FIGURE 1.2: *Fantasmagorie* (1908).

Cohl made films in the artisanal mode throughout his career: between 1908 and 1921, Cohl animated more than 250 films, which he designed, animated, and photographed single-handedly.[11] *Fantasmagorie* was the first of these handcrafted gems. Its white lines on a black background—accomplished by drawing black lines on white paper, exposing the film, and then printing the film in negative—are perhaps an homage to Blackton's *Humorous Phases of Funny Faces*, which used a black chalkboard for its images (fig. 1.2). To extend this homage, *Fantasmagorie* begins with the image of the animator's hand drawing the protagonist; the hand of the artist leaves the frame, and the drawing comes to life. Blackton's lightning-sketch performance has now been figured into the film proper—a trope that would last for decades in one form or another; the "hand of the artist" trope is probably the most common convention of early animation. The film is just over a minute long—thirty-six meters in length—and Cohl claimed it required 1,872 drawings, which is the equivalent number of frames in thirty-six meters of film. But close analysis shows that it required only 700 separate drawings, which he traced and retraced on a **light box**.[12] The difference is in the number of frames he exposed per drawing. If he had exposed one image per frame, then he would have required that many separate drawings. But Cohl decided to expose two frames of film per image, thereby cutting his work in half.[13] This shortcut, now called **shooting on twos** (or "on threes" or "on fours," depending on how many frames are exposed per drawn image), is common practice for animators hoping to cut the number of images generated; rather than sixteen drawings per second (a common projection speed in the silent era), for example, Cohl needed only eight drawings if shooting on twos.

But the most striking feature of the film is its sense of spontaneous play and metamorphosis. The narrative, such that it is, changes as the figures transform into other figures or objects. This playfulness is a product of Cohl's approach to animation: rather than meticulously plan ahead each movement, Cohl started with his first image and simply continued to draw image after image until he reached the conclusion. All the changes and transformations were products of decisions made while in the process of drawing or animating. This is now known as **straight-ahead animation**: the animator starts with little more than an intuition of how he or she will get from one point to another in the animation—instead, one animates "straight ahead" until one reaches the end. This allows for much more spontaneity in the drawing and also encourages metamorphosis as a transitional device. So this early animation addressed the problem of image generation by shooting on twos, the problem of image stability and movement continuity by tracing, and quick delivery by simplifying the graphic style and animating straight ahead.

Fantasmagorie was just the first of many films that Cohl and Gaumont produced, which were also exported to the United States, where they perhaps inspired McCay to start his own animated film. *Little Nemo*, released in 1911, owes much to Cohl in its straight-ahead aesthetic but also to lightning-sketch conventions drawn from McCay's own experience on the stage and his friendship with his neighbor Blackton. McCay designed the film to be used in his vaudeville act, but the film that was released by Vitagraph in 1911 has a long live-action prologue that emphasizes the labor of making an animated film. The opening title touts, incorrectly of course, that McCay is "the first artist to attempt drawing pictures that will move," and there is a bit of hyperbole in the rest of the prologue as well. Vitagraph actors, such as John Bunny, gather with McCay to scoff at his idea that he can make drawings move. McCay goes to a sketch board where he starts to draw his famous characters (cut to an overhead **shot** of McCay's **pixilated** hand drawing the figures on a smaller sheet).[14] The apparent quickness and confidence with which McCay draws these figures was likely a source of wonder for audiences of the vaudeville act, which the film tries to replicate. After these displays of authenticity and mastery, a title card boldly and hyperbolically declares that McCay will make "four thousand pen drawings that will move, one month from date." Bales of paper and barrels of ink are comically rolled into his office.

But the next scenes bear a closer resemblance to reality: McCay sits with his pile of drawings, the continuity of which he checks in a **Mutoscope**-like device. McCay used this device for his films as a way to check that the movement was smooth across images. Furthermore, to use this device and the camera, as we shall

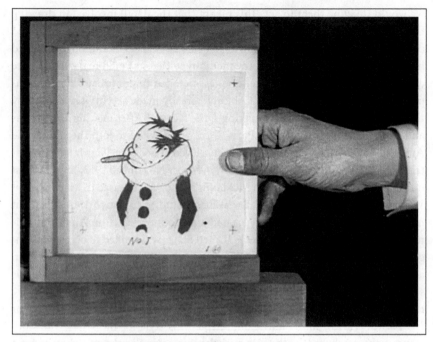

FIGURE 1.3: *Little Nemo* (McCay, 1911). McCay's hand starts the film and creates the drawing. Note the registration marks in the corners and the wooden apparatus to hold the image in place.

see, McCay had to take the extra step of mounting his drawings on stiff boards, a step that also required precise registration so that the image didn't "jump" around the screen. That is, the drawings themselves had to be precisely aligned to each other, and then they had to be mounted precisely on the board so as not to lose that registration. McCay solved this problem with small **registration marks** measured from the edge of the paper and then the boards. We can see this at the end of the prologue as McCay and the technician set up the projector to screen his achievement: McCay slips a mounted drawing into a wooden apparatus as the camera draws closer. We see the hand of the artist—now not drawing but controlling the photographic process as well—but we also see the four registration crosses at each corner (fig. 1.3). The apparatus indicates that McCay photographed his drawings horizontally, while Cohl had already decided to shoot his drawings vertically, thereby eliminating the need for a mounting board or holding apparatus for support.[15] (Photographing drawings vertically would become standard practice in the following decades.) But ensuring continuity at both stages of the process—drawing and photographing—meant that registration was a common problem for animators of all generations, even if solutions changed over time.

McCay was able to adapt or transpose his graphic style to animation—the figures in *Little Nemo* look like the figures in the famous comic strip and even act as we would imagine them to act. This meant that the detail involved in drawing these characters carried over at the cost of time: it took McCay over a year amid other projects to complete the drawings for *Little Nemo*. Cohl, though, adapted his drawing style to the needs of the medium so that he could make films more quickly; his drawings were starker and less detailed than McCay's.[16] As a comparison, between 1908 and 1911, Cohl had already made seventy-seven films by the time McCay got around to making *Little Nemo*.[17] After making animations and trick films for Gaumont in Paris, Cohl was invited to join the staff at the American outpost of Éclair in 1912; Cohl arrived at Fort Lee, New Jersey, in September 1912, started work on *The Newlyweds* in November 1912, and the first installment of the series, based on McManus's strip, was released in March 1913.[18] While mostly forgotten today—a fire at Éclair studios in March 1914 wiped out most of the prints[19]—*The Newlyweds* had a profound impact on American animation: before 1913, animation in the United States was limited to occasional single films; after *The Newlyweds*, the rush was on to create cartoon series.[20] In addition, "animated cartoons" as a phrase was used for the first time with this series, and it stuck, as well as the association between animation and comic strips, due to the number of series that followed.[21] A surviving installment, *He Poses for His Portrait* (1913), shows how Cohl adapted his style for the series. The story features the newlyweds with their misbehaving baby, Snookums, who sits for a portrait by a pretentious French artiste. In some ways, this film resembles *Fantasmagorie* in its clean white lines against a black background. It also features some startling metamorphic transitions, like the earlier film. But perhaps testifying to the collision between straight-ahead animation and the more staid approach of the comic strip, *He Poses for His Portrait* alternates uneasily between conventional, staged scenes of dialogue and more digressive, imaginative metamorphoses. As characters voice their lines, for example, the written dialogue blocks out the other characters so that there is no confusion about who is speaking (voice balloons would do the same work for later cartoons in just a couple of years), but this has the effect of stopping the action completely. Then there will be a quick, even confusing transition via metamorphosis before returning to the scene and dialogue between the protagonists. The alternation between planned and improvisational animation—between static, conventional images and quick, surreal transformations—makes for an awkward combination.

Even so, many newspaper cartoonists, recognizing motion pictures as a way to supplement their income, rushed to have their comic strip adapted for the screen via animation.[22] If hardly any new animation had been released between *Little Nemo* in 1911 and *The Newlyweds* in 1913, there were many more to come shortly thereafter, including animated adaptations of such comic strips as Bud Fisher's *Mutt and Jeff*, George Herriman's *Krazy Kat*, and Rudolph Dirks's *The Katzenjammer Kids*.[23] Among them, of course, was McCay's masterpiece, *Gertie* (1914), which was not based on any of McCay's previous strips. McCay started working seriously on *Gertie* in the summer of 1913; he took the drawings to Vitagraph Studios to be photographed in January 1914.[24] McCay used the film in his vaudeville act from January through the summer of 1914.[25] The live-action prologue was shot in November, and the theatrical version was released by Fox in late December 1914.[26] The film features a lovable dinosaur who alternately obeys and disobeys McCay's commands like a playful puppy. In his act, McCay stood to one side of the projection screen and issued commands, cajoled, scolded, and interacted with the animated dinosaur in various ways. At one point in the act, he would throw a pumpkin behind the screen at the exact moment it appeared on-screen as a treat for the beast. As a finale, he would disappear behind the curtain and reappear as an animated figure riding her huge head. Recent research has demonstrated that there was a curtain call for Gertie as well.[27] The film is an excellent example of the integration of animation and live performance that has taken many forms throughout the history of American animation.[28]

For our purposes, however, it is also a good example of the artisanal mode of production and of McCay's techniques that were to become standard or were to inspire alterations in the coming decades. McCay, for instance, continued using India ink on semitransparent **rice paper** as his drawing medium, as he had in *Little Nemo*.[29] The semitransparency of the paper allowed McCay to trace the new image over the old one, altering it slightly and therefore creating movement between frames. This was Cohl's preferred medium as well; an overlay was crucial to generating images easily for both animators—future animators would recognize the significance of this solution and improve on it with the completely transparent celluloid overlays. For their early films, Cohl and McCay eased their task with a simplified graphic design, which put their characters in the foreground without any or much of a background. Gertie, however, was more ambitious, with a full background and foreground in addition to the character. McCay therefore needed to redraw or retrace this background with every new drawing. To help him with this task, McCay hired a young assistant, John Fitzsimmons, to help him retrace the background and other elements of the image over the course of the 2,500 to 3,500 drawings required.[30] There are two stylistic consequences of tracing. First, we can notice that the lines of Gertie and the background are not stable; this effect is perhaps most noticeable in the leaves of the tree that Gertie plucks and swallows at the beginning of the film, but all the lines have this slightly unstable, shimmering quality. This is a result of tracing image after image by hand; it is inevitable that there will be slight differences in the lines from one image to the next. Animators now call this effect **boiling**, and it was nearly eliminated with the switch to celluloid and to image-generation techniques that did not rely on tracing, but we must admit that the effect enlivens the image considerably. McCay actually found it a pleasing effect: "I animated even the 'still' figures,"

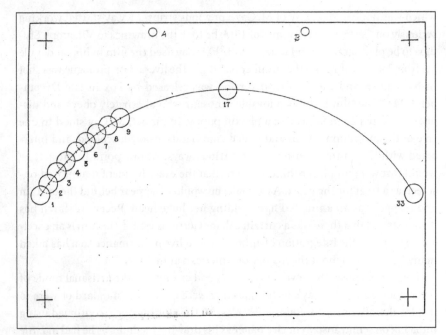

FIGURE 1.4: An illustration of McCay's "split system," which helped him plan movement along a trajectory through the use of key poses at mathematically derived points along the arc. After determining the number of poses and drawing the extremes (#1 and #33), McCay bisected the arc (#17) and then bisected that arc (#8) and so forth until the movement was fully charted (#1–9, etc.).

he once said, "which some movie cartoonists don't do. Unless all the live figures vibrate, the picture really isn't animated."[31] Second, over time tracing tends to smooth out sharp corners or edges of lines. We can see this effect in the background especially: the hills are less craggy and sharp at the end of the film compared to the beginning.[32]

Like Cohl, McCay animated *Little Nemo* straight ahead, but for *Gertie*, McCay wanted to be more precise in planning the trajectory of certain movements, as when Gertie hurls Jumbo the mastodon into the lake. He did this by deciding on the poses at the beginning of the movement and at the end and then splitting that trajectory in two and creating a key pose in the middle; he then split each of those trajectories and created key poses, and so forth, until all the poses comprising the movement were set along the movement's arc (fig. 1.4). He called this his "split system," but it is now known as **key framing** or **pose-to-pose animation**.[33] Nathan and Crafton explain: "By starting with the plan of Jumbo's trajectory laid under the paper as a guide, he started drawing the animal's body and the rock projectile at the points of Gertie's release and their distant impact with the water, and then proceeded to draw each phase of the flight. . . . McCay could thus ensure that the body diminished in proper perspective and at the correct rate on each drawing in between. Aside from improving the appearance of flights and motion in arcs, the Split System also helped tie spatial movements to the background so the objects appeared to move within the natural space of the drawing."[34] In the studio era, the key poses, or **extremes**, were set in advance by the head animator; then, the intermediate poses, or in-betweens, were often filled in by an assistant animator, or **in-betweener**. Pose-to-pose animation contrasts with the straight-ahead style. While straight-ahead animation allows or even encourages improvisation and spontaneity, pose-to-pose animation emphasizes uniformity and precision. It would become the standard approach of studio-era animation. Stylistically, we can see its effectiveness in the mastodon's trajectory into the lake: McCay's mastery of perspective allows the mastodon to diminish in size precisely as it moves along a very smooth arc. When timing and precision are important, pose-to-pose animation is the preferred method. And again, McCay checked the timing and accuracy of his poses with his Mutoscope-like flip device, which allowed him to simulate the projected movement of his images and see any errors in the order or execution of his mounted drawings.

Cohl photographed his own drawings with a Gaumont Chrono-négatif camera, which was well known for the stability of its image, making it a good choice for animation.[35] But McCay outsourced his photographic tasks to Vitagraph Studio. In this regard, McCay deviated from a purely artisanal approach by delegating the photography. But his work is still essentially artisanal in that McCay kept for himself the main task of drawing the images; even if he had an assistant, Fitzsimmons only traced the master's lines—the assistant never actually drew lines for McCay. In the true industrial mode, different animators learned how to draw in one uniform style so that they could divide the drawing tasks among them. Even if McCay delegated the photography, he still needed to prepare the images for that process to ensure stability and continuity. The registration crosses on McCay's drawing paper helped in that regard, at least during the drawing process. The images needed to be held stable for precise registration during the photography process, too. For example, the wooden holder in *Little Nemo* kept the images in place for photographic exposure. But on most **animation stands** of this era, in which the camera was placed above the drawings, the images would be held in place by registration pegs corresponding to holes punched into the drawing paper or celluloid, as well as a glass plate placed on top of the images. (An animation stand—also known as a **camera stand**—was used for to photograph the drawings, while an **animation table** was used to draw the images. Animation tables also had registration pegs, but they would often have a glass plate and light box *underneath* the drawings to aid in tracing, as opposed to the animation stand's glass plate *on top of* the images to hold them steady while they were photographed.) Cohl had already adopted this arrangement and was even using an electric drive to open the shutter of the camera as early as 1909; this would become standard in later years as the animation stand and camera became more sophisticated.[36]

McCay prepared his images for photography in another way as well: he took precise notes for the photographer about the order of images in the exposure process.[37] Why would one need such notes? Why not just order all of the images 1 to 3,500 and give them in sequence to the photographer? Two reasons: first, to cut down on the number of images generated, McCay would *reuse* certain images in a rhythmic sequence. That is, if Gertie breathes fifteen times in succession, there is no need to draw that series of images over and again until fifteen cycles has been reached. Instead, he would draw one cycle of her breathing pattern and then ask the photographer to repeat photographic exposure of that series fifteen times. This is known as "cycling," and it is a key method to reduce the number of images needed for animation. There are a number of moments of cycling in Gertie, often with a pleasing effect, as when she dances or shifts her weight between her right and left feet. Whereas in later years cycling was often merely a repetitive and dull method of extending the duration of the film cheaply, McCay used cycling to express Gertie's personality through rhythmic gesture. Second, McCay could control the *tempo* of the cycle by varying the exposure times for the drawings. For example, Gertie's breathing could appear very regular by exposing each moment in the cycle equally; or the breathing could made to appear labored by slowing down the inhalation (more exposures per drawing) and speeding up the exhalation (fewer exposures). So to make sure that the photographer knew precisely the order and timing of the exposures, McCay kept a very detailed notebook of image numbers and instructions. This became standard practice as well and is now known as an **exposure sheet**; studio animation departments would type out instructions to the photography department and send the exposure sheet along with the images to be photographed. No set of drawings would be complete without it.

Cohl and McCay took elements of the trick film and the lightning sketch and gave them narrative structure and a familiar or steady iconography;[38] in just a few short years, animators would build upon these aspects to create a set of conventions to the animated cartoon. In addition, even though Cohl and McCay worked mostly on their own, their solutions to animation problems—tracing, key framing, cycling, and so on—became the foundation for an industry. At the time, they might have been considered "secrets" of the trade. But these secrets or tips or tricks soon made their way to a new generation of animators.

The Transition to the Industrial Mode, 1914–1920

Legend has it that Cohl and McCay received curious visitors on two separate occasions. Cohl recalls that two men came to his studio in New Jersey in 1913 interested to know more about his process and techniques. Historians speculate that the pair might have been Raoul Barré and William C. Nolan, who started producing animated cartoons together at Edison studios after the success of *The New-lyweds*.[39] Likewise, John Fitzsimmons, McCay's assistant, recalls a day in 1913 when a young man paid a call to learn McCay's methods.[40] McCay was not shy; he was eager to share his tips, which he wanted to be widely known. He is said to have quipped, "Any idiot who wants to make a couple of thousand drawings for a hundred feet of film is welcome to join the club."[41] He changed his tune, however, when that same young man—rumored to be John Randolph Bray—set up his own studio, patented McCay's techniques under his own name, and then sued McCay for license infringement![42] These stories—whether they are true or not—form a primal scene for the early history of animation, in that they pit the two modes directly against each other in face-to-face meetings: the artisanal mode portrayed by innocent, open, and creative McCay versus the industrial mode played by ruthless, litigious, and derivative Bray, for example. Modern animation historians have complicated this simple cast of characters, but this portrayal was very common in early histories and retellings. These stories also offer an allegory of the relationship between enthusiasts and animators, or more broadly, amateurs and experts. Young, ambitious apprentices go to the experts to learn new techniques, the better to create an exciting economic opportunity: this is not just a story of the origins of commercial animation but also about how animation was represented in manuals, correspondence courses, the press, and fan magazines. Consistently we see animation presented as a fascinating but mysterious process that, if you have the talent for figuring it out, could bring you, too, fame and fortune. This is the story of America's fascination with how things work, and the dream of innovation, progress, and the economic gain such fascination can bring. In this section, then, we will discuss how the artisanal mode changed into the industrial mode, how the fascination with how things work—and with animation itself—shaped this emerging industrialization, and how knowledge of animation spread to experts and amateurs alike.

One thing was clear to any budding animator: the tedious and time-consuming labor of generating thousands of drawings for relatively little payoff impeded serious efforts to make money off this new form. Barré and Bray both learned that distributors made no concessions for the labor required to make an animated film: they wanted a film a month, and that was that. Bray, for example, made an animated film the old-fashioned way in 1913, *The Artist's Dream*, and showed it to Pathé, a French distribution company with branches in the United States. They liked it and gave him a six-month contract, asking for six more.[43] If he were to fulfill his contract, corners had to be cut; efficiencies had to be created. Where, exactly? The biggest problem was generating images, so Bray tackled this issue in two ways: technological innovation and in the division of labor. During the next few years, these two broad solutions would merge more closely and become the standard approach to commercial animation for decades. In terms of division of labor, Bray recognized that to deliver one animation a month—when it took perhaps twice that long to create one—would require giving up the artisan's personal control. So over the months and years following his Pathé contract, Bray hired several animators to form units within his studio, each unit of animators working on a different project. At Bray Studio, Bray himself animated the Col. Heeza Liar series for one year in 1914, while Paul Terry was in charge of the Farmer Al Falfa series, Earl Hurd helmed the Bobby Bumps series, and so forth.[44] This form of labor organization is known as the **director-unit system**, which was prevalent in the early years of the motion-picture industry at large.[45] Variations on this system would emerge at animation studios in the sound era as well: Walt Disney Studio sometimes followed a director-unit approach, although it was strongest at Warner Bros. Each unit was composed of a collection of workers who had only one kind of job: directors directed, tracers traced, inkers inked, in-betweeners drew the poses between the key frames, and so on. The **animation director** was in charge of the **scenario** and coordination among all elements of the unit, from head animators to in-betweeners to tracers, inkers, and the rest. The more units in place, the more films could be delivered as they leapfrogged each other in the release schedule.

From 1913 to 1915, Bray also developed—or appropriated—key technological innovations that formed the basis of important patents. The first of these patents, which he filed in January 1914, described the state of the art as it was known at the time. Not coincidentally, this summary included many of McCay's techniques, such as the use of tracing paper, mixing ink with turpentine to cut down on **cockling**, registration marks, and exposure manipulation.[46] To this list Bray added two innovations: (1) printing the background on tracing paper so that the background need not be redrawn with every image and (2) omitting lines in the printed background that would need to be removed anyway as they crossed or were covered by the elements of the image that would move (erasing lines is a time-consuming process). Significantly, Bray hit upon the idea of separating background from foreground in these processes. Printed backgrounds served Bray from around 1913 to 1915, when he came upon another process that would be even more useful and definitive: separating the image into different layers, each on an individual transparent celluloid sheet, known as a cel. Unfortunately for Bray, he did not discover this innovation himself but through another animator, Earl Hurd, who had filed a patent for his celluloid process in December 1914.[47] This could have been inconvenient for Bray's plans had he not had the idea to hire Hurd and join forces to form a monopoly on these key patents and licensing arrangements, which he did. Bray incorporated his studio in December 1914 and hired Hurd sometime between the summer of 1915 and the winter of 1916.[48] The Bray-Hurd Process Company was formed sometime later, perhaps in 1917; Bray filed another patent in July 1915 that incorporated both Hurd's process and the previous innovations.[49] Hurd stayed on with Bray Studios until 1920.[50] By the end of World War I, the Bray-Hurd process was widely (but not exclusively) used in American animation.[51]

FIGURE 1.5: *Tanks* (Bray Studio, 1917). The image of Bobby Bumps, who is moving at this point in the film, is a shade lighter due to the thickness of celluloid sheets.

Transparency is celluloid's primary advantage; it allows animators to separate the image into component layers, use and reuse these layers in various combinations for each exposure, and thereby eliminate the need to redraw elements of the image that stay the same from frame to frame. In cel animation, animators decide which elements of the image will receive their own transparent layer. Theoretically, there could be as many cels as image elements, but practically the animators were limited to one, two, or at most three cels; otherwise, the thickness of the celluloid discolored in the image. (We can see this effect in many early cartoons, such as Bray Studio's *Tanks* [1917], in which the moving elements are considerably lighter than the rest of the image [fig. 1.5].) Animators usually separated background from foreground; they would draw the foreground—the characters, for example—on paper and then draw the background on a celluloid layer and then lay it over the paper drawing. They could also draw the background on paper and overlay the action on celluloid, which was to become the most common practice.

In whatever way animators used them, cels became the foundation of the commercial animation industry. Why? Because in cels, the industry found a way to merge a *technology* with a specific organization of *labor*. That is, Bray and others discovered that by separating the image into discrete units, they could also divide the labor into discrete units. Bray assigned this division of labor to various elements and tasks, as outlined above, which also allowed him to pay some workers less for certain tasks than others. In addition to his animators, he hired untrained workers—usually women and adolescents, a practice that continued through the studio era and beyond—for more menial, tedious tasks, such as **inking** (retracing the animator's pencil sketches with ink), **opaquing** or painting (filling in characters or objects with opaque ink or paint), or **washing cels**, which could be reused. As Bray explained, "We worked out a system of the original cartoonist laying out the thing in pencil. Then another fellow would ink in certain parts of it. Then another girl or boy would put on color on the back of the picture."[52] Each task—from the supervisory role of the head animator to the menial work of "girl" or "boy"—was paid a different rate, allowing Bray to increase production without increasing costs. The commercial viability of American animation depended to a large extent on the availability of cheap labor paid at differential rates, made possible in the first place by the division of the image into units that could be assigned to this cheap labor.[53] Hence, the use of cels had profound economic benefits for emerging animation studios.

Cel animation had stylistic implications as well, both innovative and reifying. On one hand, separating image elements allowed an extraordinary amount of experimentation with representational choices. Some of these choices were forced; for example, it is easier to create complicated depth cues (such as shadows) for the background than for elements that move in the foreground, so cartoons often mixed different systems for representing perspective in the same image. Other conventions would develop out of cel animation, such as the duplication of legs on a character to indicate running at great speed.[54] A number of the most familiar conventions of American animation—such as the seemingly impossible expansion of an enclosed space as characters chase each other through it—are the result of the ability to separate layers and repeat elements easily. On the other hand, separating the image and dividing the labor meant not only that a single animator no longer had sole artistic control but also that all animators working on the image had to adopt the same drawing style. Dick Huemer, who worked in animation from the 1910s, recalled, "We animators inked directly on paper, which afforded us a lot of creative freedom and the opportunity to express our own techniques and individuality. . . . It never occurred to us that uniformity in appearance was a desirable thing. But this is something that the cel system later accomplished automatically."[55] The artisanal mode or single-animator, paper-and-ink approach also required stylistic uniformity—after all, *Gertie* appears to be stylistically unified—but because only one person is drawing, the work could be considered to be an expression of individual style. In cel animation, however, all individual styles must conform to the studio style, or to the style of the head animator. That is, assistant animators, in-betweeners, and even tracers had to learn how to draw the character as the head animator drew it. This was enforced through the use of a model sheet, which was a set of drawings on a single sheet that laid out the basic drawing features of the character. All animators had to practice conforming to this model. So cel animation was a major stylistic innovation, but like the economic system upon which it built, it also discouraged individuality and encouraged standardization and uniformity.[56]

Gertie's fluidity of motion and the "liveliness" of its lines were among the first stylistic casualties of commercialized cel animation. Most animation of the 1910s looks stiff by comparison. *Tanks* (1917), a Bray Studio product animated by Earl Hurd for the Bobby Bumps series, in which Bobby and his dog, Fido, build a homemade tank and wreak havoc on the neighboring farmer's fields, is a good example. We see the shading mentioned earlier, especially when Fido brings a plank and Bobby nails it on the contraption: the moving elements of the image are a shade lighter than the static elements, which were darkened by the presence of cel layers. Its apparent "stiffness" is the result of the film's emphasis on the *isolation* and *repetition* of movements. For example, the film rarely features more than one character moving at any given time; at the beginning of the film, either Fido moves or Bobby does, not both. Isolating character movements made them much easier to draw and animate, but it also gives a static quality to the whole image. Likewise, individual elements of characters—limbs, head, body—rarely move together. When the farmer drinks his moonshine, for example, only one part— his arms, his head, his hat, his feet—moves at a time. Hence there is very little **secondary action**—the movement of related parts of a character's body when a primary part moves (as in the movement of a character's torso when she raises her arm). Disney animation of the 1930s emphasized secondary action as a fundamental principle of animation, but in 1917, Bray and others were more concerned with economy.[57] Note also that the actual lines are very steady; not only was celluloid a more stable medium than rice paper, but better registration and thicker lines also contributed to the film's stolidity. Bray and other studios also made liberal use of **holds**: moments when the action stops completely and the image is completely still for a beat or two. Holds were a particularly subtle labor-saving device in early animation, but they contributed to the stiffness or slowness of cartoons. Finally, Bray cut down on the number of images by emphasizing cycling, or repetition of movement—the repeated action of Bobby hammering, for example—but the cel system had advantages for this as well. For example, as Bobby's tank plows through various fields, the movement and angle of the tank is the same over three different shots—only the background has changed from wheat to corn to pumpkins. Separating foreground and background allowed Hurd to reuse a cycle but to give it a new twist each time with a different background.

Bray patented the cel system—and any other process he could think of—to control and profit from the flow and use of this information. Those who hoped to use cels in animation had to purchase a license from the Bray-Hurd Process Company.[58] But studios were certainly not forced to use the process, and some studios opted to animate completely on paper—such as Pat Sullivan's studio, which produced Felix the Cat cartoons through the 1920s—thereby operating completely legally and avoiding the license fee.[59] Other studios developed their own techniques to animate on paper efficiently. Raoul Barré, for example, developed a **slash-and-tear system** that duplicated the cel system's major advantage—isolating and separating moving elements of the image from static ones—but without the cost of celluloid. In this system, which used heavier, opaque paper (rather than more expensive translucent tracing paper), animators drew two images: a background image on one sheet and an element, such as a character, on an otherwise blank second sheet. Then they would simply tear away the blank part of the second sheet, leaving only the character to superimpose on the background sheet, which had been designed to accommodate it. They would repeat as needed with slightly different second sheets to simulate character movement. As Crafton explains, "Success depended on accurate registration, and to ensure it, Barré used a punch to perforate the sheets so they could be stacked vertically in perfect alignment on fixed pins. This was the original **perf-and-peg** system, still in use."[60] Perforations in the paper and pegs on the animation board were to become standard features in animation studios for decades. This system was probably the closest competitor to the cel system in the silent era.

Given the variety of techniques, how did animators learn of these options? There were any number of ways to learn about animation: for experts, the patents themselves provided a wealth of information, as did the concentration and circulation of professional animators in New York City, where animation studios emerged in the 1910s (see chapter 2 for a detailed description of the circulation of animators among studios). For experts and amateurs alike, press and fan magazines, trade journals, manuals, correspondence courses, and even films themselves all were valuable sources of information about the secrets of animation. For example, the Bray-Hurd process was published in a trade magazine as early as 1916![61] Indeed, the transition from the artisanal to the industrial mode of production was supported not just by patents and cheap labor but discursively as well. That is, the transition occurred in the press and the media, as well as in the studios and the marketplace. One can hardly read any essay on animation during this period that does not focus on technique. In the American context, this fascination with how animation worked might fall under what Neil Harris called "the operational aesthetic," which he described as "a delight in observing process and examining for literal truth."[62] Nineteenth-century showman P. T. Barnum encouraged his audience to decide if his exhibits were hoaxes, but part of the fun was also trying to figure out how the hoax was accomplished. Similarly, early animated films invited the viewers to debate how they were done. Viewers knew, of course, that animated films were not literally true depictions, so it wasn't a question of doubt or even pleasurable deception as much as a sense of wonder at technical process, a wonder that seemed to spark curiosity well into the late 1920s. Hence, we see in the literature on early animation an overwhelming interest in how things works.

We see this pattern often. Reviews from the artisanal period often discussed how animation worked, usually in the most general terms. Feature articles, especially, on animation during the transitional period found it obligatory to discuss the process. The *Philadelphia Evening Ledger* in 1915 summed it up nicely: "The Cartoon Comedy: Last Mystery of the Movies."[63] Of course, we would expect *Scientific American* to solve that mystery, or *Popular Science*, but answers were just as common in *Everybody's Magazine* or *Illustrated World*.[64] The stories described the enormous amount of labor involved, of course, but also what that labor entailed, including information about tracing or (later) cels or registration and equipment, such as an animation stand. We see this in the number of film manuals during the period as well. Interest in animation seemed to surge as the novelty aspect of early cinema slackened, but manuals on general filmmaking focusing on live-action film production also usually offered a chapter or section on trick films or cartoons.[65] After 1915, the stories focused not just on the process but on industrial efficiency as well. Numerous stories about Bray and his studio emphasized his triumph over the original problem of image generation. All stories told about labor-saving techniques, but interestingly not in the detail required to actually make a successful animation; it was a rare essay or manual chapter that explored key-framing or tallying systems, which were in use since McCay, as we have seen.[66] The important thing, apparently, was the general mastery of the image by industrial means, without all the details—or perhaps more accurately, giving the reader the *feeling* of mastery.

In fact, the emphasis on scientific mastery and progress in the literature on animation matches similar themes in all sorts of popular literature of the moment. From tales of Edison, fictionalized at least since *Eve of the Future* in 1886, to the Tom Swift novels dating from 1910, American and European literature fed the operational aesthetic by insisting that one could operationalize one's scientific knowledge to solve mysteries or create a better world, or at least a better robot. In American cartoons, Rube Goldberg's contraptions encapsulated and parodied the tinkerer's compulsion, and we see that in animation of the 1910s and 1920s as well, most obviously in Felix the Cat's MacGyver-esque resourcefulness. Much writing about animation was *aspirational*; it was not so much concerned with accurate details about the animation process as giving the reader a (vague) sense of understanding and mastery. Other types of literature—correspondence courses, for example—provided more detail in order to capitalize on youthful aspirations. In the 1910s, there were numerous courses on becoming a cartoonist, and Winsor McCay even offered a lesson on animation through a correspondence course in 1919.[67] Bray himself as a youth was entranced by a **chalk talk** (an illustrated lecture somewhat like a lightning sketch); he "sent for a book of instructions, studied, and practiced by [himself]" and supplemented that with night classes in art practice.[68] Walter Lantz, an early Bray employee who went on to create Woody Woodpecker, also started with a correspondence course.[69]

One could also learn about animation at home through numerous manuals, especially after the war. Most manuals, such as John McCrory's *How to Draw for the Movies* from 1918, provide only a surface-level understanding of animation technique and are as bold as their titles about their audience and purpose.[70] These manuals stress opportunity rather than curiosity; they emphasize above all a feeling of empowerment, fortifying the pleasing dream of American bootstrap perseverance. One such chapter, "Screen Cartoons: How They Are Made," comes from a 1922 pamphlet titled *Opportunities in the Motion Picture Industry and How to Qualify for Positions in Its Many Branches*, which pretty much sums up a wide range of literature at the moment; both fictional and self-help literature fed the youthful hope that talent and know-how could translate into economic gain and Hollywood-style fame. The first and most famous manual entirely on animation, E. G. Lutz's *Animated Cartoons* from 1920, is a helpful beginner's guide to animation's various techniques, including model sheets, drawing boards, registration pegs, tracing, key sketches, extremes and intermediates, the use of cels, designing **layouts** (the setting in which the cartoon will take place), photographing the drawings, cycling, and so forth.[71] According to legend, this guide gave Disney his start by offering a step-by-step explanation of the process of making a cartoon.[72] True to the theme of industrial efficiency, it emphasizes labor-saving tactics. Apparently, the greatest skill is actually to be able to *avoid* drawing: "of all the talents required by anyone going into this branch of art, none is so important as that of the skill to plan the work so that the lowest number of drawings need to be made for any particular scenario."[73] Planning the work is paramount, so of all the skills that an animator might hope for, "his skill as a manager" ranks most highly—words that Disney apparently took to heart.[74]

If this fascination with how things work—and the American impulse to tinker and invent—is evident in fiction, patents (the number of patents filed in the United States doubled between 1900 and 1920), or even the contemporary rage for mechanical drawing (hundreds of books on mechanical drawing were published between 1900 and 1920), as well as manuals, articles, and other writings on animation during this period, it is also evident in the animated films of the late 1910s and 1920s, especially in the technical animations of Bray Studio. Announced in April 1917, this series was a variation within the popular Paramount-Bray Pictographs, a weekly one-reel magazine consisting of a split-reel cartoon and a live-action component, either a newsreel or feature. Apparently the brainchild of one J. F. Leventhal, an animator working for Bray who also had a drafting background, the films emphasized process and mechanics. Coinciding with the United States' entry into the European war, these films also stressed preparedness and satisfied viewer curiosity about the weapons of war. The first film of the series, *The Submarine Mine Layer*, demonstrated how a submarine worked via images of the machine in the water and also through sectional views.[75] Other titles included *The Aeroplane Machine Gun* (October 1917), *The Depth Bomb* (May 1918),

FIGURE 1.6: *Tanks* (Bray Studio, 1917), in which the convention of the sectional view in training films is adapted to a fiction cartoon as well.

and similar titles during the war and *How the Telephone Talks* (April 1919) and *How Movies Move* after the war.

Leventhal was the instigator, but Bray enthusiastically latched on to the idea and developed an entire unit for educational animations, which included Dean Parmelee, Jack Norling, Francis Goldman, Jameison Handy, and Max Fleischer.[76] With the outbreak of war, Bray—not one to let an opportunity pass—presented this unit's potential to the government, which immediately enlisted Leventhal and Fleischer in the U.S. Army Signal Corps, much to Bray's chagrin.[77] At Fort Sill, Oklahoma, Leventhal and Fleischer made training films for the armed forces that featured this new genre of animation, especially useful for mapmaking and demonstrating how to use weaponry.[78] Meanwhile, Bray Studios continued to present animated diagrams in the Pictographs, eventually releasing around four dozen such films between 1917 and 1920, culminating in the twelve-reel 1919 opus, *Elements of the Automobile*.[79] To depict and animate any given object or process, these technical films used many different devices, including the **sectional drawing** (or cutaway drawing), which would allow audiences to see inside a solid body. *Elements of the Automobile*, for example, shows how pistons work by "revealing" the inside of an engine. This trope even found its way to entertainment cartoons, as in *Tanks*, when we see a sectional view of the inside of Bobby Bumps's homemade panzer (fig. 1.6).[80] After the war, Bray focused his attention mostly on educational and industrial films, with Leventhal and Fleischer becoming key executives within the Bray company. Bray Studios did not survive the coming of sound, but the idea of the animated diagram caught on and became a trope of the educational film and a special darling of the visual education movement.

The transition from the artisanal to the industrial mode of production depended on the spread—but also legal protection through patents—of information about "how animation works." As animation became commercialized and monetized, we see a shift from an artisanal approach that relied on individual or communal labor and a spotty, if not outright secretive, dissemination of knowledge to an industrial approach, which featured a hierarchical organization of labor and, through patents, an official or moderately transparent dissemination of knowledge. There is not a strict division, as there was plenty of overlap and residual practice, and studios had trade secrets that were not part of the public record. But the industrialization of animation required more than patents and capitalist ruthlessness; there was much support for this industrialization in the form of essays and manuals about how animation works, emphasizing standardization and efficiency. These writings functioned to publicize and justify the cartoon-making process and align it with industrial values. Unlike the magic guild model, in which rare knowledge is valuable, the industrial model prized open and egalitarian distribution of knowledge; simple mechanical operation had value in itself as a process that the audience could grasp and understand. Animation could participate in the operational aesthetic. Indeed, this was always an important part of American animation as the process of image generation became a trope in cartoons themselves. If the artisanal period is fittingly represented by the "hand of the artist" trope (emphasizing magic and conjuring), the technical animations of the 1910s are also an interesting form of self-figuration during animation's period of transition and consolidation in that the themes of industrialization and efficiency are depicted on-screen via the animation of process. These films seem to exemplify the transition to an industrial model and align with the transition's discursive support, which came from many directions as the trade press, opportunistic authors and publishers, educators, and draftsmen capitalized on the rush toward efficiency and the American public's curiosity about how things work.

The Rise of the Studios, 1921–1928

Max Fleischer learned a number of important lessons from Bray, especially about the importance of a patent to protect and profit from information and to differentiate one studio from the next.[81] Always a tinkerer, he and his younger brother Dave developed a device in the summer of 1915 that would serve as the foundation of their fame as animators. The rotoscope, as they called it, helped to solve the problem of image generation and fluidity of movement by projecting live-

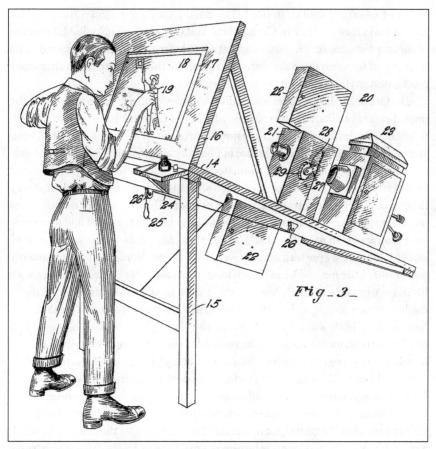

FIGURE 1.7: Fleischer's rotoscope device, as illustrated in his 1915 patent application.

action footage onto an animation table so that the animator could trace the live-action footage frame by frame and then rephotograph the drawings as animations (fig. 1.7). Max would film Dave, for example, as he danced on the roof of their building dressed in a clown's suit. (No, really, they did this.) At the animator's table, Max would trace onto paper Dave's photographic image frame by frame, resulting in a series of drawings of Dave's dance. The resulting cartoon of a clown dancing had a certain realism of movement while also obviously being a drawn animation. On the strength of this invention, Bray hired Max to work at his studio in 1916, and the rotoscope became very valuable for the wartime training films. (The potential military application did not escape Max even in the 1915 patent application, which depicts its use for semaphore training.) But after the war, Dave's clown returned in the form of Koko, a recurring character in their Out of the Inkwell series, which became popular enough that the Fleischers left Bray in 1921 to establish their own studio. Recurring characters were the bread and butter of emerging studios in the 1920s; Koko joined Pat Sullivan Studio's Felix the Cat and Disney's Alice in Cartoonland and Oswald the Lucky Rabbit as some of the most successful characters and studios before the coming of sound. This section will focus on these three studios to outline the broad trends in animation production, style, and theme during the 1920s.

The Out of the Inkwell series actually had two gimmicks: Koko the Clown, the impish central character, was rotoscoped, but he also often left his cartoon environment to bedevil his animator-creator, Max, in the "real" world. There had been animation/live-action hybrids before but only by alternating live-action and animation scene by scene. Edison's Animated Grouch Chaser series (1915), animated by Barré, for example, included live-action scenes that framed—and often had very little to do with—the featured animated cartoon. The Out of the Inkwell series was unique in its ability to make the relationship between cartoon and its creator truly interactive. In *Modeling* (1921), for example, Max draws Koko while a nearby staffer sculpts a clay portrait of, shall we say, an unhandsome man. Koko not only makes fun of the man while in the cartoon (he draws a caricature on the ice with his skates), but he eventually jumps out of the cartoon to continue his needling in the live-action setting as both instigator and victim of clay-inspired chaos. The torment goes both ways. In *Cartoon Factory* (1924), Max hooks Koko up to an electric current, torturing him as he runs. Max then sketches a drawing machine that acts as a surrogate for him, alternately tracing and erasing objects of Koko's frustrated desire. But Koko commandeers this device and draws his own scenario: Max as a live-action toy soldier Koko can control. Max-as-soldier, however, draws reinforcements in his own likeness, orders them to life, and sends them after Koko, who in turn uses the contraption to erase them en masse as they charge forward. Koko tries to get the last laugh as he uses the machine to draw a cannon to barrage poor Max into submission. But as the nearby machine shop turns out live-action replicas of Max-as-soldier one after the other, Koko retreats to his inkwell.

Cartoon Factory's title and plot recall one of the most common tropes of studio-era animation: the assembly-line motif. Countless cartoons of the 1920s through the 1950s depicted an ad hoc or literal assembly line that processes or produces people or products in startling ways. *Baby Bottleneck* (Warner Bros., 1946), for example, from the later studio era, features an assembly line that prepares babies for delivery by the stork. In *Buddy the Woodsman* (Warner Bros., 1934), lumberjacks come in for dinner, but not without passing through an elaborate face washer and dryer. *Alice's Egg Plant* (Disney, 1925) features a series of contraptions to coax and collect eggs from the hens. The motif emphasizes mechanical inventiveness, which can be funny, but also repetition, the cycling of which relieves the burden of animating it. This assembly-line motif also figures the burden of animation—the tedium of generating drawing after drawing in an assembly-line fashion—especially as animation became more industrialized. Animators latched on to this trope not only because it worked as a gag and as a reliable source of cycling but because it seemed to articulate visually both the aspirational elements of innovative tinkering—so long a part of animation's history—as well as the more mechanical, monotonous qualities of that history's struggle with image genera-tion. In the case of the Koko cartoons, the live-action element relieved at least part of the tedium of drawing. But when Koko invaded the live-action setting, he was actually traipsing into a photograph—the trick to hybrid cartoons, such as the Out of the Inkwell series, consisted in taking a photograph of the setting, using it as a background, and then overlaying a cel of the animated element. Walter Lantz's Dinky Doodle series (1924–1926) for Bray worked the same way.

Another hybrid, Disney's Alice in Cartoonland series (1924–1927), reversed the formula by having a live-action girl play in an animated setting. In that case, the technical challenge was placing the girl in these settings photographically. The best solution was a **traveling matte**: they would photograph the actor's scene, pro-ject it onto paper, trace the outline of the actor, blacken in that outline, and photo-graph that blackened shape frame by frame. Then they would create a negative of that (which would be a clear outline of the actor with the rest of the image in black) and **bipack** the negative—meaning they would have two strips of film in the same camera, perfectly aligned—in with the film used to photograph the regular ani-mation. This would produce a print that contained the animation with a black shape—a traveling matte—that moved in accordance with the original shape of the live-action actor. Next, they would print that in reverse so that the actor's shape was clear and the rest of the image black. Then they would double-print the film—laying the reversed film with the **matte** over the original live-action footage—so that the resulting film contained only the isolated image of the moving actor. Printing *that* with the animation produced an image of a live-action girl in an animated landscape.[82] If that sounds complicated, that's because it was and hence why the interaction between Alice and her cartoon friends was usually kept to a minimum.

Walt Disney, of course, established a studio that eventually dominated the animation industry in Hollywood's Golden Era (see chapter 2). While most ani-mation studios of the 1920s clustered in New York, Disney went to the West Coast. The New York animation companies included Bray Studios, the Bud Fisher Films Corporation, Earl Hurd Productions, Paul Terry's Fables Pictures, International Film Service, the Fleischer's Out of the Inkwell Films, the Pat Sullivan Studio, and half a dozen more. Studios in Hollywood included Disney, Harman-Ising, and Ub Iwerks's Celebrity Productions.[83] Animators developed different styles and themes on either coast. The New York films of the 1920s and 1930s usually featured eth-nic or working-class characters in cosmopolitan settings, while Disney and the West Coast animators emphasized animals as characters in rural or small-town and middle-class settings.[84] They differed somewhat in their approaches to pro-duction as well. All the companies were small—around 1925, Fleischer had six-teen employees, Sullivan eight, Disney ten[85]—but some, such as Fleischer and

Disney, allowed a more collaborative approach in which members of the group shared tasks, compared to Sullivan's stricter director-unit, specialized-labor model. Yet their different approaches to cartoon narrative reveal a number of variations to the industrial mode during this time. Out of the Inkwell Films promoted a collaborative, loose approach to a cartoon's story: animators had their individual scenes to work on—usually without knowing the rest of the film—but they had some say in creating new gags or story ideas beyond what Max and especially Dave had already thought up for the cartoon.[86] The semiautonomous approach contrasted with the tighter production control at Disney. While animators could contribute gag ideas—Disney famously offered bonuses for any gag actually used—the scenario was created and decided upon before animation actually began. By the late 1920s and early 1930s, Disney implemented story sketches and storyboards to illustrate what had already been established in the long story conferences—the images also exerted a degree of control over the animation process and the animators.[87]

Sullivan Studios also had a top-down approach to story construction but in a different way. Even though Pat Sullivan established the studio in the early 1920s, he was not the creative force behind Felix the Cat, arguably the most popular cartoon character of the 1920s. Sullivan's head animator, Otto Messmer, was the mind behind Felix, and he was responsible for supervising every aspect of the studio's production. The stories for the films came from Messmer's imagination and the rest of the animators in the studio only completed the work that he gave them. As Al Eugster, a young animator at the time, tells it, "Otto was all-round. Besides animating, as animators finished their scenes or sequences, he would give them more work. He would, in a sense, be directing the picture. We didn't use that term then. [The script] just came out of Otto's head and it never seemed to get on paper somehow. There never seemed to be any conference. Otto would get an idea or subject. He probably made notes, but there was no, what we call, a formal script. He would have a pretty good idea of what he wanted and he would convey it to the animator, but it seemed to be done on an individual basis."[88] Even though his approach was not formal, like Disney's, it was just as hierarchical in some ways, with Messmer as the sole arbiter and manager of the productions. In other ways, Sullivan Studios was typical of a 1920s animation studio: animation tables were all in the same room, each one fitted with glass, light bulbs, registration pegs, pencils, paper, and ink. They sketched scenes in pencil, inked over the lines, and then spent time erasing the pencil marks. (Disney used blue pencils for sketching, which did not show up on the orthochromatic film of the day.) They drew the animations entirely on paper but by the mid-1920s began using cels for the background, which they would overlay on the action. About 2,500 to 3,000 drawings were required for each six-minute film. Inkers and opaquers would finish the work before it was sent to the photographer in a separate part of the room; exposure directions were written on the sheets themselves outside the frame line.[89]

Messmer essentially functioned as the heart of the operation, exerting creative control but also directing the work to be done by the individual animators.

The system certainly worked for them: Felix was wildly popular. Part of the appeal was certainly Messmer's playful way with animation layout design. In *Felix Trifles with Time* (1925), for example, our hungry and frustrated hero bribes a passing Father Time to send him to an easier era—he obliges by sending him back to the Stone Age. There are plenty of opportunities for cycling action, as when a dinosaur chases Felix through the wilderness, but Messmer keeps it interesting by alternating the regular animation with silhouettes. When Father Time hits Felix on the head to send him back, Messmer resorted to a device he had used before to indicate "seeing stars": he quickly alternates positive and negative images of the scene to give something of a strobe effect and then animates stars against a black background, which then explode and crumble into a swirl of dust—which was accomplished by animating rock salt—before animating bows and circles and other shapes quickly against the scene. And in an earlier scene, Felix is blown to the top of a building by a tuba player—the view is from the side—but when he falls back down, Messmer drew the scene from above. By constantly varying the layout, Messmer kept the Felix cartoons fresh and inventive, unlike, say, Paul Terry's Aesop's Fables series. Messmer was similarly playful with animation conventions. To escape the dinosaur after coming to a cliff, Felix throws a boulder into the lake below; the backsplash that reaches him is shaped like an umbrella, which Felix of course uses to float down. In other films, Felix might take the question mark that appeared above his head and use it as a hook to solve that particular problem. He was especially known for his creative use of his own body parts, especially his tail, which could be used as a tool or weapon in any number of situations that called for it. This endless creativity made Felix a beloved character, the first to be merchandised successfully with dolls, mugs, clocks, and so forth.

Live-action cinema of the day also contributed to Felix's comic appeal and to that of many other cartoon characters. Animators drew inspiration—particularly gags and story ideas—from all media. While the Fleischer cartoons borrowed gags especially from the vaudeville stage, Felix the Cat shared a comic sensibility with Charlie Chaplin and Buster Keaton. Disney's cartoons owed a debt to W. C. Fields and particularly to Keaton. As Russell Merritt and J. B. Kaufman explain, "Like Keaton, Disney's cartoon characters are inveterate tinkerers, imaginative inventors of improbable devices," who shared "Keaton's ingenuity in coping with a mechanical world."[90] *The Mechanical Cow* (1927), an early Oswald the Lucky Rabbit cartoon from Disney, has a title that says it all. American animation of the 1920s continued the 1910s fascination with how things work by populating the cartoon world with ingenious contraptions of all sorts. Fleischer's "cartoon factory" whipped up a device to churn out drawings, a wish that would wait decades to be fulfilled, while the mechanical cow automatically delivers milk to needy sucklings. The history of animation could be written as a story of invisible,

magical labor—the labor that happens *between* the frames by the animators themselves or the labor that is completed *on* the frames by assembly lines, contraptions,
and objects that move and work of their own accord. This thematic intersection
of labor, comedy, and the mechanical was especially busy in live-action slap-
stick of the 1910s and 1920s, and animation of the day shared these themes and
interests.[91]

Animation adapted stylistic conventions from live-action cinema as well. Disney's late-1920s cartoons especially, but not exclusively, embraced live-action
techniques in editing and cinematography, which helped put over their gags and
story ideas. Disney and others had already adopted crosscutting, for example,
around 1924, as in *Alice's Fishy Story*, which cuts between Julius pursued by a shark
and Alice talking to an Eskimo ice fisherman to the point when Julius pops up
through a hole in the ice to interrupt them.[92] With such editing techniques, Disney and others sharpened their gags and narrative pacing throughout the 1920s.
They also included point-of-view shots, **match-on-action** edits, multiple-camera
setups (as in the *Felix Trifles with Time* examples above), simulated camera movements, and live-action transitions, such as **irises**. The number of shots multiplied
over the course of the 1920s, too: Alice comedies might have between twenty-four
and thirty-two shots per film, while later Oswald cartoons might go as high as
forty-eight shots per film.[93] *Sky Scrappers* (1928), for example, has around forty-
two shots, many examples of crosscutting, some point-of-view shots, and analytical
editing, especially cutting to a closer view. Examples of simulated camera movement include panning up the buildings as characters are lifted to the top. Irises
are used for emphasis, to focus our attention on some detail. So by the coming of
sound, the animation industry also had an established vocabulary of techniques
similar or identical to that of live-action cinema.

Animation style changed over the decade as well, if only slightly. In the 1910s
and early 1920s, when animation characters moved, only one part of their body
moved at a time—the rest of their body froze. This quirk was a result, of course,
of the separation of image elements common to the cel technique, which also made
the animation easier and quicker to produce. Secondary actions, as we have already
noted, were rare; it was not until the 1930s that the Disney studio implemented
them as a basic principle of all its animation. The common approach to character
design and movement in the 1920s would come to be known as rubber-hose style,
so called because character bodies and especially limbs were drawn to have an
elastic quality like a rubber hose. Elbows and knees were not part of cartoon anatomy during the heyday of this style. However, even with this plasticity, secondary actions were not common: when a character reached for something, only its
arm moved and elongated, perhaps; the rest of the body would freeze rather than
stretch. But especially at Disney in the late 1920s, characters begin to "squash and
stretch" more. Squash and stretch is another principle of elasticity in animation
that implied secondary action: as an object or character moved, especially in rela-

tion to the ground or gravity, it would "squash" a bit and "stretch" as it recovered or went through the rest of the walk cycle. In the mid-1920s, inanimate objects would be more likely to squash and stretch than characters; a building in *Felix Trifles with Time*, for example, rocks and squashes and stretches with the music. In *Sky Scrappers*, most of the characters stick to rubber-hose principles; as the foreman looks at his watch, his arm moves, then his hips, then his head, and then his arm—all quickly and smoothly but separately. But in the previous shot, as Oswald struggles with lifting a barrel full of water with his rope, we see that his whole body stretches and squashes and shakes with the effort, his head flattening slightly as he pulls the rope down. In Ub Iwerks's animation of Oswald, then, we have an important transitional step in animation style between the rubber-hose animation of the 1920s and Disney's **personality animation** of the 1930s and 1940s, which emphasized holistic approaches to movement that revealed character through gesture and secondary action. It's only fitting, then, that Iwerks and Disney's next character, Mickey Mouse, would usher in an entirely new approach to sound and image in American animation.

2

CLASSICAL HOLLYWOOD, 1928–1946   Susan Ohmer

The 1930s and 1940s marked the height of the Hollywood studio system. During this period, a handful of animation producers dominated the field, companies whose names we still know today. Some were units within a live-action studio, such as Leon Schlesinger's group at Warner Bros., who produced the Looney Tunes and Merrie Melodies series, or the MGM animation unit, famous for its Tom and Jerry cartoons. Other animation groups set up their own studios, including Paul Terry's Terrytoons, based in New York, and Walt Disney Productions, the first animation company to set up shop in Los Angeles. Many of the cartoon characters we continue to enjoy, characters such as Bugs Bunny and Daffy Duck, Woody Woodpecker, Popeye, Donald Duck, Snow White, Dumbo, and Superman, first appeared on-screen during this period. There were artistic innovations in animation during this time as well. Audiences could watch the first cartoons in Technicolor and the first feature-length animated films. The Academy of Motion Picture Arts and Sciences recognized the importance and popularity of cartoons by introducing a new awards category in the Oscars, for Short Subject—Cartoon, in 1932.[1] Animated films also played an important role in the history of this era. During World War II, cartoon producers crafted humorous films that made light of home-front challenges and educational films to help soldiers adjust to military life. Some cartoons even functioned as propaganda, warning Americans about Hitler or the Japanese. After the war, the industry reinvented itself again, moving into live-action and combining short cartoons into longer packages. Throughout this time, cartoon producers continually developed new business and creative strategies to respond to a changing studio system and a more complex media environment.

During this period, cartoon producers worked within a system characterized by vertical integration. Five studios (Paramount, Twentieth Century-Fox, Loew's-MGM, Warner Bros., and RKO) dominated production, distribution, and exhibition, while three smaller companies (Universal, Columbia and United Artists) produced and distributed films but did not own as many theaters as the majors. Only these eight studios, the **Big Five** and **Little Three**, maintained broad distribution networks that enabled them to negotiate licenses with theaters to screen films.[2] To remain profitable, these eight companies had to maintain a regular and reliable flow of films from their production studios to their theaters, in order, as Tino Balio notes, to feed the "maw" of exhibition.[3] Each studio, at different times and in different ways, worked with animation producers to supply cartoons for these theaters, as part of their overall mix.

Distribution contracts were essential for the survival of animation companies, but they did not guarantee screen time, for cartoons had to compete with other kinds of short films and with live-action features for a place on theater programs. The popularity of double features during this period sometimes pushed cartoons to the margins. Antitrust efforts—in particular, the **Consent Decree of 1940**—opened up new opportunities for cartoons in Hollywood's system of distribution and exhibition, but animation producers still struggled to remain solvent and profitable. To fulfill their distribution contracts, animation firms reorganized their production processes; the artisanal approaches of the 1910s evolved into more hierarchical divisions of labor that promoted efficiency and specialization. As animation became more of an assembly-line process, companies also experienced the labor strikes that were occurring in other areas of the film industry. Even with a successful short film, cartoon producers could not recoup their production costs from exhibition fees alone. This challenging economic environment spurred many animation companies to explore other revenue streams, such as merchandising their characters to reach the expanding consumer market for children. Altogether then, economic, aesthetic, social, and industrial changes in animation production during the studio era make this a fascinating period to explore and one that continues to affect the cartoons we watch today.

It's a Small World: Animation Production in the Studio Era

Many of the animators who began their careers in the 1910s went on to launch their own production companies in the 1920s and 1930s. To finance their films, cartoon producers negotiated distribution deals with small companies or with major motion-picture studios that provided either money up front or upon a film's release. Working with a major studio meant that a company's films would be distributed to large theater chains. Major studios also gave animators access to such resources as music that they could incorporate into their cartoons and use to create a distinctive identity for their films. Each animation producer wanted to develop memorable characters or styles that would attract a loyal audience. During the studio era, animation was a tightly knit world where people knew each other and each other's work, and cartoonists often migrated back and forth between employers, creating a cross-fertilization of ideas. In this period, the Disney studio and its cartoons emerged as an aspirational model and source of talent for many animation firms.

Paul Terry's Terrytoons studio was one of the stalwarts of this era. Terry began working with J. R. Bray in the 1910s before going into business with Amadee J. Van Buren in 1921 to produce a series based on Aesop's fables. In 1929, Terry left to form his own company, Terrytoons, which was based in New York.[4] Known for his frugality, Terry kept his staff on a tight schedule to meet his distribution commitment with Twentieth Century-Fox. Some animators stayed with him for decades while others grew frustrated with Terry's lack of interest in artistic innovation and left to join other studios. Bill Tytla, who went on to animate the "Night on Bald Mountain" sequence in *Fantasia*; Art Babbitt, who fleshed out the character of Goofy; and Norm Ferguson, famed for developing Pluto's expressiveness, all worked for a time at Terrytoons before moving on to Disney.[5] Terry's Aesop's Fables series of the 1920s inspired Walt Disney to pursue a career in animation, but Terry's other characters, Farmer Al Falfa and Gandy Goose, did not attract many devoted followers. In the late 1940s, however, fresh characters, such as Mighty Mouse and Heckle and Jeckle, attracted new audiences to Terrytoons (fig. 2.1).[6]

Walter Lantz began his career in the animation unit that William Randolph Hearst set up to promote the comic strips that appeared in his newspapers; then, like Paul Terry, he left to work with J. R. Bray. There he worked alongside future Disney artists Clyde Geronimi, who became one of the supervising directors on *Cinderella* (1950) and *Peter Pan* (1953), and Shamus Culhane, who went on to several other studios, including Disney, the Fleischer Studio, and Warner Bros.[7] In 1927, Lantz moved to Hollywood and became head of the animation unit that Universal had launched. There he was in charge of animating the character Oswald the Lucky Rabbit, the character that Walt Disney had developed before him. At Universal, his staff included Leo Salkin, who later joined Disney; Tex Avery, who became one of the animation directors at Warner Bros. and a director at MGM; and Pinto Colvig, who later performed the voice of Goofy. In 1935, Lantz established Walter Lantz Productions as a separately owned company under contract to Universal and with offices on their lot.[8] Inspired by Felix the Cat and Mickey

FIGURE 2.1: Paul Terry poses with Mighty Mouse, ca. 1950. © Twentieth Century Fox. Courtesy of the Westchester County Historical Society.

Mouse, Lantz sought to create a star character who could launch a series and be promoted through tie-ins and merchandising. For several years, the character of Andy Panda remained popular, but it was Woody Woodpecker, who debuted in 1940, that became his long-sought star (fig. 2.2).[9]

J. R. Bray also employed Max Fleischer, whom he met when both were working in the art department of the *Brooklyn Eagle* newspaper around 1901. They met again after World War I when Max was looking for a partner who would use the rotoscope system he had developed to reduce the work of animation and create more lifelike figures (see chapter 1).[10] In 1919, Max Fleischer used this device as the basis for a new series, soon titled Out of the Inkwell, that featured an animated Koko the Clown interacting with Max in a series of self-reflexive comic sketches. The character who became Betty Boop also emerged from the Inkwell series, and in 1932, the Fleischers introduced Popeye, the sailor man from the newspaper comics, to the screen.[11]

The Fleischers explored several possible distribution arrangements before signing an agreement with Paramount in 1929.[12] Signing with Paramount gave the Fleischers access to Paramount's music publishing business and major singers it had under contract, such as Cab Calloway and Louis Armstrong.[13] This arrangement enabled the Fleischers to incorporate the songs, movement, and personas of

FIGURE 2.2: Walter Lantz poses with a Woody Woodpecker doll, early 1940s. © Walter Lantz Productions. Courtesy Jerry Beck.

these musicians into their cartoons. In their version of *Snow White* (Fleischer Studio, 1933), for example, Koko mimics the movements of Calloway as he sings "St. James Infirmary Blues." In some cases, the combination of soundtrack and subject matter repeated racial stereotypes of the time, such as when Louis Armstrong's performance of "I'll Be Glad When You're Dead, You Rascal, You" is matched to a jungle setting (Fleischer Studio, 1932). Harlem's jazz scene in New York City inspired the Fleischers and hence much of their studio's output, which often transcended these stereotypes, even while race remained a key category for understanding representations in the early American animation industry.[14]

Music played a crucial role in the animated films that Warner Bros. released as well. In January 1930, the studio signed a two-year contract with the business executive and former press agent Leon Schlesinger to produce a new series of cartoons to be called Looney Tunes. Intended to compete with Disney's films, the films used songs from Warner's extensive music library, and their success led Warner's to contract for a second series one year later, to be called Merrie Melodies. After signing with Warner, Schlesinger set about finding animators who could create the cartoons and raided Disney and other studios for animation talent.[15] He hired Hugh Harmon and Rudolph Ising as directors, but when they left to start their own unit within MGM, Schlesinger brought in a new group of animators

FIGURE 2.3: Producer Leon Schlesinger and his "employee," Daffy Duck, negotiate a new contract in *You Ought to Be in Pictures*. © The Vitaphone Corporation 1940.

that came to include Tex Avery, Chuck Jones, Bob Clampett, Frank Tashlin, composer Carl Stalling (who had originated the early Silly Symphony scores at Disney), and voice artist Mel Blanc.[16] It was this group of artists that created Warner's most memorable characters, including Porky Pig (in 1935), Daffy Duck (1937), Bugs Bunny (1940), Tweety (1942), and Sylvester and Pepe le Pew (1945) (fig. 2.3).[17]

Metro-Goldwyn-Mayer, the film production arm of Loew's Inc., also built its cartoon unit by hiring away animators from other studios. First, MGM hired Ub Iwerks away from Disney; then, when Iwerks's Flip the Frog series was not successful, the company hired Harmon and Ising from Warner Bros. in 1933. Their Happy Harmonies series of musical cartoons used **two-strip Technicolor** but did not match Disney's in popularity, so MGM ended their contract in 1937 and put into place a new head of animation, Fred Quimby. The company then brought some of Harmon and Ising's animators in-house and made additional hires that included animators from Terrytoons and Warner Bros. In 1939, MGM reorganized the animation group again, putting in place as directors Bill Hanna and Joe Barbera and hiring Tex Avery from Warner Bros. Under this new leadership, MGM cartoons enjoyed a renaissance; its characters Tom and Jerry became the strongest rivals to Disney's and won five Oscars during the 1940s.[18]

The most successful animation production company in the 1930s and 1940s, however, was the Walt Disney Studio. Walt Disney arrived in California in 1923 with plans to continue the combination live-action and animated series Alice in

Cartoonland that he had begun in Kansas City. Within a few years, he was supervising the work of a small staff of animators, including Ub Iwerks, on the Oswald the Rabbit series for Universal. When Universal took the series away from him, Disney and Iwerks developed a new character, Mickey Mouse, who debuted in *Steamboat Willie* on November 18, 1928. The film also marked Disney's first use of sound, and the film's tightly synchronized music and movement made it a smash hit.[19] Over the next few years, Mickey's circle of friends grew to include his girlfriend, Minnie, the dog Pluto, and a continuing irritant named Donald Duck. In addition to the Mickey Mouse cartoons, the Disney studio also launched the Silly Symphony series in which the animation was built around a musical score.[20] From the beginning, Disney showed a strong interest in technological innovation. The company was the first animation studio to negotiate a contract for three-strip Technicolor and had exclusive use of the process from 1932 to 1935. In 1937, the studio won an Academy Award for the invention of the multiplane camera that enhanced the feeling of depth and dimensionality in cartoons. The Disney studio also produced the first animated feature to come out of Hollywood, *Snow White and the Seven Dwarfs*, which premiered in December 1937.

Disney's popularity in the 1930s can be seen in the series of distribution contracts that marked the progress of the organization. After working with smaller companies in New York in the mid-1920s, he signed with Columbia in 1929, one of the Little Three studios that provided production facilities and a distribution sales force. In 1932, Disney left Columbia to sign with United Artists (UA), a company that distributed films by prestigious independent producers, such as Charlie Chaplin. The UA contract offered Disney a greater advance payment for each cartoon that enabled the studio to begin producing its shorts in three-strip Technicolor. In 1936, Disney changed distributors again, moving to RKO, one of the Big Five studios. RKO was the least profitable of the Big Five and spent most of the 1930s in bankruptcy reorganization, but it owned theaters in nearly every major American city, and its New York premieres took place at Radio City Music Hall.[21] Signing Disney was a coup for RKO. To celebrate their alliance, RKO took out an ad in the trade papers announcing that "RKO Radio will have the privilege of distributing the incomparable animated cartoons of Walt Disney, in full Technicolor and with an unrivalled star list."[22]

During the studio era, then, there were many established animation producers working within or under contract to studios that aimed to produce a steady flow of cartoons to theaters. The movement of many animators from one company to another created an exchange of ideas that enriched many companies' work. Disney set the standard for technological innovation and memorable, individualized characters, but audiences also appreciated the quirky and more volatile personalities from other animation producers. Animation producers in this period aimed to meet several goals: to fulfill their distribution contracts and to create innovative characters that would sustain public interest. To do so, they developed more efficient work processes that organized animation production into discrete stages.

Modes of Production: Specialization and Efficiency

Cartoon production in the 1910s and 1920s often took an artisanal approach. Individual animators, such as Winsor McCay, created the drawings that formed the basis of their animation and perhaps employed an assistant to help them. As we saw in chapter 1, animation producers built on the Bray-Hurd patents to separate the elements of drawing and isolate the components that moved from those that did not. Moving elements, such as arms or legs, were drawn on separate pieces of celluloid, while parts that didn't move, or background images, would be drawn on other sheets of paper or on celluloid and reused when a sequence was photographed. This process of isolating only the moving parts of an image reduced the labor involved in drawing them and allowed for animation firms to divide these steps among different staff members. During the 1930s and 1940s, the tasks involved in animation became more specialized and the number of people involved in creating a cartoon greatly increased.

The introduction of sound and color into animation in the late 1920s and early 1930s expanded the methods available to create characters and stories. Animation firms competed with one another to use sound and later color creatively and to hire or train animators who could make the most of these new elements. Color and sound added additional stages to the production process and required new equipment. This increased the cost of producing cartoons, and the costs were usually not covered by rental fees. At the same time, cartoon studios needed to fulfill their distribution commitments to ensure adequate revenue. The constant pressure to innovate and to deliver cartoons on time led animation producers to increase the efficiency of their production processes. What has been described as the "old time anarchy" of production in the 1920s evolved to assembly-line methods by the 1940s.[23]

It is not always possible to trace the exact methods that different animation firms used to produce cartoons. Memoirs, biographies, and interviews with animators from the 1930s and 1940s provide some perspectives on the changes that took place in animation production during this era. Popular magazines and humorous documentaries also took audiences behind the scenes of animation studios. Technical and professional journals discussed the processes involved in animation for a more specialized audience. Both the popular press and more technical journals frequently profiled the work of the Disney studio in particular so that it came to stand for the field of animation as a whole in the public imagination. Looking at a range of sources from this period enables us to outline many of the methods that distinguish the studio era of animation production.

Paul Terry's Terrytoons studio illustrates the most basic approach to animation production in this period. Terry described himself as the "Woolworth's of animation" and prided himself on his studio's ability to churn out a cartoon every two weeks, twenty-six times a year, to meet his distribution obligation, first to Educational Pictures and then to Fox.[24] In interviews during the 1930s, Terry asserted that he created the basic story ideas for his films and then invited others in the studio to contribute ideas for gags. Together they developed a series of rough sketches that defined the characters and plot of each film. Then the cartoon's director timed the movements of characters and of individual sequences in relation to the overall timing of the cartoon. He then assigned the project to a composer, who used a **metronome** to write music in time with the beat. Once the musical score was completed, the director charted each of the sequences frame by frame and gave them to an animator, who created the drawings that brought the story to life. The animator's pencil sketches (also known as **roughs**) went to the ink-and-paint department to be inked on cells and then painted with **tempera** paint. Backgrounds that did not change from shot to shot were painted onto heavy paper using **wash colors**. When the visual elements of the cartoon were finished, studio composer Philip Scheib added the music, dialogue, and sound effects in one recording session.[25]

The stress on rapid and efficient production left little room for artistic innovation and cost Terry some of his most creative employees. Terry's cartoons used shortcuts, such as cycles and repeating animation, to simplify both the design and movement of characters and to minimize the need for complex drawings.[26] For example, in *The Timid Rabbit* (1937), a rabbit runs straight across the frame in a horizontal line as we watch trees and objects in the background cycle past more than once. In *Bully Beef* (1930), cats and mice walk, run, and gesture using the same simple movements again and again. In *The Hot Spell* (1936), we see flowers and cornstalks wilt and then revive again at the same pace and with the same type of movement. These qualities were characteristic of Disney films of the late 1920s but continue to appear in Terrytoons a decade later. As with Disney's early films, the humor in Terrytoons often derived from characters who used parts of their bodies in unexpected ways. In *Club Sandwich* (1931), a cat uses its tail to bolt a door, and in *Farmer Al Falfa's Ape Girl* (1932), a dinosaur uses its long tail to create a staircase that enables the Ape Girl to climb down from a tree. Much of the cartoons' humor resulted from these unexpected changes, rather than from character development or interaction.

This outline of the mode of production at Terrytoons points to areas where processes would change during the studio era. At Terrytoons, there was no specialized story department or artists who focused on thinking up gags. Terry himself sketched the backgrounds that established the overall look of a film, rather than assigning that duty to a specialized artist. Animators were in charge of drawing an entire cartoon from start to finish and did not have assistants to share the work. Their completed drawings went to ink and paint and then to be photographed, so the animators did not see their drawings on film until the final version was released.

At other studios, the process of developing a story idea for a cartoon was more collaborative. Dick Huemer, an animator who worked with the Fleischers and later with Disney, described the informal atmosphere that characterized animation production at the Fleischer Studio in the mid-1920s. The studio employed about ten people who worked side by side in "a very cozy cluttered place" in midtown Manhattan that was so small that people could talk from desk to desk.[27] Huemer recalls that he and Dave Fleischer would develop a story idea and gags together, and then Huemer would create the animation. Anyone on the staff could suggest a subject for a cartoon and, if it were approved, offer ideas for gags.[28] In this case, both the head of the studio and the animators themselves were involved in developing story ideas. At the Walter Lantz studio as well, everyone was invited to contribute gags to whatever cartoon was in development.[29] Walt Disney even offered a bonus if a gag was used in the film. Disney, however, insisted that gags fit the emotional and psychological structure of a character. At other studios, one animator noted, "a gag was a gag," and all that mattered was that it was funny.[30]

At both Terrytoons and the Fleischer studios, once a story was developed, it was given to an animator to draw. At the Disney studio, however, and later on at Lantz, a separate story department took the suggestions for story ideas and gags and developed a **scenario** that indicated the plot, number of scenes, characters involved, and settings. A **story sketch artist** then translated the scenario into rough pencil sketches. These sketches were linked up from beginning to end on a large board where other writers and animators could review them. Using **storyboards** enabled animators and writers to see the overall trajectory of a story and to understand the focus and purpose of each scene.[31] In this way, changes later in the production process could be reduced or eliminated (fig. 2.4).

We can see the differences in Terrytoons' and Disney's approach to gags and story when we compare films from each studio that build on similar situations. Terrytoons' *A Battle Royal* and Disney's *Moving Day* (both from 1936) begin with characters receiving a foreclosure notice, a situation that was not uncommon during the Depression. In the black-and-white Terrytoons film, Farmer Al Falfa and Kiko the Kangaroo are rudely ejected from their house and immediately see a passing carnival with a sign that offers one hundred dollars to anyone who can fight one round against the boxer One-Round Hogan. Al Falfa decides to take him on, and we see him waiting in a locker room as one victim after another of Hogan's knockout skills comes in. One-Round flattens Al Falfa, too, but Kiko takes up the challenge and succeeds in outboxing the champion. The humor in the Terrytoons film derives from the contrast between Al Falfa and One-Round and from the sight of a kangaroo boxing.

FIGURE 2.4: Walt Disney (with pointer) discusses the storyboard for *The New Spirit* (1942) with (left to right) Henry Morgenthau Jr. (Secretary of the Treasury), John L. Sullivan (assistant Secretary of the Treasury), George Buffington (assistant), Joe Grant, and Dick Huemer (Disney animators). Courtesy Michael Barrier.

By comparison, Disney's *Moving Day* maximizes the comic and animated potential of each stage of the plot. When the Sheriff pounds on the door of Mickey's house, we see the walls and the pictures that are hanging there shake in response to the banging, each in its own way. An ongoing comedic element of the film is the battle between Goofy and the piano he is trying to move. The piano slides down the ramp of his wagon, and he pushes it up, and then it slides down again. Each time, the movement is accompanied by the twanging of the wires inside that mark the piano's location and movement. This routine plays with timing in ways that recall the comic films of Buster Keaton or Harold Lloyd, whose work Disney screened for his animators. The piano starts and stops as if it had volition, and we watch and wonder what it will do next. Each stage of the story builds logically from the previous stage, and the animators maximize the gags each situation offers.

In addition to a stronger emphasis on carefully constructed stories, Disney also introduced the position of **layout artist** in 1929. This person was responsible for determining the overall composition of scenes and the size and position of characters within the space of action. In color cartoons, the layout artist might also develop a distinctive color palette for the main characters. Before this time, animators drew their own layouts and decided on the composition of the characters in their scenes without much concern with what anyone else was doing. Like the use of storyboards, this new approach to laying out a film visually created a more cohesive look and ensured consistency in character or style from one film to another.[32] This careful attention to the overall visual design of the film is shown in *Pinocchio*, for example, whose layouts by Gustaf Tenggren recall a Bavarian toyshop down to the smallest detail. The china dolls, music boxes, cuckoo clocks, and overall interior design of Gepetto's workshop create a consistent look and tone for the early sections of the film.

The introduction of sound also added new stages to animation production and challenges that animation producers met in different ways. At Terrytoons, music, sound effects, and any dialogue were recorded after the drawings were finished, but at other studios, a musical director or animation director timed the music or soundtrack for a film early in the process so that drawings could be created to fit the tempo. Walter Lantz described the process: "Let's say that Oswald is to blow a bugle-call in the middle of the scene: it must start in bar No. 5 of the music, and in frame No. 101 of the film, and in drawing No. 51."[33] The animation director then created a **bar sheet** that contained rough sketches of each scene with written descriptions of the sound and action involved. The sheet also indicated the number of bars allotted to each sequence, so both the composer and the animator could plan their work in sync with this framework. Sound effects, music, and dialogue were created on separate tracks and then combined into a composite track that was synchronized with the drawings.[34] This close coordination between sound and image can be seen in Lantz's *Hurdy Gurdy* (1929), where characters dance in synchronization to a hurdy gurdy, a piano, and non-diegetic music. At Warner Bros., the voice artists who created the distinctive sounds of Bugs Bunny and Daffy Duck were recorded after the story was finalized so that animators could fit the movement of characters' mouths to the dialogue.[35]

At Disney, the role of animation director took on great importance. This person was in charge of coordinating every phase of production on a cartoon: the tempo and pacing of the picture, the layout, backgrounds, sounds, color, and editing.[36] Animation directors "contribute ideas to the story they were going to direct while it was being written; supervise the drawing up of exposure sheets, layouts and backgrounds; give work to the animators; call for retakes; work with the musicians; attend the recordings; and approve the final prints."[37] Often these directors were animators who had worked at the studio for a long time and had absorbed the "Disney style." *Snow White and the Seven Dwarfs* lists five sequence directors and one supervising animator, all of whom had worked on Disney's short cartoons earlier in the 1930s. By giving trusted, longtime employees this responsibility, Walt Disney ensured that the studio's distinctive vision of characters and stories would be maintained. We see this continuity in the careful sequencing of *Snow White*, where actions are set in the Queen's castle, the dwarfs' diamond mine, and their cottage, and each environment is presented in rich detail.

By contrast, at the Warner Bros. animation unit, directors were encouraged to develop a unique, individualistic approach, rather than a studio style. Animators including Chuck Jones, Bob Clampett, Frank Tashlin, and Tex Avery developed such memorable characters as Pepe Le Pew, Wile E. Coyote and Road Runner, and Sylvester and Tweety.[38] Warner Bros. cartoons are known for their humor, and often the object of that humor was Disney. There are several Warner Bros. cartoons from this period that satirize Disney characters, plots, or even specific films. In *Falling Hare* (Clampett, 1943), Bugs Bunny is reading *Victory through Air Power*, a book that Disney adapted for the screen that same year. *Pigs in a Polka* (Champin, 1943) satirizes both the classical music of Disney's *Fantasia* and Disney's 1933 short *The Three Little Pigs*. *Corny Concerto* (Bob Clampett, 1943) mocks the highbrow culture of Disney's *Fantasia*. The film opens at "Corny-gie Hall" and features Elmer Fudd as concert conductor, whose clothing and accent ("the whytmic stwains of a haunting wefwain") make fun of the host Deems Taylor and conductor Leopold Stokowski in the Disney film. Like *Fantasia*, *Corny Concerto* includes several short films, such as "The Blue Danube," which makes fun of Disney's *The Ugly Duckling*. The plot lines are similar: a black duck thinks its mother is a swan, and the mother rejects him. In the Disney film, we feel the emotional pathos of the little lost duck; in the Warner Bros. version, by contrast, the mother swan smacks the little duck violently and does not welcome him into her family until he saves her other ducklings from vultures.

Once the animation director assigned a project to an animator, the process of drawing the cartoon began. Most animators of the studio era broke down sequences of drawings into key poses, or extremes, and in-betweens. In this system, a sequence of drawings would be numbered 1 through 9, for example, and the lead animator would create drawings 1, 5, and 9 as points of reference. Then an assistant, or in-betweener, would fill in the drawings in between. MGM animator Joseph Barbera described how, at that studio, the head animator created drawings 1, 5, and 9; then the assistant animator created drawings 3 and 7; and finally the in-betweener completed drawings 2, 4, 6, and 8.[39] This system enabled the senior animator to concentrate on "salient spots in the course of the action where a definite change in the position of the character takes place."[40] Disney animators often specialized in particular characters and developed a sense of their personalities and framework of action. Animators sometimes created model sheets for characters that showed them from different angles and in different sizes so that the animation team would have a consistent point of reference for their drawings. We can find short documentaries about character design from Chuck Jones and recent Disney animators on YouTube.

At Fleischer, Terrytoons, and the Lantz studio, animators were expected to produce a certain quota of animation each week. At the Disney studio, however, there was no quota; animators were encouraged to review and redo their work until it passed muster with the animation director and often with Walt Disney himself. After an animator completed a sequence of drawings, the images were filmed in black-and-white and then screened on a **Moviola** in "sweatbox" sessions where other animation staffers were invited to critique the footage. The animator could then revise the footage before it was sent to the ink-and-paint department. This use of **pencil tests** to check animated scenes while they were being developed was unique to the Disney studio, according to animator Shamus Culhane, who worked at both Fleischer and Disney. Culhane felt that animators at other studios could not take that much criticism and review, but he believed that these pencil tests were a key way that Disney developed the studio's style.[41] The extra features on DVDs of *Snow White* include pencil tests for that film that enable us to see animated sequences at this early stage.

After the drawings were completed, the animated sequences were sent to the ink-and-paint department, which could range from a staff of one or two people to several dozen. This stage was common to animation studios in this period, though the complexity of the process varied. At Disney, for example, the paint lab maintained a library of 113 separate hues with seven values ranging from light to dark for each hue, totaling nearly 800 colors.[42] The wide range of choices here resulted from the shift to Technicolor, first at Disney and then at other animation producers in the 1930s. This vast array of colors also reflects Disney's belief that color could play a dramatic and psychological role in film, by creating visually distinct characters who moved through spaces defined by carefully placed, brightly colored objects.[43] The character of Jiminy Cricket in *Pinocchio* (Disney, 1940) illustrates the ways in which Disney animators used color to create detailed costumes and facial expressions that enhanced a character's believability.

Once the drawings were inked onto sheets of celluloid and painted, they could be synchronized with the composite recorded track. At the Fleischer studio, the musicians and Dave Fleischer attended these recording sessions, while at Disney, the director of animation participated and could also order retakes.[44] The process of sound recording changed over time and differed at each studio. At all of the studios during the first years of sound recording, and at Terrytoons even afterward, all the different kinds of sounds were played and recorded at the same time. At Lantz and at Disney, the music was recorded first, and then sound effects and dialogue were recorded on separate tracks before the three were meshed together.[45] The introduction of sound to animation in the late 1920s meant that animators planned an entire film with sound in mind and designed characters and key plot points in relation to beats of music.

During the 1930s, the number of people employed at animation companies greatly increased. At Disney, the staff grew from less than a dozen people in the late 1920s to over 1,200 by 1940 and at Fleischer, from less than ten employees in the 1920s to over six hundred by the late 1930s.[46] To accommodate these expanding staffs, animation producers built much larger studios. The Fleischers moved to Florida, where they built a new studio in Miami in 1938.[47] Warner Bros. built new quarters for its animators that were affectionately nicknamed "Termite Terrace" for the other occupants who shared the space. Disney built a new and expansive studio in Burbank, California, designed "for optimum per capita production . . . a smooth and efficient production flow line—a sort of picture assembly line."[48] These larger spaces provided room for the more complex work processes involved in animation, yet they also changed the ways that employees interacted with each other, often increasing the distance between them (fig. 2.5).

Animators who began their careers in the 1920s, such as Shamus Culhane, felt that there was a clear path to move ahead in the field. For many, working in ink and paint was the first rung on the ladder for an animation career. A would-be animator could begin washing cells and then inking drawings onto celluloid, before moving into animation as an in-betweener or assistant. Over time, however, ink-and-paint departments came to employ women only and were not seen as a means to advance into animation.[49] As the steps involved in animating a film increased, the organizational structure of animation firms became more complex. Animation historian Harvey Deneroff has noted that the 1930s "was a period that saw the establishment of an increasing number of separate departments . . . each often with its own manager and assistant manager."[50] In this increasingly structured environment, it was harder to move ahead or to move from one department to another. Managers focused attention on broader systems of production, not necessarily on individual career paths.[51]

In Hollywood during the 1930s, studio employees with different kinds of expertise began to unionize or form craft guilds. The Screen Actors Guild was certified as a bargaining agent in 1937 and the Screen Writers' Guild in 1938.[52] In 1940, union organizers approached animation studios. MGM and Warner animators voted to organize without a strike, but at Disney, employees walked out in May 1941 and continued striking through the summer until the union was recognized.[53] An earlier strike at the Fleischer studio in New York in May 1937 lasted most of the year and permanently changed the relationship between the Fleischer brothers and their employees.[54] These strikes were a visible reminder of the changes animation studios and staffers experienced during the studio era, as production processes became more complex and specialized and animation firms developed more elaborate organizational structures.

The 1930s and 1940s marked the era of full animation in Hollywood. Cartoons became more like live-action films, with star characters, more structured stories, and camera movements and framing similar to those used in live-action.[55] Characters became personalities whose bodies maintained their physical integrity and moved naturalistically. At Disney, the goal was truly to create "the illusion of life."[56] As historian Giannalberto Bendazzi notes, "the time of bell towers kneeling

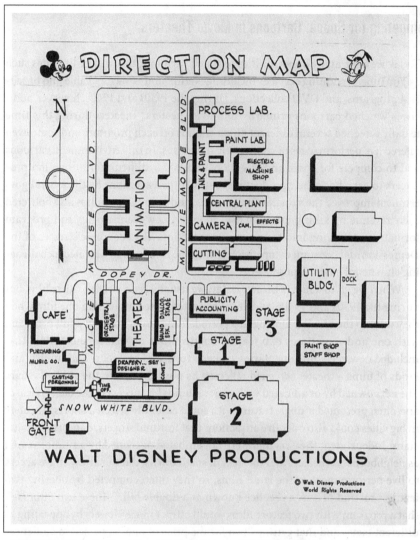

FIGURE 2.5: "Direction Map" to Disney's Buena Vista (Burbank) campus. © Walt Disney Productions.

to avoid being hit by planes, or big toes transforming into ballerinas at the sound of a flute had gone forever."[57] Animation firms planned their films carefully to ensure consistency and an efficient work process, using storyboards, exposure sheets, and model sheets, and drawings and soundtracks were designed to fit precise tempos. The number of staff members increased, as did their areas of expertise, and the space of production expanded to accommodate the larger number of people and projects. In this dynamic environment, cartoons not only competed with each other; they competed against live-action films for space in American movie theaters.

Competing for Space: Cartoons in Movie Theaters

Today we have many opportunities to watch cartoons, through online sites such as YouTube, streaming services including Netflix and Amazon, cable and broadcast programs, and DVD collections. During the 1930s and 1940s, however, audiences watched cartoons primarily in movie theaters. Theaters during this time usually screened several different kinds of films on each program, and some even offered live performances or contests for free prizes. In this environment, cartoons had to compete for space and attention, and it was difficult for animation producers to earn back their production costs. Antitrust actions by the federal government improved the situation for cartoons, and animation studios also bolstered their revenue by selling merchandise, adopting new technologies and program formats, and moving into feature film production. The economic stresses of the Depression and constant competition within the film industry created a challenging climate for cartoon producers.

When we go to a movie theater today, we usually see a single feature film, but during the 1930s and 1940s, audiences expected to see more than one film when they went to the movies. During this period, film theaters offered a full program, with one and sometimes two feature-length films, as well as short films that included newsreels, documentaries, comedy reels, and cartoons. The number and kinds of films a theater screened reflected its position within the studio system. Theaters owned by or affiliated with major studios had access to the latest releases and often presented a single feature with some carefully selected shorts. Theaters in big cities could also offer live attractions that featured singers, dancers, or musicians. Independent theaters that were not affiliated or owned by a studio, as well as neighborhood theaters and theaters in small towns, did not always have access to live performances or the latest films, so they often competed by offering two features instead of one, a practice known as a double bill.[58] These exhibitors felt that a program with two feature films would attract more viewers by appealing to different tastes and that getting "two for the price of one" appealed to audiences suffering amid the Depression.[59] By the end of the 1930s, 75 percent of motion-picture theaters in the United States screened double bills, while the remaining 25 percent played single features with selected shorts.[60]

Theaters that programmed double bills also presented shorts, but the time required to screen two features often left little time for them. *Variety* found that, in theaters that adopted a double-bill format, screening times for the entire program increased from two hours to three or more, driving out shorts.[61] Cartoons occupied a prominent place in bills at first-run theaters but had to compete for space at houses that featured double bills.[62] And films weren't the only attraction on double bills. During the Depression, theaters often added promotions and con-

FIGURE 2.6: Two theaters—two policies. The Capitol's "Two Big Features" program leaves no room for shorts. The Elsinore's traditional program includes a Paramount Popeye cartoon (*The Daily Capital Journal*, Salem, Ore., January 23, 1937).

tests with prizes to attract audiences. Producer Walter Lantz complained, "What with double features, Bank Night, Keeno, automobile giveaways, country store, gas range contests, etc., the short subject has been taking a beating." Sometimes a theater owner couldn't screen the shorts he had rented because, according to Lantz, "his double ran too long or one of the games of getting-something-for-nothing interfered"[63] (fig. 2.6).

In part because of this uncertainty, cartoons rarely earned back their cost of production. Double-feature theaters could not or would not pay high rental fees for shorts they did not have time to screen.[64] Exhibitors also complained that they could not absorb the number of short films studios turned out. During the 1935–1936 season, for example, studios released 750 short films, but only about one-third of them were booked enough to cover their negative and print costs.[65] Throughout the 1930s, there was a large gap between what it cost animation studios to make a cartoon and what they earned from rental fees. By 1940, production costs had increased by 38 percent in two years; labor costs were up 25 percent;

and raw stock cost 20 percent more—but rental fees remained the same as they were in 1933.[66] *Variety* did the math and concluded that even Disney's popular Silly Symphonies and Mickey Mouse cartoons could not break even from rental fees alone.[67]

Since producers of animated shorts could not recoup their production costs through rental fees, most turned to merchandising and other forms of promotion to bring in additional revenue. They built on strategies developed in the 1920s that used film stars to sell consumer goods.[68] Cartoon characters promoted every kind of merchandise imaginable, including books, pins, toys, balloons, door-knob hangers, records, shoes, stationery, clothes, dishes, and pajamas.[69] In describing the campaign to support its since-forgotten character Scrappy, Columbia Pictures said it intended "to sell Scrappy by building him into the life of juvenile audiences everywhere. With its tremendous number of merchandise licensees, it is Columbia's boast that armies of children eat, sleep, wear and live Scrappy in a 24-hour a day promotion that never ends."[70] Some of this promotional activity was coordinated through clubs aimed at children. In the 1930s, there were over three hundred Popeye Clubs from coast to coast that Paramount claimed attracted a quarter million young fans.[71] Disney in particular won applause for its ability to integrate the timing of new films with the release of new consumer products. The head of the company's licensing division, Kay Kamen, published regular catalogs listing all the merchandise available for the company's films and characters. In 1938 alone, one hundred manufacturers contracted with Disney to produce licensed merchandise.[72]

The inability to recoup production costs from rental fees also pushed cartoon producers to innovate. Trade papers suggested that some of the changes introduced in this period, including sound and color, resulted in part from the need to compete with double features, as *Film Daily*, for example, announced in its headline "Short Subject Producers Pioneered in Color to Offset Double Features."[73] Warner Bros.' switch to using oil paints instead of watercolors for backgrounds, new methods of photography and music scoring at MGM, and even Disney's development of the multiplane camera were portrayed as efforts to remain competitive in the double-feature environment.[74]

Some animation producers in this period began to develop feature-length films. In December 1937, Walt Disney released *Snow White and the Seven Dwarfs*, the first animated feature to come out of Hollywood. The film was an enormous box office success, grossing eight million dollars during its first run, and its popularity inspired Disney to plan an ambitious slate of other feature-length productions, including *Pinocchio* (1940), *Dumbo* (1941), and *Bambi* (1942).[75] Features were more profitable than short cartoons because animation companies could charge the higher distribution fees that full-length films commanded and could set more conditions on their exhibition. In its distribution agreements for *Pinocchio*, for example, Disney specified that the film had to be exhibited as a single feature and not as part of a double bill and that the rental fee would be 50 percent of the gross.[76] Other cartoon producers followed their lead: the Fleischers debuted *Gulliver's Travels* in 1940 and *Mr. Bugs Goes to Town* in 1941, but these films did not match Disney's success at the box office, and their failure led Paramount to cancel its distribution agreement with the Fleischers.[77]

The situation of cartoon producers improved with the signing of the Consent Decree of 1940. During the 1930s, film studios required theater owners to rent films in blocks of five, rather than individually, and often before they had even seen the films, a practice known as **blind bidding**. Exhibitors argued that they screened double features as a way to use up films of inferior quality that distributors forced them to rent. For this reason, some cartoon producers felt that blind bidding and **block booking** made it more difficult for short films, such as cartoons, to gain screen time. In response to complaints from independent theater owners, the federal government carried out several investigations during the 1930s as part of the Roosevelt administration's antitrust efforts.[78] In 1940, the government issued a consent decree that required studios to offer blocks of no more than five feature films and to allow exhibitors to see them in advance.[79] Another provision of the decree stipulated that distributors could not force theater owners to rent short films as a condition for obtaining features. These provisions meant that the 1940 antitrust decree improved the status of cartoons in several ways.

To avoid charges that they were forcing shorts on exhibitors, distributors decided to sell them separately and organized separate sales forces to promote them.[80] The *Motion Picture Herald* found that "because of the consent decree's proviso that shorts can no longer be forced with features, the majors are going out to actually sell shorts, with special plans and promotions."[81] Even though the decree did not require distributors to screen shorts in advance, some began to do so. Warner Bros. held special trade shows for shorts, including cartoons, and Paramount offered sneak previews of its upcoming season of shorts and shared information about audience reactions with exhibitors.[82] Exhibitors had long urged distributors to give shorts the same level of publicity that features received, and finally they responded.[83] Distributors began to offer theater owners press books, display material, mats, and newspaper campaigns. The *Motion Picture Herald* noted that "in many cases, this is the first time in a long, long time, if ever, any such effort has been made in behalf of the short subject."[84]

Paramount, the studio that distributed the Fleischers' Superman and Popeye cartoons, illustrated this new attitude toward cartoons. On April 30, 1941, the studio took out a four-page ad in *Film Daily* to outline the steps it was taking to promote its cartoons (fig. 2.7). A letter from the general sales manager to exhibitors in the United States and Canada announced that Paramount had created a separate sales department for short subjects and newsreels and was conducting a nationwide survey to find out what kind of shorts exhibitors wanted to. The studio planned to change its production program to meet those interests. Paramount

FIGURE 2.7: Paramount promotes its Fleischer cartoons to exhibitors. *Film Daily*, April 30, 1941. Courtesy Media History Digital Library.

also allocated more money for national publicity and exploitation and set up special departments in those divisions exclusively for shorts.[85] As a result of the consent decree, then, studios that distributed cartoons launched intensive efforts to promote them.

In this new environment, distributors found that it was easier to promote shorts with familiar names because they had a large pre-sold audience.[86] The new exhibition circumstances favored cartoons that featured popular characters in established series, such as the Fleischer Brothers Superman and Popeye characters and Disney's Mickey Mouse and Donald Duck.[87] Superman and Popeye, for instance, had built a loyal following from readers of newspaper comics and comic books, radio dramatizations, merchandise, and children's clubs.[88] Trade papers often pointed to the Disney studio as setting the paradigm for this level of promotion. Some of its cartoons were timed for release during changes of season or for holidays, and the studio organized merchandising tie-ins and promotions weeks ahead of time.[89]

Despite their popularity, cartoons faced many challenges during the 1930s and 1940s. The popularity of double bills meant that cartoons had to compete for space at many movie theaters. Animation studios did not earn back their cost of production from renting films to exhibitors, so they added color and music to attract audiences and packaged their shorts into feature-length programs known as **pack-**

age films. Merchandise promoting cartoon characters also opened up new revenue streams, and government antitrust efforts spurred studios to promote cartoons with more energy and creativity than ever before. To control costs and keep theaters supplied with films, cartoon companies also carefully examined their work processes to increase efficiency. During the 1930s and 1940s, animation production became a highly specialized and very controlled environment.

Animation and World War II

World War II created challenges for animation studios but also inspired them to find creative ways to support the war effort. Famous characters, such as Mickey Mouse and Donald Duck, did their part in films and special projects for the military. Cartoon studios changed their work processes to cope with shortages of raw materials and the loss of male staffers to the draft. In the early 1940s, most animators were male, and many of them were draft age. As the war expanded, more and more studios lost trained staff members to the military. The Disney studio alone lost nearly one-third of its top personnel to the service.[90] The shortage of men meant that women were asked to take on greater responsibilities within animation production. During the war, women received opportunities to work as inbetweeners, for example, rather than only in ink and paint.[91] Thousands of new soldiers needed to learn their responsibilities fast, and the government turned to cartoons for a new kind of training film. The widespread use of animated films for instruction during the war led some producers to think about a new kind of visual education after the war. As with World War I (see chapter 1), both in the United States and overseas, the function and importance of animation expanded during wartime.

Even before Japan's attack on Pearl Harbor in December 1941, some cartoon producers were already involved in the war efforts of other countries.[92] The Disney studio offers an exemplary illustration of the range of ways that animators became involved. In April 1941, Lockheed commissioned the Disney studio, its neighbor in Burbank, to make the employee training film *Four Methods of Flush Riveting* and later screened the film for government executives. On the basis of that film, according to *Fortune* magazine, the Canadian government commissioned Disney to develop films that would boost the sale of war bonds and savings certificates in that country. Films such as *All Together, The Thrifty Pig,* and *Seven Wise Dwarfs* featured well-known Disney characters, including Donald Duck, Pinocchio, and Snow White, marching and singing in support of Canada. The success of these films in turn led U.S. Secretary of the Treasury Henry Morgenthau to commission *The New Spirit* (1942), a short in which Donald Duck demonstrated the need to pay income tax to support the U.S. war effort (see fig. 2.4).[93] During this same period, according to the *Los Angeles Times*, Disney was also producing twenty-five short films for the Navy that taught how to distinguish U.S. planes from those of the enemy.[94] It is estimated that these military contract projects accounted for as much as 93 percent of the studio's output from 1942 to 1945.[95]

To complete such a wide range of projects, Disney and other studios had to ramp up the pace of production. During the 1930s, the studio took up to three years to create one of its cartoon features, but by the end of 1943, it could create a full-length film in only two to three months.[96] To speed up the pace of production, the studio extended its work week from five days to six, and the entire staff worked three hours of overtime on Tuesday and Thursday evenings.[97] In 1940 and 1941, Disney also created individual production units for each of its characters in order to improve efficiency and concentrate expertise. One group of animators focused on Donald Duck cartoons, while others focused on Goofy or Pluto. These units enabled animators to focus on particular stories and characters and to work with a group of colleagues consistently. The director of each of these units gave Walt Disney weekly reports so that he could track the progress of each of their projects.[98] Disney was not alone in changing its work processes. Walter Lantz started to undertake time and motion studies in 1944 to develop an incentive plan to speed up production.[99] Hugh Harmon at MGM and Leon Schlesinger at Warner Bros. also closely analyzed their production methods to speed up the production of government films.[100]

These detailed assessments of work processes enabled studios to shorten the time it took to create an animated film. At the Lantz studio, for example, animators used paper **cutouts** instead of watercolors for backgrounds to eliminate complex designs. Lantz's animation staff also used the rotoscope more often for sequences that involved human movement.[101] The Disney studio reused and reworked footage from its earlier films for the Canadian war bonds projects. In *Seven Wise Dwarfs* (Disney, 1941), the dwarfs march directly from the diamond mine to the bank to buy war bonds. The soundtrack was changed as well so that the dwarfs sing, "Heigh ho, heigh ho, we all must help, you know." Similarly, *The Thrifty Pig* reuses sequences and music from Disney's 1933 hit *The Three Little Pigs*. This time the practical pig argues, "We'll be safe from the Big Bad Wolf if you lend your savings." Disney also used diagrams, simple color block backgrounds, and fewer drawings altogether to shorten production time.[102]

These changes enabled the rapid production of training films the military needed. The opening frames of *Four Methods of Flush Riveting*, for example, announce that the film displays the "quickest and cheapest" method to apply animation to national defense training. The film explains how to rivet pieces of metal together so that the bolts do not stick out and cause the plane to drag in the wind. The film uses simple diagrams with little movement except for arrows and numbers added to illustrate its points. A male voice-over provides all the explanatory information, rather than complicated drawings. *Stop That Tank!* (Disney, 1942) uses music, bright colors, and a caricature of Hitler to engage its audience. While Hitler babbles, written titles on the screen translate the sounds he makes into semi-coherent English. After three minutes of humorous animation, the film switches to live-action footage that uses voice-over to explain how to operate an anti-tank rifle. Close-ups draw attention to specific features of the weapon. At Disney, the layout and special-effects departments faced significant challenges. Films about torpedoes or ships often involved parts that moved in different directions and at different rates of speed, which meant multiple camera exposures for each scene. The special-effects department had to combine live-action, animation, and sometimes three-dimensional models in one shot.[103] One studio writer summed up the general challenge Disney faced by noting that "before December 7th, we were concerned chiefly with making Mickey Mouse cleverer, Donald Duck more captivating. Now it is our job to help simplify the mass production of men and implements for war."[104]

Other films aimed at military personnel discussed how to maintain personal health and hygiene on the war front. In 1945, Hugh Harmon, formerly of the MGM animation unit, released the Commandments for Health series for the Navy. Featuring Private McGillicuddy, films in the series explained the importance of clean drinking water and mess gear, latrine safety, personal hygiene, and the need to avoid native foods, for "many native foods contain poisons more treacherous than a Japanese warlord." The films were in black-and-white and used minimal movement. The action proceeds in short four- to five-second sequences linked by cuts or **wipes** that replace the continuous movement of traditional animation. A male voice-over provides humor and a note of sarcasm as it gives advice.[105] Similarly, Walter Lantz's *Enemy Bacteria* (1945) reminds doctors of the importance of scrubbing up before surgery. The film features Mel Blanc as the voice of germs that encourages doctors to take shortcuts in their routine. "What's a few thousand germs more or less?" But the audience soon learns that taking such a shortcut can lead to the patient developing a serious, disabling infection.[106]

In addition to these productions for the U.S. government, cartoon producers continued to produce entertainment shorts for home-front audiences that featured famous characters in war-related situations. Disney's *The Vanishing Private* (1942) employed the traditional "hand of the artist" motif to show how Donald Duck makes himself disappear when he tries to disguise a tank with camouflage paint. The Fleischers' Superman cartoons portrayed the hero combatting threats at home and abroad: industrial saboteurs in *Destruction, Inc.* (1942), the Japanese in *Japoteurs* (1942) and *The Eleventh Hour* (1942), and Nazi collaborators in *Jungle Drums* (1943). MGM director Tex Avery satirized both Disney's three little pigs and Adolf Hitler through the character of Adolf Wolf in *Blitz Wolf* (1942). Other films evoked the war without making it the focus of the narrative, such as William Hanna and Joseph Barbera's *The Yankee Doodle Mouse* (MGM, 1943), in which Tom and Jerry chased each other with objects that mimic airplanes and jeeps. In some films, anti-Japanese attitudes veered into racism. Such shorts as *Bugs Bunny Nips the Nips* (Warner Bros., 1944) caricatured the Japanese in pejorative terms.[107]

In addition to entertaining audiences, some of these cartoons also reminded viewers how they could support the war effort. Lantz's *Ration Bored* (Universal, 1943) stressed the need to conserve gas and tires by showing Woody Woodpecker doing the opposite. He attempts to fill his car's gas tank by siphoning fuel from cars in a used car lot. One of them happens to be a police car and a chase ensues.[108] Terrytoons' *All Out for V* (Twentieth Century-Fox, 1942) showed various forest creatures working together to collect scrap metal, manufacture equipment, and prepare against bombers. One animal paints a blackout curtain over cottage windows and even the crescent moon. *Scrap for Victory* (1943) showed soldiers calling home directly from a battleground to request more scrap metal, and the home front responds by collecting everything from toothpaste tubes and fishhooks to birdcages.[109]

In 1941, Nelson Rockefeller, the Coordinator for Inter-American Affairs, invited Walt Disney to serve as a goodwill ambassador for the United States in South America.[110] The invitation enabled Disney and some of his animators to travel to several countries in Central and South America to collect ideas that could serve as the basis for cartoons. The extended trip is documented in the documentary *Walt and El Grupo* (Disney, 2010), which shows the animators drawing and painting the dances, costumes, and scenery of Mexico, Argentina, Brazil, and other countries. Their work became the basis of two feature films, *Saludos Amigos*, (Disney, 1942), a package of four short films, and *The Three Caballeros* (Disney, 1944), which combined animation and live-action to show Donald Duck enjoying Latin culture and Latin women. For today's critics, the films invoke stereotypical attitudes toward Latin culture, treating it as an exotic Other, yet they also attest to the international recognition that the Disney studio enjoyed in the early 1940s.[111]

The training and propaganda films that animators developed during World War II earned the admiration of the government and the public.[112] Animators' efforts to educate military personnel and civilians demonstrated that cartoons could entertain as well as inform. By 1944, as the war in Europe was drawing to a close, short films, such as cartoons, had begun to replace the second feature on many double bills.[113] Raw material shortages, combined with the block-of-five limit in the consent decree, reduced the number of feature films that studios released and opened up space for cartoons in many theaters. During the war, first-run theaters in major cities adopted a policy of running a single feature with carefully selected shorts, and by the end of 1945, second-run neighborhood theaters had begun to follow this practice as well.[114] There were also more contracts stipulating that certain films must be played as singles and requiring shorts to accompany them.[115] By the end of 1946, first-run theaters in large cities were showing more single-feature bills than at any time in the previous five years, a situation that favored short films.[116]

Building on this momentum, animation producers announced ambitious plans to make more cartoons—and more cartoons in color—than ever before.[117] Exhibitors and distributors supported them by increasing advertising and publicity budgets and by licensing animated characters in a variety of merchandise items.[118] By January 1945, bookings for short films were running 15 to 20 percent ahead of previous years.[119] To meet this demand, some animation producers, including Fleischer and MGM, announced plans to expand their staff.[120]

Despite this enthusiasm for cartoons, technical and financial challenges continued to plague cartoon producers. Even though exhibitors were eager to screen more cartoons, there were substantial delays in delivery. A shortage of photographic equipment and raw stock, combined with bottlenecks at Technicolor labs, meant that in 1944–1945 many short film producers fell six months behind in their releasing schedules.[121] Exhibitors continued to refuse to pay higher fees for short films. The ongoing gap between the cost of making cartoons and the rental fees they earned widened even more during the war. Cartoon shorts that cost $12,500 to produce in 1941 cost $26,000 to $35,000 in 1946, double or triple the cost, but rental fees increased by only 15 percent in that time. Animation producers absorbed price increases for raw film stock, color processing, new equipment, and salary increases for musicians and guild craft members, but rental fees barely budged.[122] Although animation studios increased the efficiency of their work processes during the war, the changes were not enough to compensate for cost increases at every stage of production.

The continuing inability of animation producers to earn back their costs and the uncertainty around antitrust decisions created an environment that led to dramatic fluctuations in cartoon production. In August 1946, Disney announced that it would lay off 450 employees, nearly half its staff.[123] A few months later, in November 1946, the studio announced that it was thinking of dropping shorts altogether because they could not bring in more rental income.[124] At the end of 1946, both Paramount and RKO announced that they were going to reevaluate the cost and quality of the short films they distributed.[125] Walter Lantz, the president of the Cartoon Producers Association, gave an interview to the Associated Press in which he said that the cartoon field "was on the verge of extinction."[126] After the Hollywood box office peaked in 1946, ticket sales to all films fell off by 30 percent in 1947 and continued to drop in 1948.[127] In early 1948, MGM cut its payroll by 40 percent, Columbia fired 25 percent of its employees, and RKO shut down production for a week.[128] Paramount stopped releasing its Little Lulu series, and Columbia discontinued its Screen Gems cartoons.[129] In 1948, *Film Daily* reported that the number of cartoons produced annually had dropped by half over the previous year.[130] Soon the writing was on the wall: **theatrical shorts**, including studio-era cartoons, would become a thing of the past. But commercial animation in the industrial mode did not disappear after the demise of the theatrical model; it simply adapted its mode of production to meet the economic constraints and distribution venues available to it. This transformation would become known as limited animation.

3

LIMITED ANIMATION, 1947–1989   Kevin Sandler

1946. The moment, according to Charles Affron and Mirella Jona Affron in *Best Years: Going to the Movies, 1945–1946*, that "Hollywood enjoyed the spectacular popularity guaranteed by its unrivaled position in the entertainment industry and by the advanced stage of its own artistic and industrial development."[1] Certainly, it was the most successful year in the Golden Age of Hollywood, the period generally considered to have lasted from the birth of sound in 1927 through to the late 1950s. Movie attendance peaked at 90 million customers a week as roughly 60 percent of Americans viewed some combination of a feature film, newsreel, short subject, and, of course, an animated short. The bulk of animated theatrical shorts in the studio era was produced by houses affiliated with or owned by the major vertically integrated, and often financially solvent, film studios. A spectator in 1946 might have stumbled into a theater screening the RKO-distributed Walt Disney short *Donald's Double Trouble* (King, 1946), the Warner Bros. short *Baseball Bugs* (Freleng, 1946), the MGM Tom and Jerry short *The Milky Waif* (Hanna and Barbera, 1946), or any other cartoon from Twentieth Century-Fox (Terrytoons), Universal (Walter Lantz), Columbia (Screen Gems), and Paramount (Famous Studios).

Besides Paramount's releases of George Pal's stop-motion puppet animation (Puppetoons), the cartoons of this period were essentially all hand-drawn animation on transparent sheets of celluloid, or cels. By employing an assembly-line system of mass production—as described in chapters 1 and 2—to produce this form of animation, the studios unwittingly naturalized the superiority of full animation over another stylistic tendency in cel animation: so-called planned or limited animation. In *Art and Motion*, Maureen Furniss distinguishes between a full and limited animation aesthetic around four criteria: "the movement of images, the metamorphosis of images, the number of images, and the dominance of visual and aural components."[2] In general, she states, full animation involves constant movement accomplished by creating approximately twenty-four images for each second of running time, what is known as "on ones"—to match the standard twenty-four-frame-per-second projection rate for motion-picture films. Full animation also employs a metamorphosis of shapes—movement along the x-axis (horizontal), y-axis (vertical), and z-axis (toward and away from the foreground), where characters frequently change proportions. In contrast, limited animation features much less shape-shifting and fluidity in character movement. This aesthetic also tends to include a higher number of cycles—the re-looping of a series of movement—as animation is done on threes (eight images per second), fours (six images per second), or even higher to reduce the number of drawings required. Extensive camera movement, such as panning over or **zooming** into the artwork, often enlivens an otherwise still image; as in the early period (see chapter 1), holds were used liberally in limited animation. Given these differences, full animation typically placed a greater emphasis on visuals to achieve narrative clarity, while limited animation relied to a much greater extent on sound, such as dialogue, music, or voice-over narration.

The Big Five and Little Three's control over the film industry's distribution and exhibition sectors in the domestic marketplace papered over the expensive production of full animation during the studio era. However, within a couple of years after World War II, the American movie industry went into an economic tailspin that would lead to the gradual demise of the theatrical animated cartoon (see chapter 2). Throughout the 1950s and into the 1960s, the studios did one or all of the following things regarding their animated shorts: they closed their animation units, curtailed their yearly animation output, or employed greater use of limited animation techniques as a means of reducing labor costs and cutting production costs.

In the wake of these transformations in the market, limited animation became more or less the dominant approach to commercial animation production in the United States, particularly in television. Instead of depicting the full range of motion as full animation frequently did, limited animation aimed at reducing in-betweening and the overall number of drawings and relying more on abstraction, symbolism, camera techniques, holds, cycles, and other labor-saving devices.

New production houses, many of which employed former studio animators, sprung up to create innumerable television series and commercials that used limited-animation cel techniques as an aesthetic choice, economic necessity, or a combination of the two. At the same time, the limited style proliferated in movie theaters, being adopted by Hollywood studios (e.g., Disney and Warner Bros.), smaller production houses affiliated with Hollywood studios (e.g., UPA and DePatie-Freleng), and independent companies (e.g., Hubley and Ernest Pintoff), whose shorts were nominated for—and sometimes won—Academy Awards. While several of these companies had a presence in both the television and theatrical markets, the bulk of animation production during this time was for television. As Paul Wells notes, "Arguably, animation as an industry only survived in the United States because of its albeit 'reduced' presence on television." Disney, Fleischer, and Warner Bros. made some use of limited animation during the studio era, but it became ubiquitous in U.S. television between 1947 and 1980. An examination of the key animation houses of this period, especially United Productions of America (UPA), Hanna-Barbera, Jay Ward Productions, and Filmation, reveals the industrial and institutional conditions that gave rise to cel-based, limited animation.

The Emergence of Limited Animation on Television

The transformation of the U.S. motion-picture industry and the emergence of tele-vision as a new technology of entertainment after World War II forced producers to adjust or abandon long-standing organizational and aesthetic principles of full animation cultivated during the studio system. The limited mode of cel animation—one associated with the restriction of character movement, simpler or formulaic character design, and abstract or minimal background design—certainly provided a solution to budgetary constraints faced by several 1950s film and television producers. However, limited animation had a political dimension as well. The Disney strike of 1941—an early sign of the labor troubles to come—did much to alienate animators not just against a mode of production or division of labor but against an approach to animation: specifically, Disney's idea of what animation should be. Two former Disney employees, John Hubley and Zachary Schwartz, penned a manifesto to this effect in 1946; the pair had become employ-ees of the left-leaning United Productions of America (UPA) after making train-ing and industrial films during World War II. They declared: "We have found that the medium of animation has become a new language. It is no longer the vaudev-ille of pigs and bunnies. Nor is it the mechanical diagram, the photographed charts of the old 'training film.' We have found that line, shape, color, and symbols in movement can represent the essence of an idea, can express it humorously, with force, with clarity. The method is only dependent upon the idea to be expressed.

And a suitable form can be found for any idea."[3] Limited animation became that "suitable form" for UPA and other studios principally as part of a larger modernist project that spread throughout the industry in the early to mid-1950s. Simultaneously, other companies, such as Television Arts Productions or Terrytoons, embraced this stripped-down form of cartooning more for commercial rather than aesthetic or political reasons.

The nascent medium of television was a haven for the more commercial approach to limited animation. A few series emerging during the early days of television reveal the first efforts at determining the tools, techniques, and division of labor that would constitute animation production for television. *Tele-Comics* (syndicated, 1949, then as *NBC Comics*, 1950–1951), which holds the distinction as one of the first cartoon series produced for television, has virtually no animation. Distributed by Vallee Video (entertainer Rudy Vallee's company) and produced by a former film executive (Don Dewar), former Disney animator (Jack Boyd), and a veteran newspaper cartoonist (Dick Moores), the fifteen-minute-long series consisted of four three-minute serialized stories under such titles as the detective drama *Danny March* or the prizefighting saga *Kid Champion*. Filmed sequentially as a series of comic-strip drawings using voice-over narration and dialogue with an occasional animated effect, this **stop-and-go technique**, as it was known, employed several cost-effective storytelling strategies that would become common to limited animation: camera pans and zooms to add movement, the reuse of drawings, and reliance on sound effects.[4] *Winky Dink and You* (CBS, 1953–1957) offered only slightly more animation in its Saturday-morning time slot. Created by New York advertising "mad men" Harry Pritchett and Edwin Wyckoff and produced and hosted by Jack Barry (who would later host such game shows as *Twenty-One* and *The Joker's Wild*), *Winky Dink and You* was a low-tech children's series that featured the cartoon adventures of a star-headed boy named Winky Dink. The action was interspersed with in-studio comic sketches and antics. The boys and girls at home were asked by Jack Barry to help Winky Dink out of an inescapable situation by drawing whatever the character needed (e.g., a door, ladder, or parachute). Children accomplished this via a fifty-cent "Official Winky Dink Kit" available through mail order from CBS; they placed a transparent cellophane screen covering, or "Magic Window," over the television screen, drew the necessary apparatus with the "Magic Crayon" directly over it, and then cleaned the screen with a "Magic Cloth."[5] Only thirty or so different, often recycled drawings made up the animation in an episode of *Winky Dink and You*, largely now considered to be a crass experiment in children's programming. Nevertheless, *Winky Dink and You* served as an early example of the symbiotic relationship between limited-animation production and marketing, a marriage soon to be dominated by breakfast cereal and toy companies by the end of the decade.

Crusader Rabbit (syndicated, 1950–1951) and *Tom Terrific* (CBS, 1957–1959) served as a primitive template for the economics and aesthetics of limited anima-

FIGURE 3.1: A single drawing to suggest Crusader's motion of painting the name of a ship in *Crusader Rabbit* (1950–1951).

tion on television that would take hold in the late 1950s. Jay Ward and Alex Anderson wrote and sketched the black-and-white *Crusader Rabbit* at their company, Television Arts Productions Inc., from Ward's garage in San Francisco, along with theatrical "novelty" short subjects producer Jerry Fairbanks, who handled the postproduction (filming, editing, sound) from his Los Angeles studio. Fairbanks also secured the Carnation Milk Company as a sponsor and then sold the show to individual NBC stations with built-in commercials, a method known as **spot-marketing**. After a series of test screenings throughout 1949, *Crusader Rabbit* finally premiered on August 1, 1950, at 6:00 P.M. on station KNBH (NBC Hollywood) in Los Angeles (fig. 3.1).[6]

Starring a smart, pugnacious do-gooder rabbit and his big, dumb, strong sidekick Ragland "Rags" T. Tiger on several "crusades" for truth and justice, the satirical *Crusader Rabbit* featured five-minute serialized episodes with cliffhanger endings as narrator Roy Whaley usually concluded each installment with the ominous phrase, "Uh-oh, this looks like the end of our heroes." The show's miniscule budget of approximately $2,500 for a nineteen-and-a-half-minute cartoon set great constraints on its design and movement during the early days of television. "At the rock bottom prices the networks or stations were able to pay for programming then," stated Fairbanks, "we had to develop shortcuts. *Crusader Rabbit* was very limited. They often contained fewer than four cels per foot compared to ten times or more for full animation. [A foot of animation is equal to the length of sixteen frames of 35-mm film. Or one second of animation equals twenty-four frames or one-and-a-half feet of 35-mm film.] We would simply plan a story line so we could reuse some of the animation with a different background."[7] For instance, a single pose of Crusader or Rags would often last up to five seconds without additional animation. And even then, said Ward biographer Keith Scott, "Movement was mainly limited to stationary cutout figures with mouth movements, eye shifts, and various changes of expression created on cel overlays."[8] Such elements are clearly evident in a twelve-second shot toward the end of the first episode of the second crusade, "Crusader Rabbit vs. the Pirates." After Crusader and Rags discover a newspaper clipping stating, "Pittsburgh Pirates Stronger Than Ever!" the narrator informs the viewer, "Of course, to hunt pirates one needs a seaworthy vessel, so our two friends quickly set about fashioning one from materials provided by the garbage scow." However, just a single drawing of the ship's construction accompanies this narration. The only movement in the shot comes from a four-frame animated cycle of Rags sawing a mast followed by a camera tilt and pan across that drawing to a motionless Crusader painting the name of the ship, the "Robert E. Leak." The overall effect of shots like this in *Crusader Rabbit*, as Ward himself notes, is one of an "animated comic strip," and indeed, the series does feel more like the narrated storyboards of *Tele-Comics* than a cartoon itself.[9]

Eight years later, the cartoon serial *Tom Terrific* exhibited many of the same tendencies as *Crusader Rabbit*. Produced by the Terrytoons studio, bought by CBS-TV in 1955, each of the twenty-six episodes contained five installments and ran once per day, Monday through Friday, exclusively on the network's daily, live-action children's series *Captain Kangaroo*. Unlike its theatrical Terrytoons predecessors, *Tom Terrific* had greatly diminished resources, forcing the newly installed studio head Gene Deitch to devise and implement cost-cutting animation strategies for this series about an energetic, gee-whiz boy who could transform himself into anything thanks to his magical, funnel-shaped "thinking cap." In his book, *How to Succeed in Animation*, Deitch recalls the simplified and threadbare style of the transparent, black-and-white drawings against a sparse background in *Tom Terrific*: "I wanted to use as much real animation as possible, taking advantage of the large Terrytoons staff of animators, and save money on the everything else. I went so far as to eliminate opaquing the cels, letting Tom and the other characters be transparent, and making the backgrounds simple enough so it wouldn't matter."[10] The prominence of full animation above any other aesthetics in *Tom Terrific* is present in chapter 1 of "Robinsnest Crusoe." In this episode, Pittsburgh the Pirate—apparently, a popular pun of the day—captures Tom and Manfred with a trawler and brings them aboard his ship. The song and dance number between Pittsburgh and his parrot contains no instrumental accompaniment, few or zero background drawings of the ship, and sparse black-and-white outlines of the characters (fig. 3.2). Occasionally, though, their dance performance tends toward fuller animation, an aesthetic forsaken in *Crusader Rabbit*. Despite not having elaborate budgets and time for full animation, Deitch's

FIGURE 3.2: A full animation dance number in an otherwise limitedly animated *Tom Terrific* (1957–1959).

cost-saving aesthetics, like those of Ward and Anderson for *Crusader Rabbit*, demonstrated a range of possibilities for television series creation under the limited mode of production. By the end of the 1950s, independent producers embraced and refined cost-saving "shortcuts" for their own series: the energetic narration, zany sound effects, dynamic camera movements (zooming, panning, shaking), expressive musical score, witty dialogue, and resonant vocal performances, in addition to the standardized cycle moments, close-ups, reaction shots, and mouth and eye movements.

At the same time that independent television producers and theatrical animation units gradually employed more limited-animation tools and techniques as cost-cutting measures for cartoon comedies and adventures, another simplified animation style influenced by mid-century modernism spread throughout the film and television industries during the decade. The arrival of this modern art sensibility to style, content, and technical construction in the American animated cartoon—present even in *Tom Terrific*—is generally attributed to United Productions of America. In their early union and governmental work during World War II, UPA's left-leaning employees, many of whom had fine arts ambitions, experimented with storytelling and design, partly as a result of economic constraints but often in direct philosophical contrast to the fluidly animated, rounded realism of Disney and the hyper-violent anarchy of Warner Bros. "UPA's cartoonists," Dan Bashara observes, "built their reputations by agitating for a simple, bolder graphic approach to animation not because it was less expensive, but because it was better suited to its time, and to the social, cultural, and visual concerns of America in the postwar era than was Disney's three-dimensional, flesh-and-blood naturalism."[11] Such traditional studio animation tended toward comic-strip simplicity in terms of drawing and characterization, wrote Hubley, and it was his hope that artists could "exploit the primary property of animation—the symbolic condensation of transformation of energy—to describe with great sensitivities the complexities of the inner self."[12] UPA's insistence on adapting limited-animation techniques for the purposes of psychological insight rather than entertainment aligned with a new postwar modernity; Bashara further argues that its approach echoed an earlier modernist moment known as precisionism. Its graphic principles—blurring abstraction and representation—lent UPA's limited animation a distinctive look: "hard-edged, simplified forms; bold, unmodulated colors; an evacuation of detail; a minimalist environmental surround often reduced to geometric patterns or even a flat color plane; the avoidance of rounded, centerline character design; and a relaxed (at best) implementation of Renaissance perspective."[13] Other aesthetic hallmarks of UPA's style included shooting on fours and eights rather than on ones and twos, drawing strong expressive poses rather than animating squash-and-stretch motion, and erasing spatial distance between characters and background rather than reproducing more traditional approaches to perspective. The result: animation techniques subordinated to a sparser, abstract, modern design.

UPA's most celebrated theatrical short, *Gerald McBoing Boing* (Cannon, 1950), demonstrates its use of the limited mode to advance a new visual language of animation in the modern art style. Originally created by Theodor Geisel (better known as Dr. Seuss) for a phonograph record, *Gerald McBoing Boing* tells a story, through rhyming couplets, of a little boy who emits sound effects, such as "Boing! Boing!" each time he opens his mouth, much to the chagrin of his parents, doctor, and teacher. Rejected by his peers, Gerald runs away from home only to be discovered by a radio station owner, who hires him to perform all the effects for a radio drama. Now that his speech impediment is a benefit to society, Gerald becomes a celebrity and is cherished by his parents. Distributed by Columbia Pictures, *Gerald McBoing Boing* partly communicates the emotional stakes of its drama through the utter simplicity—and cost-saving measures—of its production design. Flattened character designs and stripped-down layouts (the barest of outlines define Gerald and his surroundings), borderless backgrounds (no walls, floors, ground levels, or skies despite the presence of rugs, window, chandeliers, and snow), and stylized, limited movement (little in-betweening in posture, talking, and walking) are streamlined but expressive. For its pictorial representation of space, Robert "Bobe" Cannon developed a "continuous path of action," as designer Bill Hurtz explained, using a lot of "camera tricks in lieu of animation. We were very sensitive to the means the camera afforded us," he said.[14] For instance, at one point Gerald runs away from home, his journey

FIGURE 3.3: Modernist limited animation in the Academy Award–winning theatrical short *Gerald McBoing Boing* (1950).

sparsely indicated only through single props against a neutral background: his window, the fence of his yard, a forest tree, a town light post—all in a single, time-compressed, five-second shot, before cutting to his arrival at a railroad crossing sign (fig. 3.3). All the while, Gail Kubik's pulsating and dissonant woodwind-and-horns score and Jules Engel's and Herb Klynn's color scheme of a black-and-blue snowy background accentuates Gerald's distress. On one hand, this approach to rendering four different moments within a single shot meant that the filmmakers did not need to redraw backgrounds and layout. On the other hand, it is a conscious, graphic application of modernist techniques as foreground action and background design together overtly communicate a pointed, emotional value well beyond what classic Hollywood animation was capable.[15] In addition, rather than "pigs and bunnies" as characters, here a human boy overcomes his "disability" to become a valued member of society. That year, *Gerald McBoing Boing* won the Academy Award for Best Short Subject—Cartoon, establishing UPA as a force in animation and heralding a shift toward the limited mode in the industry dominated by modern art sensibility in the 1950s.[16]

Soon enough, UPA innovations in modern art would be adopted by Warner Bros., MGM, and even Disney in a variety of media. For instance, Disney's theatrical shorts *Toot, Whistle, Plunk and Boom* (1953) and *Paul Bunyan* (1958), theatrical features *Sleeping Beauty* (1959) and *101 Dalmatians* (1961), three space-travel television episodes of *Disneyland* (1954–1958), and the redesigned Mickey Mouse commercials for American Motors Nash automobiles all embraced a modern look uncharacteristic of the studio. However, UPA's commitment to using limited animation to advance modernist principles ultimately could not be financially sustained. Despite Columbia paying UPA $27,500 (and later $35,000) per seven-minute cartoon—comparable to a Warner Bros. short and more than a Walter Lantz release—the artists' total commitment to quality made almost every film go over budget due to revisions and other costly changes. UPA was even forced to sell back part their 25 percent share of ownership of each cartoon to Columbia to make up the difference.[17] Had it not been for UPA's thriving commercial studio in New York and its economical and successful star-driven Mr. Magoo series, it is unlikely the studio could have created the small legacy of modern art films it is widely recognized for in the early 1950s. By the time Gerald McBoing Boing last appeared as Tiny Tim in UPA's prime-time *Mr. Magoo's Christmas Special* (NBC, 1962), the mode of production in the film and television industry had changed for animation. Story, layout, and backgrounds that once took six weeks each for a UPA theatrical short, remarks Adam Abraham, were now all completed in two and a half weeks' time.[18] What proved to have the most profound impact on the industry were not theatrical cartoons grounded in modern art and personal expression but low-budget commercial television series using limited-animation techniques that primarily targeted children.

Hanna-Barbera and Limited Animation for Television

The mid- to late 1950s witnessed the loosening grip of the studio style of full animation as the major studio-distributors either closed their animation shorts units or drastically cut costs by reducing the number of releases, firing personnel, or employing more limited-animation tools and techniques. Despite the dwindling theatrical shorts marketplace and because of the developing opportunities in television, established studios adopted the limited mode to varying degrees for their animated theatrical features while newly created independent studios produced limited-animation cartoons. The popularity of theatrical cartoons packages on television among children throughout the 1950s would ultimately attract the most interest from television producers, sponsors, and ad agencies given the industry's growing investment in children as consumers. *Crusader Rabbit* and *Tom Terrific* served as the prototypes for these new series as broadcasters looked for fresh, low-cost programming sources with sponsorship to replace or compete with the syndicated packages of old theatrical shorts, such as Popeye and Bugs Bunny. One company became the symbol for limited animation's commercial viability and aesthetic deficiency: Hanna-Barbera Productions, so successful with MGM's Tom and Jerry series during the studio era, now had to reinvent themselves to break into the television market.

The need to create limited-animation production for television arrived surprisingly swiftly for William Hanna and Joseph Barbera. Despite having won seven Academy Awards for their fully animated Tom and Jerry series in the 1940s and 1950s, MGM decided to shut down their animation unit in May 1957 shortly after nineteen of the film studio's twenty in-house productions posted a combined loss of nearly $16 million for the 1956–1957 season.[19] Given the high costs of producing a slate of seven-minute cartoons per year at $35,000 to $40,000 each, the financially troubled studio realized it could earn more money reissuing its old cartoons to theaters and television rather than producing new ones. In a last-ditch effort, Hanna and Barbera submitted a six-page memo to MGM on how they could retain the unit for television production by cutting costs in half through a system of much-reduced animation: fewer drawings, less painting and inking, and less camera work but still maintaining the same quality background art. MGM's rejection of this demonstration model, recalls Hanna, meant that "producing animation for television was not only our brightest prospect, it was our *only* alternative."[20]

A 1956 deal indirectly launched H-B Enterprises, a television venture jointly owned between Hanna, Barbera, and MGM director George Sidney, whom they befriended on the film *Anchors Aweigh* for which they had furnished Jerry Mouse as a dancing partner for Gene Kelly. Earlier that year, NBC had bought a package of color Screen Gems cartoons from Columbia Pictures, which now used the Screen Gems name for its television subsidiary after closing its own theatrical animation studio in 1946.[21] Screen Gems vice president of sales John H. Mitchell looked for an original television property to bookend these less appealing, older theatrical shorts for a Saturday-morning series. Unhappy with the crude limited animation done for Sam Singer's *Pow Wow the Indian Boy* (1957) that Screen Gems distributed to CBS's *Captain Kangaroo*, Mitchell turned to Hanna and Barbera to do better with the same budget. The result was *Ruff and Reddy*: a color, serialized adventure of a smart and steadfast cat (Ruff) and his brave but not particularly bright canine pal (Reddy). Hanna and Barbera originally pitched the series as a full-animation prospect to MGM but now proposed it at one-tenth the cost of a theatrical short with a budget starting at $2,700 for five, five-minute cartoons. The show's economics permitted only a few drawings per foot of film, about 1,500 colorless outline drawings in pencil test per five-minute episode compared to 25,000 to 40,000 drawings for a Tom and Jerry cartoon.[22] Debuting on December 14, 1957, as the opening and closing acts for a hosted kids show of the same name with General Foods as a sponsor, *Ruff and Reddy* became a hit the following spring as H-B Enterprises successfully demonstrated the feasibility of producing original low-cost animation for television.

The time-saving and labor-saving techniques developed for *Ruff and Reddy* by H-B Enterprises—reincorporated as Hanna-Barbera Productions in 1959— would serve as the studio's mode of production for the next three decades, covering such series as *The Huckleberry Hound Show* (syndicated, 1958–1961), *The Yogi Bear Show* (syndicated, 1961–1962), and *Scooby-Doo, Where Are You!* (CBS,

1969–1971). Given the dismissive connotations of the term "limited animation" with poor quality and unartistic work produced in the more minimalist *Crusader Rabbit* manner at the time—for example, *Ruff and Reddy* contemporaries such as *Bozo: The World's Most Famous Clown* (syndicated, 1958–1962) and *Spunky and Tadpole* (syndicated, 1958–1961)—Hanna-Barbera first described their economical system to the press as **planned animation**.[23] The company also tried to position their method as different than, if not superior to, full-animation techniques. For an article in the *Los Angeles Times* on the series premiere of *The Flintstones* (ABC, 1960–1966), Hanna spun the overall advantages of planned animation: "Take the Disney method—the old movie method. It tried to mirror life. We don't. We spoof reality but we don't mirror it. Our characters don't walk from a scene, they whiz. Movements that took 24 drawings under the old movie system take us four. We just keep the story moving."[24] Longtime H-B animator Jerry Eisenberg does not even recall the term "planned animation" being used around the studio; to him, Hanna-Barbera simply produced limited-animation cartoons.[25] While Hanna-Barbera's cartoons may have been more skillfully designed and animated than other studios, given the number of former MGM and later Disney and Warner Bros. artists on staff, "planned animation" was more a name change and marketing ploy than a real change in production technique. Like its competitors, Hanna-Barbera still had to rely heavily on close-ups and reaction shots, standardized expressions and gestures, repeated cycles of movements and backgrounds, canned soundtracks of music and sound effects, camera movements over static, simple graphic forms, and compartmentalized character designs for a medium demanding a large amount of animation for a relatively small amount of money in a short period of time.

If planned animation signified anything specifically at Hanna-Barbera, it referred to a highly economical and efficient mode of production that streamlined their earlier production methods for full theatrical animation. Stages from storyboarding to animating to soundtrack recording each had to be "planned" in advance to accommodate the much-reduced budget and time limitations per cartoon. Barbera described one such adjustment as simply "[taking] away much of the second half of cartoon production, keeping the finished product more like pose reels, closer to the roughs that he used to produce with such velocity at MGM."[26] A **pose reel** merged a recorded soundtrack with dialogue to a carefully timed compilation of layout drawings, story sketches, and extreme poses—those critical positions of an animated character that depict the extreme accents in its expression or mood, or extreme points in its path of motion. Hanna-Barbera delivered to the network or syndicator essentially these pre-visualized pose reels or nicely illustrated sequences of drawings that suggested a cartoon's action and humor but with little of the time-intensive cel animation, ink-and-paint, and camera work done in the later stages of full-animation production. "We reasoned that by animating only key poses and selected drawings that dramatized or emphasized the cartoon's dialogue," stated Hanna about this process, "we could artfully reduce the overall amount of drawings used in a television cartoon and still produce the convincing illusion of movement in the film."[27] Accordingly, a good percentage of the production budget would be thus allocated to versatile voice-over work and well-written scripts to carry the story in lieu of in-betweening action. Renowned artists Daws Butler and Don Messick—both worked with Hanna and Barbera at MGM—performed the major character voices for the studio's cartoons until the mid-1960s, including *The Huckleberry Hound Show*, *The Quick Draw McGraw Show* (syndicated, 1959–1961), and *The Yogi Bear Show*. Michael Maltese and Warren Foster, the top story men for Chuck Jones's and Isadore "Friz" Freleng's animated short units at Warner Bros., served as Hanna and Barbera's head writers after 1960. These contractual employees kept costs down for Hanna-Barbera while standardizing the voice work and stories for their cartoons.

To evoke a sense of movement or action around these key scenes propelled by dialogue, Hanna-Barbera introduced some efficient animation shortcuts. For instance, instead of redrawing an entire figure for each cel as one did in a fully animated scene, only those body parts that move in planned animation are redrawn: an arm, leg, hand, mouth, or eye (recalling the slash-and-tear technique of early animation—see chapter 1). Characters in the early cartoons, explains longtime Hanna-Barbera animator Iwao Takamoto, all tended to wear neck adornments—bowties (Huckleberry Hound), scarves (Quick Draw McGraw), or neckties (Fred Flintstone)—"so the head could be easily separated onto its own cel without a seam line" while the rest of the body remained intact on another cel. A similar logic, Takamoto states, also applies to the characters' muzzles being of different color from the rest of their face, allowing for only the mouth to be animated.[28] Generally, for any other character movement beyond a walk cycle, Hanna-Barbera had all action take place outside the frame. Scooby-Doo co-creator Joe Ruby, then a sound editor in the early 1960s, remarked: "[Hanna-Barbera] wouldn't show an action. For instance, [a character would] say, 'I am going to go teach him a lesson.' And they would zip off scene and then you would have screen shakes. And that's where we came in. We had to create sound effects that would sound like something was funny happening off scene. And then they would cut to the aftermath of the sound which was a funny picture. So you got the effect that something was happening but they never had to animate it."[29] Such character design—static key poses combined with animated heads to emphasize the cartoon's dialogue—and character action occurring offscreen cut production costs and time immensely.

Additionally, Hanna-Barbera, like other animation and live-action television producers at the time, relied on stock music libraries to economize planned-animation production. Unlike the studio era when such cartoon composers as Carl Stalling produced new seven-minute scores for each cartoon on average every ten days, Hanna-Barbera needed twenty-two minutes of music from a composer for a half-hour show. Be it a seven-minute segment of Augie Doggie and Doggie Daddy from *The Quick Draw McGraw Show* or a thirty-minute single-story-line *Jetsons* episode, a considerable amount of underscore music and sound effects material was required on a weekly basis for several Hanna-Barbera shows from the late 1950s through the 1980s.[30] For the early series, such as *Ruff and Reddy* and *The Huckleberry Hound Show*, musical director and theme composer Hoyt Curtin relied on generic recordings or **needle-drops** licensed from the Hi-Q library of Capitol Records written and arranged largely by William Loose and his collaborator John Seely. "We saved a lot of money that way," said Hanna. "Our editors used to listen to their library of music and pick out things. I remember going down to the Capitol Tower myself to pick out music."[31] For example, "Sheriff Huckleberry," in the first season of *The Huckleberry Hound Show*, opens with "TC-204A: Wistful Comedy," a stock musical cue in the Theme Craft series that underscores the Monument Valley backgrounds while narrator Don Messick intones about the "never-ending battle over good and evil" in the Old West. As Hanna-Barbera became more successful and their budgets increased, the studio phased out the Hi-Q library, and Curtin composed his own melody sets for the series, first for Hanna-Barbera's only theatrical cartoon series, *Loopy De Loop*, in 1959, and then prime time's *The Flintstones*, the Snagglepuss and Yakky Doodle elements of *The Yogi Bear Show* (first aired in 1961), and then for all remaining new cartoons until 1986, except for 1963–1973 when the primary musical director was Ted Nichols.[32] These oft-repeated cues would serve as the musical foundations of Hanna-Barbera shows to follow, a practice, notes Daniel Goldmark, that "helped to *define* the sound of television cartoons" for the next thirty years.[33]

The enduring success of *The Flintstones* certainly helped to establish Hanna-Barbera's dominance in television animation for some time. As the first animated series on television to go beyond the six-or-seven-minute cartoon format, the thirty-minute situation comedy *The Flintstones*, stated Hanna, "required that we retool a lot of our production methods."[34] For non-prime-time syndicated series, such as *The Huckleberry Hound Show* and *The Yogi Bear Show*, all of Hanna-Barbera's animators worked on every show, a system facilitated by the aesthetic homogeneity amid the series and the studio's assembly-line process of animation. Barbera recounts that animators got paid for each foot of film produced, providing "[them] incentive to work at a blazing pace, using all the effective shortcuts their experience commanded."[35] For *The Flintstones*, Hanna-Barbera instead assigned a special corps of writers, artists, animators, and other personnel to work specifically on the series. What amounted to a director-unit production mode (as from the studio era) could not be accomplished, though, on a *Huckleberry Hound* budget; the 8:30 P.M. Friday night slot for *The Flintstones* required greater storytelling sophistication to reach adult audiences than did Hanna-Barbera's syndicated cartoons aimed primarily at children. Consequently, and with financial support from a growing merchandising business and sponsorship from Winston

Cigarettes (Reynolds Tobacco Company) and One-a-Day Vitamins (Miles Laboratories), *The Flintstones* was budgeted three times higher than other Hanna-Barbera shows, at a cost of $65,000 an episode, making it one of the most expensive half-hours on television at that time.[36]

Despite having a higher budget, many of Hanna-Barbera's planned-animation techniques are still present in *The Flintstones*; drawings are still generally shot on twos, and the amount of animated movement is proportionate to the studio's non-prime-time series. However, given four main characters—larger than any cast in the shorter cartoons—and a greater variety in character design and background layout to accommodate more complex storytelling in each episode, *The Flintstones* required more shots and scene changes and therefore extra expense than Hanna-Barbera's syndicated series. Factor in a whole new cue library from music director Hoyt Curtin, first-rate voice talent, and funny scripts to support a satirical vision of a *Honeymooners*-like prehistoric family, and the $65,000 budgets comes into view. For instance, a single writer, Warren Foster, storyboarded and wrote the majority of the first season's twenty-eight episodes after Hanna and Barbera realized they could not write, record dialogue, *and* direct a new episode each week as with their previous programs.[37] Even so, additional sitcom writers had to be hired, and, more than likely, additional artists were needed to turn their stories into storyboards. Furthermore, to meet the deadline of a thirty-minute cartoon per week for twenty-eight straight weeks, Hanna-Barbera had to pay several key animators on staff (e.g., Ed Love, George Nicholas, and Carlo Vinci) to design the characters, all of whom animated in their own style or "off model" from Ed Benedict's original drawings.[38]

Hanna-Barbara sustained this production model for six seasons on *The Flintstones* and likely applied it for its next two prime-time series using the same house style—*Top Cat* (ABC, 1961–1962) and *The Jetsons* (ABC, 1962–1963). Poor ratings led to their cancellation after a single season, but the same cannot be said for *The Adventures of Jonny Quest* (ABC, 1964–1965), Hanna-Barbera's most atypical and ambitious of its four 1960s prime-time series. Inspired by such novels as *Doc Savage* and such radio serials as *Jack Armstrong, All-American Boy*, *Jonny Quest* was Hanna-Barbera's first action-adventure series, requiring expensive new layouts, backgrounds, locations, music, and character models each globetrotting week for its twenty-six-episode season. "It takes four people to lay out *The Flintstones* and 30 to lay out *Johnny*," stated Hanna about the ambitions for the series. "The ratio is more than 4 to 30 for the backgrounds. Two animators are needed for every one on every other show."[39] Also driving up the cost of *Jonny Quest*'s production methods were its aesthetic choices, designed and developed by *The Outlaw Kid* and *The Saint* comic artist Doug Wildey. Fantastic, technological stories of demented scientists, electrical monsters, and oversize carnivorous lizards featuring realistic human characters and action sequences gave *Jonny Quest* a lavishly illustrated visual and live-action dramatic feel unlike any television animated cartoon before it, approaching full animation in artistic ambition and detail.

This kind of quality, however, was prohibitively expensive. Furthermore, nobody at Hanna-Barbera—the writers, animators, or layout people accustomed to the techniques of planned animation—understood how to draw convincing human figures, faces, gestures, and attitudes. They eventually had to bring in other artists from the world of comic books to do some of the writing and artwork, such as Alex Toth and Warren Tufts, which in turn created a wildly uneven aesthetic in *Jonny Quest*. For instance, Wildey recounts how the sequences involving Bandit, the comic-relief bulldog of the series designed not by him but by Hanna-Barbera layout artist Dick Bickenbach, were shot separately from the rest of the show by other in-house artists. In the "Shadow of the Condor" episode, "Bandit's running along in this courtyard, and the condor swoops down and picks him up and drops him into a pond. This is easily handled by the cartoon guys, the guys who can draw funny dogs, because it's Bandit, he's in motion, and there's no one else in the scene. If any so-called 'funny-dog' type artist had trouble with the condor, then one of the layout artists, who can draw realistically, would work that condor, we could bring him down on a vertical panel, and the dog would take care of itself"[40] (fig. 3.4).

These cartoony "Bandit moments" of run cycles, **cel reversals**, and other planned-animation techniques contrast with Wildey's realist aesthetic of mountain passes, aircraft design and shading, and special-effects explosions in the aerial dogfight sequence later in the episode. Such incongruities in the mode of production on *Jonny Quest*, particularly given the pressure to make airdates on a twenty-six-episode season, led to budget overruns and a huge financial loss of more than $500,000 for Hanna-Barbera.[41]

Despite Hanna-Barbera's innovations, some television cartoon series producers viewed the company as a symbol for limited animation's aesthetic deficiencies. In particular, Jay Ward, of *Crusader Rabbit* fame, unreservedly rejected the studio's planned approach to limited animation. Along with head writer, coproducer, and voice talent Bill Scott at Jay Ward Productions, Ward designed a series around similar personalities like Crusader and Rags T. Tiger to be the antithesis of Hanna-Barbera in terms of style and sensibility. Premiering on ABC on November 19, 1959, *Rocky and His Friends* (later known as *The Bullwinkle Show*) featured an omnibus of stories including the scrappy Rocket (Rocky) J. Squirrel and his dopey sidekick Bullwinkle J. Moose in two four-minute cliffhanger chapters, the humorous reimaginings of "Fractured Fairy Tales," the time-traveling tales of "Peabody's Improbable History," and the poetry recital "Bullwinkle's Corner."[42] These off-center, irreverent satires of fables, history, melodrama, current events, and the television apparatus itself were in sharp contrast to the cartoons of Hanna-Barbera or even its forebears Disney, Warner Bros., and UPA. As Darrell Van Citters puts it in *The Art of Jay Ward Productions*, "there was no effort to mimic

FIGURE 3.4: The "cartoony" Bandit moments that contrast with the realist aesthetic in the action-adventure series *The Adventures of Jonny Quest* (1964–1965).

reality, no interest in predatory/prey relationships, and no pretense about making art. [Jay Ward Productions] made an adventure series without action, produced animation that was written to be heard rather than seen and had characters routinely break the fourth wall. What made it to the screen seemed to have broken all the rules of classic animation and looked like nothing from any other cartoon studio. Humor drove *everything* there."[43] To be sure, Ward's array of cultural references, intellectual jokes, hyberbole, outlandish plots, and shameless puns served very different comedic purposes than the more slapstick-oriented work of Hanna-Barbera. By no means though did Jay Ward's work "[break] all the rules of classic animation," as it partook of many of the same production shortcuts for limited animation as Hanna-Barbera, including the illusion of on-screen action and a heavy reliance on dialogue for narration. Even some Hanna-Barbera characters, from Huckleberry Hound to the animals powering prehistoric technology in *The Flintstones*, were known for turning to the viewing audience to make comments and asides. Jay Ward merely presented other cost-saving variations in the limited mode of cel animation production for television, the same as other companies and series at the time, such as Soundac's *Colonel Bleep* (1957–1960) and Television Arts' color reboot of *Crusader Rabbit* (1959).

Where the two studios noticeably differed was in character design, layout, and timing, as Jay Ward definitely showcased more aesthetic variety in its many segments of *Rocky and His Friends* than Hanna-Barbera did across all its output until *Jonny Quest* in 1964. For Ward and designer Al Shean, limited animation meant "cycle animation that was to be *well drafted*," not the planned, standardized approach that characterized Hanna-Barbera.[44] These disparate approaches are quite visible when comparing the first episodes of two series from these studios: Jay Ward's "Missouri Mish Mash" (1961) from the newly retitled *The Bullwinkle Show* and "Oinks and Boinks" (1961) from Hanna-Barbera's *The Yogi Bear Show*. "Missouri Mish Mash" contains thirteen different individualized characters in strong unique poses from head to toe conveying personality and meaning, from the elongated dopiness of Bullwinkle Moose to the sharply angled features of Fearless Leader to the stocky bravado of Rocky the Flying Squirrel. "Oinks and Boinks" presents an interchangeable set of body poses and simplified facial expressions common to Hanna-Barbera in only six different characters (Yogi Bear, Boo Boo, the Three Little Pigs, and the Big Bad Wolf). Each of them has a necktie, bowtie, or handkerchief, with three characters bearing the same little pig design. Compared to the dynamic perspective, staging, and backgrounds that situate the Rocky and Bullwinkle cast in "Missouri Mish Mash," "Oinks and Boinks" is largely a series of reused character walk and run cycles and talking heads over different backgrounds, what Bill Scott calls "Hanna-Barbera palsy"[45] (fig. 3.5). Furthermore, the Ward series has more scene changes and is faster paced than Hanna-Barbera's work, leading to more drawings per cartoon. "Missouri Mish Mash" contains almost as many shots (seventy-two) as "Oinks and Boinks" (eighty-three) despite being roughly half as long (3:29 vs. 6:45, minus credits and introductory material). "That's why we cut so often," said Scott about his studio's distinctiveness. "It gave a form of motion to the show, even though the animation within those scenes was pretty damn limited. Whereas Hanna-Barbera might do a segment in 150 scenes, we would do it with 300."[46] And lastly, while stock music indiscriminately underscores every scene in "Oinks and Boinks" and largely all scenes in Hanna-Barbera's output, "Missouri Mish Mash," like many of Ward's cartoons, features voice-over work in lieu of a background music track for aesthetic and cost-saving purposes. William Conrad's frantic narrator—like that of Edward Everett Horton in "Fractured Fairy Tales" and Bill Scott in "Peabody's Improbable History"—is fundamental to the breakneck pace and meta-reference humor; for example, in the opening sequence of this Rocky and Bullwinkle segment, his narration sets the story ("You know things are usually pretty peaceful in Frostbite Falls, Minnesota. . . . Most of the time the citizens just sit around swapping yarn") or impedes the action ("Other Frostbite Fallsians play lazily at Tiddlywinks as they. . . . Aren't you fellas going to play?").

The greater efficiency and homogeneity of Hanna-Barbera's operation can also be attributed to another sharp difference between its mode of production and that

FIGURE 3.5: Standardized character design and layout in the "Oinks and Boinks" episode of *The Yogi Bear Show* (1961–1962).

of Jay Ward's: the division of labor. All of Hanna-Barbera's work was produced in the United States during the 1960s while the actual, hand-drawn animation of *Rocky and His Friends / The Bullwinkle Show* and its next series *Hoppity Hooper* (ABC, 1964–1967) took place in Mexico City at Val-Mar Productions, a studio newly built for the purposes of the earlier series. Ward outsourced production to Val-Mar—renamed Gamma in 1960—in order to take advantage of tax breaks and cheaper labor costs. In doing so, argues Tom Sito in *Drawing the Line*, outsourcing effectively divided John Randolph Bray's animation assembly line into two divisions: "the perceived creative areas such as direction, storyboarding, animation, and art direction—labeled '**above the line**'" and performed in Los Angeles, "and the more labor-intensive areas not perceived as creative tasks—assisting, inking, painting, backgrounds, checking, and camera—labeled '**below the line**'" and performed in Mexico.[47] While American animation talent was hired at Val-Mar on short-term contracts, with some being Disney-trained Mexican nationals, most of the staff was unskilled and had to be hired and taught from scratch. To further complicate matters, trade restrictions made such supplies as cels, pegboards, paint, and camera light bulbs difficult to obtain, and language barriers led to production delays and substandard craftsmanship, particularly in the first season, when budgets for five minutes of animation were about half of

Hanna-Barbera's ($1,600 vs. $3,000).[48] As a result, *Rocky and His Friends* episodes are often sloppily animated, suffering from bad sound quality, scratched cels, shoddy camera work, poor mouth syncs, inconsistent character models, and other production problems.[49] The work at Val-Mar gradually improved, and budgets more than tripled to $26,000 per show in its second season, establishing *Rocky and His Friends* as the first successful **runaway production** in television animation.[50]

Rocky and His Friends / The Bullwinkle Show was just one of the many original television cartoon series that followed in the wake of the many successes of Hanna-Barbera by the early 1960s. Like Hanna-Barbera, each studio had its own mode of production to deal with the economic demands and deadlines of the mass medium. Total TeleVision, one of the larger studios during this boom in limited cel animation, shared Ward's outsourcing studio in Mexico for *King Leonardo and His Short Subjects* (NBC, 1960–1961), *Tennessee Tuxedo and His Tales* (CBS, 1963–1965), and *Underdog* (NBC, 1964–1967). Cambria Studios, beginning with *Clutch Cargo* (syndicated, 1959), photographed what creator Clark Haas called "motorized movement," a combination of live-action, comic-strip drawings, and basic animation techniques to cut corners in order to produce a thirty-minute episode at only $18,000. One method unique to *Clutch Cargo* and Cambria's ensuing series *Space Angel* (syndicated, 1962–1964) and *Captain Fathom* (syndicated, 1965) was the studio's patented process known as Syncro-Vox, superimposing live-action human lips over animated cels to eliminate the high cost of lip animation and subsequent voice synchronization. Also borrowing the filmed comic-strip panel aesthetic of *Tele-Comics / NBC Comics* was *The Marvel Superheroes* (syndicated, 1966), a half-hour series from Grantray-Lawrence Animation consisting of three serialized adventures from five separate components (Captain America, The Incredible Hulk, Iron Man, The Mighty Thor, and Sub-Mariner). Like Cambria, Grantray-Lawrence found its own resourceful solution to a miniscule budget of $18,000 ($6,000 per six- to seven-minute segment) per episode: xerography, a relatively new production method that eliminated the time-consuming hand-inking stage in the animation process by using Xerox machines to photocopy pencil sketches directly onto animation cels.[51] For *The Marvel Superheroes*, these xerographic pencil sketches not only were based on actual Marvel Comics stories but were drawn by several of their best artists so that many of these compositions presented fully articulated, extreme poses of action that remarkably gave the illusion of motion despite the lack of any actual animation beyond minimal eye, hand, and mouth movements in the series. Cofounder Robert Lawrence likened the production to "animat[ing] a book" with the promotional material advertising it as "exactly as they originally planned."[52] Xerography—minus the artistic detail found at the inking stage of *The Marvel Superheroes*—would become a standardized tool in the mode of production for Saturday-morning cartoons by the end of the decade, saving millions in production costs for the studios, including Disney, which used it for its feature film *101 Dalmatians* (see chapter 6) (fig. 3.6).

FIGURE 3.6: Advertising for *The Marvel Superheroes* (1966) promoting the series "exactly as they originally appeared" in the comic book, made possible through the technology of xerography.

Other companies rebooted streamlined and simplified television versions of fully animated, theatrical cartoon series: Trans-Lux's *Felix the Cat* (1959–1961), UPA's *The Mr. Magoo Show* (syndicated, 1960–1961), King Features' *Popeye the Sailor* (syndicated, 1960–1962) and "Krazy Kat," a segment of *Beetle Bailey and Friends* (syndicated, 1962–1964). For *Felix*, the comic illustrator and show creator Joe Oriolo had voice actor Jack Mercer speak very slowly in order to consume film footage for the show's miniscule $5,000 budget per four-minute episode.[53] And Oriolo, as it was widely known, would send scenes back to the animators, most of them former Fleischer employees, for containing too many drawings if they couldn't fit under his door.[54] As for *Popeye*, King Features produced an astronomical 220 limited-animation television entries in two years, compared to Fleischer Studios' and Famous Studios' earlier production of 230 theatrical shorts for Paramount in almost twenty-five years. To manufacture these cartoons at such a breakneck pace, King Features hired several different studios, including Rembrandt Films, an animation company housed at the Bratri v Triku studio in Prague, Czechoslovakia, and run by former Terrytoons and UPA director Gene Deitch. He divided the *Popeye* work with studios in Zagreb, Croatia, and Rome, Italy, and the "Krazy Kat" work with Artransa Film Studios in Sydney, Australia.[55]

Rembrandt Films was one of those production houses that had a presence in both the television and film markets when limited animation became the dominant mode of production in the 1960s. In 1961, MGM contracted with Rembrandt to revive the Tom and Jerry franchise for the theatrical market at one-fourth the budget ($10,000 vs. $40,000 each) that MGM had once offered to Hanna and Barbera. The result of this thirteen-episode commitment was a Czech-style Tom and Jerry that had little in common with either its fully animated ancestors from the studio era or the limited-animation film or television cartoons of the period. The Czechs, as Deitch discovered, had a diametrically opposite approach to the realistic style of personality animation: "The mouths did not move as they spoke dialog, and the eyes did not really look. There was no great consideration to weight, or the laws of physics. There was no real development of character. All of those things were secondary to a symbolic approach to storytelling. They felt that American animation left nothing to the imagination; that we 'shoveled it to 'em.' They preferred to *suggest*, to mime."[56] To further complicate matters, Deitch's staff had never seen a Tom and Jerry cartoon—they had little to no access to Western entertainment being behind the Iron Curtain—so he primarily did all the storyboards, layouts, key poses, writing, and directing on the series while his staff did the animation, music, and sound effects. This blend of national styles exhibited many traditional limited-animation techniques but with a bizarre, crazed vitality: stories take place in a nightmarish range of odd locales, such as a nineteenth-century whaling ship or Nairobi jungle; the animation has more spastic, fluid-to-stilted movement in them; sound effects carry a disturbing amount of reverb; background paintings are done in a stilted, angular, modernist style; the soundtrack interpolates composer Scott Bradley's original Tom and Jerry themes with a quirky orchestral and electronic musical score and eclectic voice work ranging from mumbling to goofy prattle performed by Allen Swift. In the end, said Deitch, "I put a lot of emphasis on sounds and atmosphere and music and the very richness of the image to compensate for what we were not so good at." This was an apt description of a mode of production for Tom and Jerry cartoons far different than what came before with Hanna and Barbera or after with Chuck Jones, a result of MGM's 1963 partnership with the director's new production company, Sib Tower 12, which housed many members of his recently fired, Hollywood-based animation unit at Warner Bros.[57]

By the mid- to late 1960s, Saturday morning became the principal home of newly produced and previously aired limited animation series as well as older, fully animated theatrical cartoons. This exile, as Jason Mittell describes it in *Genre and Television*, led to the establishment of a kid-only generic category "Saturday morning cartoons." He argues that several cultural assumptions linked to the cartoon genre fueled this industrial shift away from the adult audience: that kids will gladly watch recycled and repeated programs, that kids cannot discern quality of animation, that cartoons should not address "adult" subject matter, and that cartoons are "harmless entertainment."[58] In light of a more hands-off approach to the television industry by the Johnson administration and the success of recycled animated shows on Saturday morning, any residual affiliation of television cartoons with social satire, an educational mission, and the mass audience ended. "Cartoons became stigmatized as a genre *only* appropriate for children" writes Mittell;[59] the networks followed suit, shortly discovering that new series targeted at children, particularly *The Beatles* (ABC, 1965–1967), delivered the largest audience. Of greatest significance, though, was the batch of shows on CBS known as "Superhero Saturday." Established by their director of daytime programming, Fred Silverman, this lineup of action-adventure programming—returnees *Mighty Mouse Playhouse* and *Underdog* followed by newcomers Hanna-Barbera's *Frankenstein Jr. and The Impossibles* (1966–1968) and *Space Ghost and Dino Boy* (1966–1968), Filmation's *The New Adventures of Superman* (CBS, 1966–1967, 1969–1970) and Format Films' *The Lone Ranger* (1966–1969)—catapulted CBS from third to first place; *Space Ghost* alone posted a 55 percent audience share.[60] As the first network executive to take Saturday morning seriously by generating ideas, supervising scripts, and overseeing storyboards, Silverman changed the business of children's television.[61] Prior to his involvement, recounts Filmation's Lou Scheimer, "Kellogg's or General Mills would come in with a show, produce it, give it to the networks, take two commercials out of it, and the networks had no control over the body of the show."[62] Now CBS, NBC, and ABC would be buying directly from the studios, giving the networks complete control over Saturday morning's purse strings for each of their four hours of programming from 8:00 A.M. to noon. Yet under this marketplace arrangement, the mode of production for limited animation would go rather unchanged on television throughout the 1970s. Hanna confirms: "Outside of the transition from inking to photocopying, there were no real significant technical or artistic changes in the production process within the cartoon industry."[63] As a result, Saturday morning, largely the only place where any new cartoons landed outside of prime time, became a graveyard of formulaic stories, uninspired artwork, and shoestring budgets—season after season.

Saturday Morning in the 1970s

From 1967 into the early 1980s, the three major networks programmed a massive amount of new or returning made-for-TV animation series and theatrical animation shorts packages from 8:00 A.M. to noon on Saturday morning, with some extending their animated offerings until 2:00 P.M. on Saturday and also into Sunday morning. A common practice of repackaging existing series during this time misleadingly sold viewers on a new "season" of cartoons primarily so the networks could mix in reruns from the first season at a lesser cost than paying for the production of an entire season.[64] The result of such practices, wrote Charles Solomon, was that "animation became a cheap way of filling large blocks of time, instead of an entertainment or an art form. In the never-ending search for quantity, quality was gradually compromised out of existence."[65]

Several new competitors to Hanna-Barbera—Rankin/Bass, DePatie-Freleng, and Filmation—met this unprecedented demand for new product on Saturday morning, but their entrance into the market failed to change the mode of production for limited animation on television. Low budgets and tight deadlines hampered these studios as well, leading them to develop their own set of tools and techniques for animation production to service their individual artistic approaches. Of these studios, Filmation, second to Hanna-Barbera in animation sales to the networks in the 1970s, managed to create a unique, economized look to its cartoon output. Filmation relied on a **stock animation** system of close-ups, long shots, and other sequences involving movements of its characters to cut costs, a method initially developed on its first Saturday-morning series, *The New Adventures of Superman*. CBS was only paying them $36,000 an episode originally, $9,000 less than Hanna-Barbera was receiving, to animate humans and humanoid superheroes, widely considered to be more difficult and thus more time-consuming to do than funny animals or cartoony figures.[66] The use of rotoscoping, a process invented by Max Fleischer (see chapter 1) and used in his own *Superman* cartoons in the early 1940s, provided one solution for this approach. More photorealistic and fluid than other Saturday-morning cartoons, *The New Adventures of Superman* and its rotoscoped stock was subsequently referenced, reused, and traced over for other DC superhero segments in *The Superman/Aquaman Hour of Adventure* (CBS, 1967–1968), *The Batman/Superman Hour* (CBS, 1968–1969), and later in *The New Adventures of Batman* (CBS, 1977).[67]

Eventually, Filmation established a Stock Coordination Department to manage all the studio's stock scenes, models, and backgrounds in books for the artists to reference. Stock material—run cycles, dialogue poses, and so on for the lead characters—would be assembled before production even commenced, because Filmation expected a certain ratio of stock animation to new animation per episode.[68] The *Filmation Layout Manual* describes the procedure for stock animation, or "S/A," stating, "The *Stock Coordination Department* will track down any *S/A material*, be it from shows currently in production or shows that are completed and located elsewhere. This is to enable us to keep track of all the scenes and to keep a copy on hand for future use if needed."[69] For example, *The Brady Kids* (ABC, 1972–1973) featured an enormous amount of repurposed animation from *The Archie Show* (CBS, 1968–1969), only this time with different cel paint. In any given episode, the rock band performances are all frame-by-frame animation replacements, as are most of the poses for Mop Top, the dog sidekick in *The Brady Kids* that was almost identical to Hot Dog, his counterpart in *The Archies*.[70] On the other hand, Filmation built a unique set of scenes for its stock animation system with *Tarzan, Lord of the Jungle* (CBS, 1976–1980) and *The New Adventures of Flash Gordon* (NBC, 1979–1982). In the end though, despite a few attempts to break formula with the educational *Fat Albert and the Cosby Kids* (CBS, 1972) and adult-skewing *Star Trek* (NBC, 1973–1974), Filmation, like all the other studios, could not escape the network strictures and economic realities of Saturday morning: cheap programming, states Scheimer, for the networks, who considered the base audience to be six-year-olds.[71]

Several industrial forces were responsible for the cheap, substandard, and indistinguishable limited-animation cartoons aimed at children during the 1970s. Some of the blame can be initially attributed to the red tape, language barriers, and untrained workforce inherent to runaway production, especially in the work of Hanna-Barbera.[72] According to Hanna, the studio began subcontracting work overseas with *The Funky Phantom* (ABC, 1971–1972) due to cost savings and the scarcity of skilled animators, background artists, and other laborers in Hollywood to complete all the network orders during the Saturday-morning boom.[73] For instance, the second-season episodes of *The New Scooby-Doo Movies* (CBS, 1972–1974), animated in Hanna-Barbera's newly formed studio in Australia, often feature different character models, voice synchronization issues, and other quality control matters. Overseas production alone, however, does not fully explain such errors, as Filmation, Hanna-Barbera's chief competitor, never employed runaway tactics for its cartoons. CBS, NBC, and ABC imposed incredible production constraints on *all* the studios for their Saturday-morning fall schedule. The networks required them to produce a full season of sixteen or more shows in only six to eight months; new series were ordered in March, animators and support staff were hired in April, and the episodes were due each week from September through December or January.[74] "Under that pressure," states David DePatie, "there's just no way to develop quality."[75] The seasonal nature of television work that left many animators unemployed for four months a year further compounded these quality control issues. "The prospect of being well paid for half a year and unemployed for the remainder," says Grossman, "discouraged younger talent from entering the field and encouraged producers, in a crush for employees, to look for more and cheaper labor overseas."[76] With a diminishing pool of studio-era animators and domestic animators, "they knew exactly where to take a shortcut yet still keep the overall show looking good," states Sito. Given that, according to animator Gerald Baldwin, "At the peak of a production season there was so much work to be done in so little time that just about any 25-cent sub-contractor could pick up an episode," it is not surprising that Saturday morning cartoons suffered in quality.[77] The studios attempted to address all these issues (runaway production, four-month employment, and a reduction in an experienced labor force) with other assignments, such as commercials, features, and prime-time specials, as well as internal training programs and free external classes for budding animators. Still, Hanna-Barbera came under fire from Motion Picture Screen Cartoonists Local 839 in Southern California in early 1977 for pushing its animators to work faster to meet deadlines, leading to a strike at the studio later that year.[78] Strikes by Local 839 in 1979 and 1982 failed to improve working conditions or the quality of limited animation into the 1980s.

However, several prime-time television specials defied the trend of the formulaic action-adventure and character comedies on Saturday morning in the 1960s and 1970s. *Rudolph the Red-Nosed Reindeer* (NBC, 1964), *The Little Drummer Boy* (NBC, 1968), and *Santa Claus Is Comin' to Town* (ABC, 1970) were some of many seasonal holiday specials produced by Rankin/Bass (Arthur Rankin Jr. and Jules Bass) under their patented Animagic process. This labor-intensive, three-dimensional, stop-motion technique used a special kind of puppetry made largely of plastic, cloth, wood, and armature whose parts animators, working in Japan, would move one frame at time. Every movement was a frame, says Rankin Jr., and each shot would take one to two minutes to accomplish depending on the number of characters and the action they were performing. At twenty-four unique frames a second, a fifty-minute special, such as *Rudolph*, would requires approximately 72,000 moves, which, run together, creates the whimsical, herky-jerky effect that was the Animagic Rankin/Bass aesthetic.[79]

There were also specials that used cel animation, most notably a spate of programs based on Dr. Seuss books, such as *Dr. Seuss' How the Grinch Stole Christmas!* (CBS, 1966) and *The Cat in the Hat* (CBS, 1971), as well as the annual Peanuts specials based on Charles M. Schultz's comic-strip characters, such as *A Charlie Brown Christmas* (CBS, 1965) and *It's the Easter Beagle, Charlie Brown* (CBS, 1974). The budgets for the Peanuts specials were never large, originally only $76,000 for a half hour—just three times the amount of a single Saturday-morning episode.[80] However, directors Bill Melendez and later Phil Roman had the luxury of longer production schedules without any network interference to create an animation approach that used limited resources creatively. Following a tradition learned during his years at UPA of letting design dictate the style of movement, Melendez applied an aesthetic of strong posing, flat perspectives, and bold use of color to the specials that preserved the minimalistic look and feel of the comic strip while keeping expensive animation costs down. For example, the Red Baron fighting sequence in *It's the Great Pumpkin, Charlie Brown* (CBS, 1966) creates emotional tension through a flatness in visual space largely composed of three aesthetic elements: a single fully animated but sparsely drawn image of Snoopy, wearing his World War I flying ace costume aboard his doghouse; air combat sound effects; and an expressionistic use of color for its watercolor sky backgrounds and for Snoopy himself. Although barely employed in this sequence, voice acting in the Peanuts cartoons was equally treated cost-effectively and stylistically. Melendez voiced Snoopy and later Woodstock himself, while children less expensively supplied the voices of the main characters, not adults, as was common practice at the time. For adult voices, states Melendez, a musician would listen to an actor read dialogue and then play a trombone to shape a musical line to mimic the inflection of the person's voice.[81]

Unlike most Saturday-morning cartoons, cost-saving aesthetics contributed to rather than detracted from the nuance and expressiveness in limited-animation work, an artistic choice reinforced by Melendez's equitable approach to labor. He paid his animators for their time spent on each foot of animation, states animator Dave Brain, rather than total feet of animation produced, the industry standard for most employees: "In some studios, you have the problem of animators making friends with the production manager so they get simple scenes they can do quickly because it's all paid at the same rate. But Bill had figured out a fairer way, and that was to rate the scenes. A good average scene, maybe a half shot so you didn't have to deal with the whole body, moderate animation—that would be paid at the rate per foot times 1.0. If there was a little bit more to draw, 1.5. If you got a scene with four characters, you might get to multiply that rate by 3 or 4."[82] Furthermore, Melendez did not compile a library of movements and music cues to reuse in each Peanuts special as was commonplace in Saturday-morning cartoons; animators redesigned the characters and backgrounds from scratch every time—even similar walk cycles or football kick misses by Charlie Brown. Vince Guaraldi composed a unique jazz score for each special—performing the signature "Linus and Lucy" theme over and over. The result of these efforts was an intimacy and sincerity rarely seen with limited animation on television. As Andrew Stanton, the director of *Finding Nemo* (2003) and *Wall-E* (2008) remarked, "What I always find surprising about [Melendez's] work was you never felt like you were being denied something. It was the best, most positive definition of 'limited animation' there could ever be."[83]

Other companies developed different time- and labor-saving devices for cel-based television cartoons, most notably those Japanese studios employing the limited animation style known as anime, which was widely syndicated in edited form in the United States during this time. In *Anime's Media Mix*, Marc Steinberg describes how Japanese animation studios, facing the same economic and temporal constraints of producing television as their American counterparts, found a practical and aesthetic solution in the still images of manga (comics) that would minimize the number of drawings and lengthen their on-screen duration.[84] Cohering as a style in famed writer Tezuka Osamu's adaptation of his manga series *Astro Boy* (*Tetsuwan Atomu*, 1963–1966), followed by several other manga-inspired series, such as *Kimba the White Lion* and *Speed Racer*, anime developed unique stylistic traits setting it apart from UPA, Hanna-Barbera, Filmation, and other U.S.-based studios producing limited animation. They included the elimination of intermediate drawings in walking and talking, still-image close-ups of characters' faces, single foreground images pulled across backgrounds (or vice versa), and short shot lengths in lieu of character movement.[85] The result of this particular approach to television animation is not the illusion of cinematic motion that traditionally characterizes Hanna-Barbera and others but an "experience of motion and immobility, movement and poses," states Steinberg—a "motion-stillness economy."[86]

Efforts like those of Melendez and Osamu were rare from the mid-1960s to the end of the 1970s on U.S. television. Television cartoons, mostly clustered on Saturday morning, were indistinguishable from one another. Formulaic stories, careless artwork, clumsy editing, threadbare background design, and sloppy sound recording failed to meet the standards of creativity reflected in the best of the 1950s and early 1960s series. However, given that the power dynamics and financial relationships between the networks and production companies had changed by the mid-1960s, such animation studios as Hanna-Barbera and Filmation were at the mercy of the networks for the types of stories they got to tell. As Amanda Lotz has argued about the network era, "Film studios and independent television producers had only three potential buyers of their content and were thus compelled to abide by practices established by the networks."[87] These strictures, shaped by internal censorship, external pressures, corporate greed, and cultural assumptions of animation's audiences, forced an industrial mode of production that countenanced homogenization and ratings above comedy, art, or anything else. John Kricfalusi, the creator of *The Ren and Stimpy Show* (Nickelodeon, 1991–1995), who got his start on Filmation's *Super Friends* (ABC, 1980–1982) and *The Tom and Jerry Comedy Show* (CBS, 1980–1982), expressed it best when he said, "Working on these cartoons showed me that it would take a lot more than talent to get cartoons to be funny again. The whole production system had to be turned around so that good ideas could actually make it to the screen."[88]

For all of its aesthetic deficiencies, limited animation kept an industry alive long enough for younger apprentices, such as Kricfalusi, to acquire the experience necessary for this production system to be turned around in the 1990s. The rise of cable outlets fragmented the television marketplace, allowing veteran animators, such as Kricfalusi with *Ren and Stimpy* and Tom Ruegger with *Animaniacs* (Fox Kids and Kids WB, 1993–1998), to break free of formulaic stories while still using some of the same cost-saving techniques as Hanna-Barbera and Filmation. Today, most television animation, such as *The Simpsons* (Fox, 1989–present), *South Park* (Comedy Central, 1999–present), *Archer* (FX, 2009–present), and others, owe much to this legacy, in that they are primarily dialogue driven and use limited-animation techniques even if the stories are more inventive and adult-oriented than what we find in the heyday of Saturday-morning cartoons.

4

INDEPENDENT ANIMATORS AND THE ARTISANAL MODE,

1947–1989   Alla Gadassik

Independent animation, particularly in its artisanal handmade form, is often described as the most artistically expressive and personal approach to filmmaking—the greatest opportunity to exercise individual authorship and directly shape the entire look of a film.[1] A solitary animator can design and control every aspect of the frame, even personally draw the images or move all of the models. Moreover, the tactile traces of the artist's hand on paper or its impressions in clay form an intimate physical bond between the filmmaker and the film, similar to the connection between painters and their brushstrokes on a canvas. As the first chapter in this book demonstrated, many early animators invoked the tradition of fine-arts authorship by including scenes of their hands sketching on a blank canvas, deliberately staging a proprietary relationship between the filmmaker and the drawn figures (see chapter 1). The narrative structure of such self-reflexive cartoons often pitted the animator against the characters, suggesting that the animated world held its own independence; yet the films still made the implicit claim that the animated figures originated as personal extensions of the artist, as playful or naughty progeny released into the universe.[2] Throughout the twentieth century, animated characters frequently served as avatars for their animators, whose gestures guided the characters' design and movement.[3]

This belief in animation as a distinctly personal form of filmmaking never waned among animation artists, even during the so-called Golden Age of studio production, when labor was divided and shared among numerous departments and hundreds of people, making individual authorship increasingly difficult to demonstrate. Many an oral history and auction-catalog entry has taken pains to assess and prove the contributions of individual artists to one animated sequence or another. As such, even when the postwar decades saw the decline of classical theatrical animation in the United States, they simultaneously ushered in a period of expanded independent animation. Taking advantage of increasingly compact lower-budget cameras and more affordable film stocks, as well as new sources of funding and film distribution, an astonishing number of talented artists from different backgrounds took up and revitalized the artisanal mode of animation production that recalled the art form's early years.

This chapter maps out the blossoming American independent animation scene throughout the postwar decades, asking why the artisanal mode thrived during this period and how this mode shaped recurring visual techniques that appeared in the works of various filmmakers. At the price of eliding individual differences and omitting some noteworthy figures, the chapter combines and draws on the works of three different groups of artists that established the independent tradition in the postwar period and defined its most exemplary graphic qualities. The first group includes filmmakers who primarily defined themselves as fine artists rather than cartoonists or animators, most of whom were closely connected to avant-garde cinema circles and many of whom worked in other media besides film. Their work is most frequently referred to as "experimental animation" or "absolute animation," though both terms can be misleading.[4] The second group includes filmmakers who began their careers in the studio animation system but became disillusioned with this mode of production and left to pursue independent work. A majority of these animators were drawn to independent work because they were interested in discovering new graphic approaches that allowed for more unorthodox types of narratives and unconventional character development. These filmmakers generally described their work as "personal animation" or "independent character animation," and they had a more direct relationship to classical studio animation. The third group of filmmakers loosely defines a younger generation of independent animators, who were influenced or inspired by their predecessors in the immediate postwar period. These filmmakers came of age in the politically charged 1960s and 1970s, often attended some of the first university animation programs in the country, frequently studied under mentors from the first two groups, and benefited from newly established paths of exhibition and distribution. Their bodies of work, which defined the most prolific 1970s and 1980s, often resist clear divisions between "experimental" and "character" animation traditions, since many of the filmmakers played with different approaches throughout their careers. Another distinguishing feature of this third group is the prevalence of women filmmakers. Women faced institutional barriers and pressures that excluded them from many creative positions in studio animation during the classical period, and a gender disparity persists to this day. Shifting societal norms and expanded funding opportunities made the independent route more feasible for women in the 1970s and 1980s. This means that for women animators these decades marked only the beginning, not the end, of a so-called golden age.[5]

One major thread that connected all three disparate groups was a commitment to maintaining an intimate and direct relationship between the animator and the animated image—a relationship that could be spiritual, physical, or psychic but that had to draw directly on the animator's experience, including the experience of animating itself, in the design and composition of the film. Whether this meant animating images directly by hand or basing a film's composition on one's philosophical perspective of the world, the independent path allowed filmmakers to impress onto the actual graphic language of a film their own breath, bodily rhythm, spiritual mythology, or autobiographical memory.

However, the solitary artisanal mode of production came at a price, not only in terms of limited financial support but also in terms of the high labor demands of animation. The actual process of animating still demanded an immense amount of time and corporeal effort—an inescapable material constraint that fostered the growth of the studio system in the first place. As animation instruction manuals and promotional behind-the-scenes materials love to emphasize, a single minute of a hand-drawn or clay-animated film requires hundreds of images and poses, or thousands of hours of delicate work. The studio method of production resolved this labor demand by breaking down the work into various stages and tasks and then disseminating the different tasks among a collective of trained artists. This system was complicated and expensive, but it also allowed for a speedier delivery of films and a more polished result. Independent animators striking out on their own had to figure out their own strategies for generating moving images in mass quantities, without spending their entire lifetime and life's earnings on a single film. For all the lofty aspirations toward fulfilling an individual vision and achieving creative freedom, the major challenge of being an independent animator was recognizing one's own material and temporal finitude and using it as an indisputable point of departure for artistic exploration. The range and diversity of answers to this challenge cannot be adequately covered even in a single book, but here I propose the two most common strategies that postwar independent animators developed in tackling the labor constraints of artisanal production. First, independent animators embraced the visible roughness that characterized fast-paced work, including the incompleteness of sketched lines, the emptiness of unfilled canvases, and the unruliness of their chosen materials. Second, animators found different techniques and tools for automating the process of generating repeating images. Both of these broader strategies indelibly shaped the kinds of films and visual styles that predominated during this period.

Leaving the Artist's Studio and the Cartoon Factory

Before looking closely at specific animation strategies, it is important to understand what motivated and supported the challenging path of independent production in this period and what types of different approaches and philosophies made up the rich tradition of American independent animation. The first group of filmmakers pioneering the artisanal mode of production in the immediate postwar years consisted of artists who came to the cinema with a background in the fine arts and who typically approached the moving image as a synthesis of music, dance, sculpture, and painting. During the 1940s and 1950s, these filmmakers included accomplished avant-garde artists who immigrated to the United States from abroad (e.g., Oskar Fischinger and Len Lye), American-born artists trained in Europe or mentored by European artists (e.g., Mary Ellen Bute, Robert Breer, Dwinell Grant, John and James Whitney, and Lawrence Jordan), and artists active in emerging American avant-garde circles like abstract expressionism, pop art, or Beat culture (e.g., Harry Smith, Stan VanDerBeek, Jordan Belson, and Hy Hirsh). Most often, these artists were drawn to animation techniques because of the opportunity to manipulate abstract audiovisual forms without relying on naturalistic conventions of representation. For all these animators, the ideal of artistic solitude and proximity to the film image played a very important role in animation's appeal and aesthetic potential.

This is especially true for filmmakers who turned to animation after working in musical composition or painting, two disciplines that continued to emphasize the role of the artist as a singular visionary. For instance, Oskar Fischinger described his painstaking approach to painted animation as a process of spiritual seeking, which demanded the same level of sustained attention and ambition afforded to performance and fine artists: "The creative artist of the highest level always works at his best *alone*, moving far ahead of his time. And this shall be our basis: That the Creative Spirit shall be unobstructed through realities or anything that spoils his absolute pure creation."[6] Fischinger, a German-born filmmaker, moved to the United States to escape the Nazis' escalating persecution of avant-garde artists but found himself unable to conform to the American animation industry and struggling to secure funding for his films. He blamed this largely on Hollywood's studio production model, which inserted so many barriers between the animator and the final image that it weakened or diluted distinct voices. He wrote:

The cartoon film is today on a very low artistic level. It is a mass product of factory proportions, and this, of course, cuts down the creative purity of a work of art. No sensible creative artist could create a sensible work of art if a staff of co-workers of all kinds had his or her say in the final creation—producer, story director, story writer, music director, conductor, composers, sound men, gag men, effect men, layout men, background directors, animators, inbetweeners, inkers, cameramen, technicians, publicity directors, managers, box office managers, and many others. They change the ideas, kill the ideas, before they are born, prevent the ideas from being born, and substitute for the absolute creative motives only the cheap ideas to fit the lowest among them.[7]

Fischinger's sentiment was shared by many other experimental animators working in the United States, who viewed their work in film as an extension of art, rather than as a storytelling medium or a commercial endeavor. The New Zealand–born artist Len Lye, also a World War II émigré to the United States, similarly considered filmmaking to be an art form best suited for independent work. Like Fischinger, Lye could not subscribe to the commercial assembly line of mainstream cartoon production because he saw animation as an opportunity to escape the rigid system of narrative filmmaking, which perpetuated repetitive techniques and stifled artists' ability to explore their own kinesthetic sensibility. Lye made most of his films by painting or scratching images directly onto film celluloid, in part because these cheaper, more modest materials (celluloid, inks, and scavenged etching tools) gave him the opportunity to take intuitive risks, make mistakes, and explore visual effects that might never have been tried in a commercial setting. Speaking about his choice of such a **direct animation** method (also known as **cameraless animation**), Lye noted: "To me, discovery is something that is a workout on imagery I haven't seen done before, and that I haven't done before and one that I can make click for me. . . . I've been reduced to painting *on* film, or scratching film, not that I want to, but because I want to deal with the *control* of three dimensional motion. In direct film, if I can make something wiggle in a way that is fascinating to me, I'll take three months messing around with it."[8] Working outside of the commercial production model gave filmmakers the benefit of controlling their own projects and time, as well as the luxury to abandon some experiments and doggedly pursue others. However, independent work also came at the enormous expense of having no infrastructure for funding and fewer distribution opportunities.

Fortunately, independent animators *did* find a small and growing audience during this period. Many filmmakers gained international exposure via newly founded film festivals and exhibition programs. In the summer of 1949, the Belgian film critic and curator Jacques Ledoux organized the Festival International du Film Expérimental and Poétique, dedicated to gathering and exhibiting new experimental films that explored the lyrical and poetic dimensions of cinema. The Grand Prix at this event was awarded to Oskar Fischinger's *Motion Painting No. 1* (1947), an animated film made with painted oils on acrylic glass. *Motion Painting No. 1* defies conventional expectations of an animated film. Over the course of nine months, Fischinger recorded successive brushstrokes of vibrant and evolving paintings, allowing the numerous instances to come together on a single filmstrip and produce an accelerated changing graphic surface. Pointillist dots, twisting spirals, and rectangular dashes emerge and overlap to the sounds of a Bach concerto, creating a multilayered canvas that gradually morphs into new compositions and color palettes. As each brushstroke and each painted figure covers and irreversibly alters preceding layers, the film performs a fluid artwork, whose life becomes animated in the process of projection (fig. 4.1). For Fischinger, this kind of animation could only be possible with the work of a solitary artist, who was allowed the extensive duration required for making gradual changes that would add up into a harmonious pulsing unity. Although Fischinger made numerous groundbreaking films throughout his career, *Motion Painting No. 1* received the widest exhibition and circulation for decades, partly due to its recognition at the Belgian festival. It also played frequently in some of the first experimental cinema programs in the United States, where it reached and inspired American filmmakers, including John and James Whitney, Jordan Belson, and Harry Smith.

A similar case occurred with Len Lye's work after the second installment of the Belgian festival, this time titled the 1958 Brussels Experimental Film Competition. The second prize was awarded to Lye for his *Free Radicals* (1958), a film made by etching lines and figures directly into unexposed film celluloid. The success of *Free Radicals* in Brussels was not enough to attract viable commercial investments for Lye, but as with Oskar Fischinger's film a decade earlier, the prize helped solidify his place in avant-garde film history. The Brussels competition invited and promoted numerous other American filmmakers, who worked occasionally (or exclusively) with painterly and graphic filmmaking techniques: Mary Ellen Bute, Robert Breer, Hy Hirsh, Stan Brakhage, and Francis Thompson. Many of these names would become synonymous with the history of American experimental animation. Expo '58 was also an important catalyst for the formation of the International Animated Film Association (Association International du Film D'Animation, or ASIFA). ASIFA's influence and importance was discussed in this book's introduction, along with the newfound exhibition opportunities made available to independent animators in the United States.

As the number of fine artists working with animation techniques grew during the postwar period, they were joined by classically trained character animators, who had become disillusioned with the studio production system. Throughout the 1950s and 1960s, mainstream studio animators increasingly echoed Oskar Fischinger's disparaging conclusion that the studio model stifled aesthetic experi-

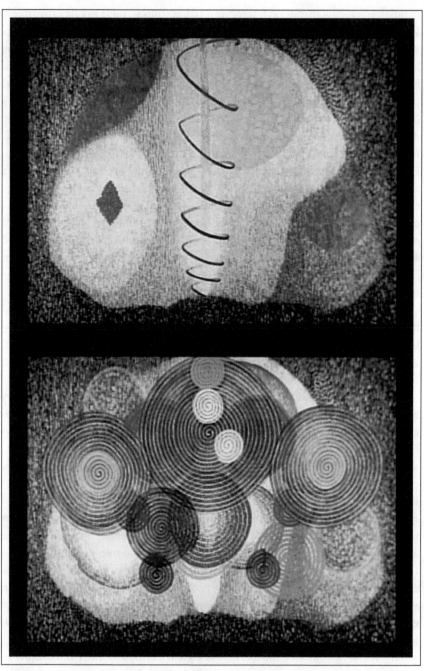

FIGURE 4.1: Still frames from Oskar Fischinger's *Motion Painting No. 1* (1947).

mentation. During this period, large animation studios, most notably the titanic Walt Disney Company, continued to promote the classic myth of the animator as a unique artistic visionary, whose creative genius is merely implemented by the labor force that he expertly manages. It did not matter that Walt Disney himself hadn't animated a single sequence of his films for decades; both the company and the public treated the studio's cartoons as the direct manifestation of Disney's imagination.[9] Perpetuating this myth meant that most of the people actually designing and animating the films received limited creative license, few motivational incentives, and very narrow credit for their work. As the filmmaker Faith Hubley noted about the Disney structure, "there's animation, the craft, and there's animation, making the whole film. In the Disney studios the craft people were the animators. Disney knew exactly what he was doing when he emphasized the craft separation so that nobody would have the film-making power; that's not only a political observation, it's an artistic one. People who did animation would start at Disney as little apprentices and spend fifteen years learning to do 'in betweens' and if they lived long enough or were lucky enough to become animators, they would think they were on a pinnacle."[10] Collectively founded studios, such as United Productions of America (UPA), which worked with a more limited labor force and strived for more internal flexibility, hoped to invigorate the industry, but many of the same tensions over authorship remained. As a result, numerous mainstream animators broke off to form their own small production houses or independent companies.

The careers of Faith Hubley and her husband, John Hubley, a former Disney background painter and layout artist, are exemplary in this regard. After the conclusion of the famous 1941 Disney strike, John Hubley was among the many disillusioned animators who never returned to the studio. For several years, he was a chief figure at the UPA studio, but his past history of labor activism landed him on the Hollywood blacklist during the McCarthy-era House Un-American Activities Committee (HUAC) hearings. This major professional blow motivated Hubley to form his own private company called Storyboard Productions. Soon thereafter, John Hubley married Faith (née Elliott), a talented film assistant and aspiring film editor, who herself was shut out of creative roles in the studio system, in part due to the pervasive institutional gender bias. Together the couple established Storyboard headquarters in New York and went on to produce an impressive range of award-winning films inspired by their own autobiographical experiences and personal artistic interests—an approach to filmmaking that Faith Hubley described as "working from the interior out."[11]

The Hubleys' film *Moonbird* (1959) is a great example of their philosophy of working from the interior out, since the film is based on tape recordings of the couple's two young sons engaged in nighttime play. The boys' amusing rambling conversation about catching a magical "moon bird" and bringing it home becomes a soundtrack for an adventurous expedition through a backyard garden, which

FIGURE 4.2: Still frames from John and Faith Hubley's *Moonbird* (1959).

in turn morphs into a journey through a mysterious forest. With *Moonbird*, the Hubleys took familiar narrative tropes of studio animation—the fairytale journeys of Disney's films and the loose-association structure of television cartoon gags—and applied them toward a film that begins with the specific microcosm of their private family life and expands outward into a portrait of childhood imagination. The film's layered composition style (animated foreground figures and painted backgrounds are partly blended using photographic superimposition), as well as its monochromatic palette of deep blues, rendered in inks and loosely smeared paint strokes, establish a dreamlike nocturnal atmosphere that stands in stark contrast to the bright and well-polished images produced by large studios (fig. 4.2). In all, just four artists were involved in designing and animating *Moonbird*, a number that would be laughable by mainstream production standards.[12] Yet in 1959, this very personal film became the first independently produced work to win an Academy Award for an animated short, ending decades of unchallenged studio dominance and announcing a new period of stylistic experimentation.

John and Faith Hubley's path was mirrored by many other filmmakers, who began their independent work by leaving well-regarded careers at mainstream studios. The majority of Disney's most promising artists who didn't return after the strike went on to establish their own private production houses, take freelance contracts, or find more creative control in positions at smaller studios. Some animators also accepted teaching posts, founding or directing new animation programs that would foster later generations of independent artists.[13] Many seminal independent animators born in the postwar decades have credited the preceding generation for invaluable mentorship and inspiration to pursue their own work.

The departure of so many classical studio animators for smaller production companies and the ubiquity of pioneering animators in prominent teaching roles completely changed the landscape of American animation, demonstrating that the studio model was no longer the only path for aspiring filmmakers. Independent work also became more financially feasible in the postwar decades. A basic drawn animation stand, which includes a **light box** for image tracing and a rotating **animation disc** for image repositioning and registration, has always been possible to construct relatively cheaply on one's own. By the 1950s, however, filmmakers could also buy smaller and more portable film cameras, which they could rig to record the images and which would also have a better image registration than prior models of amateur cameras. (One popular choice was a Bolex camera shooting 16-mm film.)

Even when making films with relatively modest means, independent animators still had to financially support their own work. Some filmmakers got by on teaching positions or a handful of scarce art grants, but for most artists, the independent path meant living in poverty (an unfortunate fate that awaited such visionaries as Mary Ellen Bute and Harry Smith) or taking on freelance work and commercial projects. In fact, the explosion of small animation houses and independent animators in the second half of the twentieth century was made economically possible by the growth of several commercial and industrial sectors that commissioned short animated pieces. Chief among these were three growing television markets: media advertising, children's television, and educational television—all of which viewed animation as a streamlined and eye-catching graphic language that could effectively deliver information to viewers. Other sectors that hired independent animators included the burgeoning special-effects industry, specialty television channels like MTV, the medical industry, and the military. Combined, all of these potential clients required short made-to-order projects, which was the perfect fit for small companies and freelance artists. It was therefore not uncommon to see the name of an airline company, a children's TV show, a science-fiction film, or a rock band video nestled in a filmography of an underground or experimental animator. By the late 1970s and 1980s, one was hard-pressed to find an independent animator who was not also a sole owner, cofounder, or chief creative director of a small production company.

Collectively, these different career trajectories represented the resurgence of the artisanal tradition after decades of commercial studio standardization that divorced most animators from the visual products of their labor. For filmmakers coming from fine-arts backgrounds, such as Oskar Fischinger, the artisanal mode represented vital solitude and aesthetic control, making room for the extensive duration and experimentation required to compose a moving image and ensure its harmonious integrity. For animators coming from studio backgrounds or trained in classical animation, such as the Hubleys, independent work opened the door to a more personal approach to filmmaking, often reflected in the autobiographical themes and idiosyncratic visual styles of their films.

Motivated by a wide range of artistic philosophies, these disparate animators nevertheless faced similar challenges in navigating the economic, material, and temporal pressures of animating alone. The opportunity to single-handedly compose and organize every single part of a film frame might sound appealing and rewarding, but when faced with having to recreate much of the same frame again . . . and again . . . and again, for twelve or twenty-four frames per second, the endeavor suddenly turns into a staggering physical and psychological climb. The demands of solitary production risk pushing the tedium of animation to an unbearable extreme. Moreover, the imperative to continuously repeat many of the same unchanging lines and poses runs counter to what attracted most animators to this art form in the first place, which was the opportunity to improvise and play around with movement. So how did independent artists address this paradox between the ideals of independent animation and its material realities? The remainder of this chapter will look more closely at two of the most common aesthetic strategies that filmmakers developed in tackling the constraints of their chosen mode of production.

Embracing the Rough Freehand Line

In hand-drawn animation, the task of single-handedly controlling stability of an image over time is nearly impossible, since this would require absolute precision in recreating all drawn lines that the animator wants to stay in place for any duration longer than a single frame. Even with the steadiest hand, the properties of the chosen pencil, the grain of the selected paper, the physical tremor of the hand as it redraws and shifts the lines—all insert differences between any two strokes, which in rapid projection turn into a wobbling or pulsing line that the animation industry refers to as boiling. The boiling effect stems from the basic materials of hand-drawn animation (the penciled outline and the paper canvas), but one can add the challenges of coloring and painting backgrounds, keeping smudges or creases away from individual sheets, or preventing materials from deteriorating under thumbprints and hot lamps.

A key objective of the studio cel-animation system was to eliminate the idiosyncratic traces of working with pencil, inks, and paper, which would otherwise insert inconsistencies between the frames and disparities among the numerous people assigned to each sequence. The graphic design of a scene might have been intended to look painterly and stylized, but the actual traces and brushstrokes that produced each image were to become inconspicuous, allowing for a sense of stability and continuity in a sequence that included many distinct contributors. A key step in achieving stylistic continuity was a multitiered process of cleaning up animators' pencil **roughs**—their early loosely animated sequences—by retracing them with more solid figure outlines and then inking those contours onto the cels with very fine, even strokes. The job of "running cleanup" was a common entry-level position in the industry, as aspiring animators trained their hands into collective submission by straightening out and ordering the more impressionistic freehand sketches of the lead animators. A lead animator's more tentative and messier drawn lines would become more polished and solidified in the subsequent cleanup and inking stages.

The adoption of transparent animation cels further helped maintain clean lines, because one could apply the inked outlines and the painted fills on reverse sides of the same cel, avoiding possible overlap and preventing color bleeding. Another common entry-level position in an animation studio was the cel polisher, whose main responsibilities involved cleaning stray hairs and dust particles from cel surfaces. The cels also eliminated the opacity and texture of paper, which resisted layering and attracted irreversible thumbprints and creases. In other words, the graphic precision and stylistic consistency of a studio-made film depended on minimizing the personal inconsistencies of its numerous makers and maximizing the transparency of the raw materials of animation. Such a transparency of materials and gestures would be virtually unattainable in solitary work, and many of the filmmakers turning to the artisanal mode of production chose instead to embrace the errant line and the textured surface that characterized individual freehand work. The studio's production "problem"—disparities between one animator's working tendencies and another's or unwanted deviations between one individual drawing and the next—became a welcome point of departure for the artisanal mode. The same kinds of graphic traces that studios associated with unpolished work or rough pencil tests would become central design elements in independent animation. Such embraced roughness included blank or unfilled canvas areas, loosely wandering and clustered lines, incomplete or nonexistent figure outlines, looser textured brushstrokes, and visible artifacts produced by the chosen materials.

For example, Robert Breer's *A Man and His Dog out for Air* (1957) begins with a frame that looks as though it might belong in the supply closet of a cartoon studio: an opaque white page with a penciled *X* that recalls an off-kilter crosshair registration symbol. Instantly, however, the crosshair spins to become an asterisk, contracts into a tightly wound ball, expands into a series of angular arms, bends and floats upward into a cloud formation with the briefest suggestions of a winged form, elongates into a bipedal creature, and so proceeds onward in a constant series of transformations. At times, the lines cohere to form the appearance of a single shape moving against a background; at other times, they disintegrate into broad patterns that crisscross the surface and extend beyond the visible edges of the frame. In the final seconds of the film, the playful lines finally come together

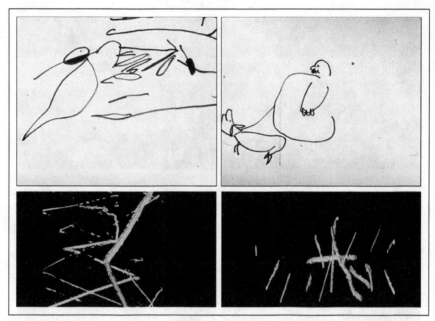

FIGURE 4.3: (top row) Still frames from Robert Breer's *A Man and His Dog out for Air* (1957); (bottom row) still frames from Len Lye's *Free Radicals* (1958).

into a rotund figure of the titular man walking a dog around the rectangular perimeter of the frame (fig. 4.3).

Re-watching the film with this final animated figure in mind, we could interpret the endless series of freehand metamorphoses as a chain of visual impressions from the artist's walk through a cityscape, but we can also think about the line itself as an animated companion that the animator takes for a stroll around the corners of the canvas. The film embraces the wavering qualities and ambiguities of the pencil line, as well as the possible inconsistencies that arise during drawn repetitions of figures from one frame to the next.[14] The line's elasticity and simplicity make for a raw physical element, which can be shaped and reshaped into a wide variety of forms without a clear predetermined goal in sight. The rapid pace and gestural variety of transformations from one frame to the next prevent the line from becoming just an invisible *out*line of figures. One gets the sense that its various incarnations might have surprised even the artist when he first projected the finished sequence of drawings.[15] A similar effect is achieved with the use of rough scratched marks in Len Lye's *Free Radicals*. Wiggling and pulsing against the black canvas of film celluloid, the slight differences among successive lines generate rotating and dancing autonomous figures (fig. 4.3).

John and Faith Hubley's *Windy Day* (1968) also embraces the inconsistent curves of a drawn line, as well as the textures of paint and paper, to render sensory impressions and flights of imagination. Produced as a sort of sequel to *Moonbeam*,

FIGURE 4.4: (top row) Still frames from John and Faith Hubley's *Windy Day* (1968); (bottom row) still frames from Marvin Newland's *Bambi Meets Godzilla* (1969).

Windy Day is based on recordings of the animators' two young daughters playing out various fantasy scenarios and speculating about the future. Loose freehand ink lines, as well as splashes of water-based paint, set the scene and establish the characters but also leave enough visual ambiguity and empty space in the frame to merely imply rather than definitively show some of the imagined details that the girls act out (fig. 4.4). Faith Hubley noted that the roughness and imperfection of the visual design was not only an acceptable price of limiting production to a smaller group of artists but also a deliberate departure from the polished look of studio-made animation: "It was the beginning of eliminating the hard-cel and the hard-line that I've always felt was ugly. And cel-animation is, was, inhibiting. One would have to have a certain kind of skill to do it as handmade mass production. I'm not a specialist in it; I just know I hate it—I hate the way it looks and I don't like the feel of it. I hate the hard edge and I don't see why anyone should learn to be tidy. I am a bit of a slob and I like a free-flowing line and texture. That was our contribution . . . using improvisation to liberate animation from itself, and to go to watercolors and to paint pastels."[16] In *Windy Day*, as the girls' conversation rapidly shifts in and out of various story elements or between earnest playacting and reflective commentary on their real lives, the lines also improvise to follow their patterns of thought. Some scenes are illustrated in more substantial detail, with shading and cross-hatching that evokes the sophisticated designs John Hubley made for the UPA studio. But others give only a hint of a little head and arm or dissolve ink lines in splotches of paint or abandon outlines for lightly suggested silhouettes of objects. The textures and inconsistencies of outlines create a graphic language that conveys the sense of unrestrained abandon and visual exaggeration of childhood play. Another clever and easily overlooked technique in the film is the use of different opacities of paint to lend the blank paper an effect of receding depth and reticulated density. As the inks run into the paper fibers or alter in saturation from one brushstroke to the next, the emptiness of the untouched blank paper begins to suggest a thick mist, a mysterious fog, or the titular wind rustling the boil of the animated lines and breathing life into the scene.

Faith Hubley's definition of the free-flowing line as a device of improvisation was echoed by many other animators, for whom the process of continuously drawing and redrawing lines did not intend to execute a preassigned look but to create a system for open-ended discovery. Independent animators were more likely to animate without planning out a full sequence or gestural arc in advance. This philosophy of proceeding forward and deciding on changes from frame to frame, sometimes described as straight-ahead animation, was rarely employed in studio production. Lynn Smith described working with crayon pencils directly at her animation stand as an opportunity to work out a visual idea, rather than as a technical process of turning storyboards into pre-planned sequences: "There was a dynamic energy that happened. I get an idea when I'm working under the camera. I come to the animation stand with a plan and with a method of actually completing the shot, but as I'm working, the excitement of drawing and erasing, and drawing and erasing, or using the cutouts—other ideas happen."[17] Accepting the less controlled and more erratic personal line, as well as embracing the emptiness and texture of an untouched canvas, allowed animators to generate more images independently and to rely on simple variation and visual suggestion, rather than meticulous detail. Just a few loosely jumbled doodles and a single horizon line in Fred Wolf's *The Box* (1967) are enough to suggest a disheveled bearded man slumped behind a bar, and a soft gray watercolor wash with scattered ink droplets at the end of the film suffices to turn the canvas into a torrential downpour for the concluding joke. In Sara Petty's *Furies* (1975), crisp and confident pastel lines edged against receding blue and black patches suddenly morph into the fluid contours of sleek and powerful felines. Mischievous penciled characters in Kathy Rose's *Pencil Booklings* (1978) break apart into beautifully coordinated shape-shifting figures and then reassemble into their previous forms. A cartoonist's marker in Bill Plympton's *Drawing Lesson II* (1985) produces a sentient "magic line" that takes the viewer on a wobbly, meandering journey through heartbroken memories.

For animators trained in the fine arts, the imperative to recreate the same freehand lines across numerous frames challenged their dexterity and virtuosity, but it also pushed them to abandon unnecessary ornamentation in favor of emphasizing the most essential graphic qualities of movement. As animator George Griffin notes, even the most basic tool for drawing, the pencil, can become a mode of discovery: "To 'pencil in' is to suggest a provisional state. A pencil drawing is a 'draft,' an incomplete sketch, a work in progress stabbing at an idea. A pencil stroke may be erased, smudged, scratched, overdrawn, reworked with limpid pentimenti: a discursive, ruminative practice, or a bold spontaneous gesture. Like speech, a sketch is a restless combination of declarations and demurrals, components of a herky-jerky rhythm of communication."[18] Beyond the fluid lines of pencils and paintbrushes, experimental animators also employed more unruly materials, such as crumbling charcoal, dust, pastels, and unorthodox drawing surfaces, to add depth and texture to otherwise restrained animation techniques. Even in the most technically masterful and precise examples of independently drawn animation, one can detect the impulse toward unexpected graphic transformations—a desire to disrupt compositional integrity in favor of an erratic surface and a line with a mind of its own.

For other independent filmmakers, particularly those still invested in narrative structure and character animation, a rougher line would also become a symbol of deliberate technical crudeness and self-reflexive irony—a defiant affront to the romantic ideals and naturalism of classical drawn animation. The indie festival classic *Bambi Meets Godzilla* (1969) by Marv Newland captures, in a brief ninety seconds, the stripped-down graphic style and irreverent attitude toward the classical studio style that characterized a younger generation of animators. The film begins with a penciled profile of a young fawn, recognizable only by his outline, a few spots on his hide, and enlarged black eye with a glint. Positioned against a bare horizon dotted with flowers, Bambi repeatedly raises and lowers his neck, wags his small tail, and occasionally shuffles one leg. The entire scene has the look of a basic animated pencil test, drawn with fairly minimal differentiation between frames and looking like a very stiff imitation of Disney's iconic young deer. As the seconds tick away, the animal repeats the same simple loop that no longer holds much interest, whereas a string of humorously pompous credits with Newland's name establish a developing gag, taking proud ownership over a visually underwhelming project (fig. 4.4). Suddenly and without warning, as the fawn mechanically raises his neck and looks up for the sixth time, a large scaly and boxy paw drops rapidly into the frame and crushes the animal's body. Godzilla's destructive stomp is accompanied by the low clang of the final chord from "A Day in the Life" by the Beatles, which squashes the previous pastoral soundtrack and reverberates for the remainder of the film. Together, the intrusion of the rock-'n'-roll soundtrack and Godzilla's foot gleefully interrupt Bambi's animated romanticism.

Like a classic cartoon chase gag, the film sets up a clear promise (a meeting between Bambi and Godzilla), stretches anticipation toward tedium, and then delivers a violent twist that betrays established expectations (in this case, the expectation that Godzilla's entire body, presumably scaled down to Bambi's size, will enter the frame from the side and initiate a fight). The film executes its premise by pushing limited animation to its extreme, and the extended credits of the first half seem both proud and apologetic for the production efforts that went into the drawings. Made by a single and primarily self-taught student filmmaker, working alone at his desk, the animated image depends more on concept, pacing, and pop cultural references than on fluidity or sophistication of movement that would demand significantly more drawings and elaborate effects.

To animation historians, the film's introduction of a giant dinosaur might suggest a reference to early artisanal modes of production, as if it weren't Godzilla but Winsor McCay's famous Gertie the Dinosaur, who came back from the margins of the frame to claim her dominance over the cute mammals that replaced her in the public's imagination. However, whereas Winsor McCay framed Gertie, and by extension the early animated cartoon, as a miraculous feat of human ingenuity made possible by modern technology and immense labor, Marv Newland's film suggests just the opposite: that animation can develop even without sophisticated proprietary tools, polished lifelike movements, or months of precise drawing. On the contrary, animation could embrace its own limitations, turning even the crudeness of simple pencil drawings into a virtue.[19] Despite its modest origins and ambitions, *Bambi Meets Godzilla* struck a chord with other animators, precisely *because* it was so antithetical to the aspirations of mainstream studio animation. Unsurprisingly, the film's short duration and violent irony also made it popular with later Internet audiences.

Mounting frustration with the stylistic sterility and polished naturalism that studio animation often demanded of its artists is palpable in the works of later independent animators, such as Ralph Bakshi, Bill Plympton, and Don Hertzfeldt. For these animators, workings on the margins of the studio system, the rough animation test and the simplified line were an economic inevitability but also an opportunity to break free of the stylistic codes and storytelling formulae of mainstream production. Ralph Bakshi, as the first of these figures to independently achieve financial success and recognition, left the more conservative codes of television cartoons to embark on independent films with mature content, graphic violence and sexuality, **B-film** genre tropes, and characters living on the social periphery. For Bakshi, the constraints of animating on the fly in a smaller independent studio became synonymous with the rebellious energy and aggressive attitude of his projects: "I made my feature films with no pencil tests, no storyboards, no retakes, no **color keys**, no character designers, no special effects department, nothing, zip, nada—because we had to. When I was young, I had a dream—and a rage over Disney's insistence that nothing worked on the big screen unless it was perfect—redone and reworked until it was flawless. I always thought the difference between my films and the Disney ones was the difference between rock n' roll and a symphony."[20] Many independent animators running their own small production companies still maintained aspects of the studio animation mode, frequently hiring teams of animators for projects they directed. However, whether they were truly working alone or collaborating in smaller groups, postwar animators interested in more artisanal approaches found different ways of embracing and exploring the imperfections, accidents, and open-ended surprises that occur in the process of roughly drawing and redrawing an image.

Expanding Mechanical and Electronic Reproduction

Freehand drawing and improvisation were integral to the aesthetics of artisanal animation in the United States, but it would be misleading to characterize this tradition as a turn to unmediated traces of the artist's hand. Aside from the obvious fact that the majority of animators relied on cameras to capture their handiwork and produce moving images, many of them also frequently took advantage of other devices for mechanically or electronically reproducing graphic forms. In the expanding field of postwar independent animation, the overwhelming production demands of making repeated images alone inspired different technical solutions to reduce or make the most of the gestures that an animator needed to perform—not just by cutting down the frames and trading kinetic fluidity for graphic dynamism, as limited animation would in part propose, but by finding new ways to automate the process of image generation.

The most deceptively simple strategy to make the most of an animator's gestural work and limit unnecessary repetition is to take advantage of the camera's inherent properties as a sequential image-capturing and animating device. In classical drawn animation, including many of the independent films featured in the preceding section, filmmakers typically produce multiple separate images, either on paper or other canvases, before a camera is used to photograph all of the images and assemble them into a sequence. In other words, the camera enters the scene when most of a sequence's component frames have already been made. However, it is also possible to animate by making changes to a single image or composition, as one would do with an evolving painting or a puppet scene, while periodically recording the sequential steps, thereby creating the components of a sequence *while* filming it. Oskar Fischinger's film *Motion Painting No. 1*, mentioned at the beginning of this chapter, is exemplary of this approach. Since *Motion Painting No. 1* was made by painting with oils on acrylic glass and recording sequential strokes, one could simply describe the film as a sped-up documentation of the making of a painting (one way of interpreting the film's title). And yet the process of separately photographing the different stages in a painting's metamorphosis creates a moving image that appears to be animated of its own accord.[21] This approach to animation is typically called animating **under the camera**, because every increment of the process occurs concurrently with filming the results; the actual production process physically happens almost entirely underneath or in front of a periodically recording camera.[22] Under-the-camera animation paradoxically brings handmade animation closer to live-action filming, because the camera is not used to assemble many disparately generated images into a continuous sequence but rather to excise static snapshots from a continuous process that is occurring in front of the camera.[23]

Animating by altering a single surface demands planning, meticulous detailed work, and long stretches of uninterrupted concentration. However, it is a different type of work than recreating or redrawing an entire composition for each tiny incremental movement. Almost every gesture and impression made by an animator working under the camera results in concrete animated movement on screen—if anything needs to stay the same between frames, it is simply left untouched.[24] The actual labor of generating a sequence requires less time for physically reproducing the same lines and shapes. A helpful way to grasp the difference in production demands between classical drawn animation and under-the-camera animation is to think about the materials left over from each approach: after completing a sequence with the classically drawn animation approach, one is left with piles of backgrounds, cels, and drawings; after completing a sequence with the under-the-camera animation approach, one is left with only the image that was finished and filmed last.

Traditional cel-animation supplies are less suitable to under-the-camera animation, which requires materials that can be arranged more freely between frames. If a filmmaker relies on the standard inks and paints, then each stroke needs to dry in place and has to be covered up with subsequent strokes and layers. To get around the delays of literally watching paint dry, many artists have sought out more flexible alternatives, which could be selectively erased or altered. Popular options have included mixing paints with chemical retarders to keep it wet, so it can be spread or wiped off a surface; selecting hard low-absorbency surfaces, such as glass and plastic, that maintain paint fluidity; using charcoals and pastels that can be selectively erased; or animating with small objects and particles that can be shifted around. Several such techniques appear together in Douglass Crockwell's early *Glen Falls Sequence* (1937–1946), a compilation of different tests that Crockwell (an illustrator better known for his commercial posters of wholesome Americana) made over nine years of experimenting at home, trying to develop and patent a cost-effective animation process.[25] *Glen Falls Sequence* features dreamlike landscapes and biomorphic images made by applying wet paint onto layers of glass, by sculpting melted wax and plasticine, by repositioning cutout paper shapes, and by animating small objects that appear to be pastel stubs. Some of the compositions were painted with detailed brushstrokes, while others were applied with fingertips or air blown onto inky water. As the animator added or released pressure from the firm surface, the paints mixed and blended together with each step, creating soft gradations that took on fleshy and organic forms. Crockwell described the animated images generated with this method as "four-dimensional traces objects leave in space during the course of their existence," which is a description echoed by numerous other experimental animators.[26] Animating by manipulating a single surface creates a sequence that visually captures the temporal lifespan (fourth dimension) of that surface, which also includes and incorporates the traces of the animator's labor.[27]

Some under-the-camera animators abandoned ink and paint entirely, in favor of more malleable materials. Caroline Leaf's student film *Sand, or Peter and the Wolf* (1969) was the first American film to use sand as its primary material.[28] By experimenting with a light box in her Harvard University animation class, Leaf discovered that pushing grains of sand around the surface formed different barriers to light, which could be used to make moving silhouette shapes and add various levels of transparency. The composition is quite malleable, because the sand can always be shifted into new arrangements. Since the technique works by restricting light and forming solid silhouettes, it is particularly suited for simplified and iconic shapes, such as human figures or easily identifiable animals and objects. The density of the sand grain can also be manipulated to form dispersed clusters, which is effective for evoking more amorphous particle formations, such as water, clouds, and smoke. Soon after completing her first film, Caroline Leaf moved to Canada to work at the National Film Board, but her approach to **sand animation** (and later paint-on-glass) was picked up by other artists working in the United States. *Sandman* (1973), by Eli Noyes Jr., is a good example from this period, arranging sand particles into dancing stick figures and breaking them apart into dreamlike clouds and patterns. The film secured Noyes a commission to produce a series of popular sand alphabet segments for *Sesame Street*.

Non-hardening clay and plasticine, used by film animators since the turn of the twentieth century, reemerged as popular artisanal animation materials, straddling the line between more traditional puppet animation and under-the-camera graphic approaches. Eli Noyes Jr.'s *Clay* (1964) shifts between these modes, first using plasticine as a pliable two-dimensional canvas, pinched and scratched under the camera to form different relief patterns, and then repositioning the material in front of the camera for sequences of more three-dimensional **clay animation**. This back-and-forth interplay between the voluminous extension of the material and the flattening effect of the camera's photographing process is also explored in Art Oakley's impressive student film *Gumbasia* (1955), which led to funding support for his popular clay animation series *Gumby*.

Since each gesture applied to an image animated under the camera alters the ongoing composition, the process is simultaneously destructive (the production of each frame destroys the integrity of the previous frame) and generative (each stroke and alteration emanates directly from the image that directly preceded it). Animating under the camera makes it extremely challenging, if not impossible, to redo an earlier frame or retroactively add new in-between frames, as one can more easily do with a compilation of drawings. As Caroline Leaf described her experience: "Working under the camera takes a special kind of nerve, because you can't go back to make changes. It's like a performance in slow motion. You develop a system for remembering movement as you are making it, and you have to feel it intensely."[29] Once an image has been repainted or reshaped, the previously recorded frame is gone. Such a unidirectional method of destroying and creating, or erasing and adding, would not be acceptable to studio animation producers, not only because it is too difficult to parse out and distribute one sequence across a collective of animators but also because one cannot fully standardize and repeat the evolving series of images. Digital technology has gone a long way toward changing the irreversibility of under-the-camera techniques, but going back to redo frames is still frequently more demanding than going with the flow and figuring out creative ways to keep moving forward.[30]

Embracing the camera saved a lot of redundant and tedious work for independent animators, but it also challenged them to respond to the distinct properties and constraints of their chosen materials. In addition to its irreversibility, the process of altering an image under the camera is never completely precise and often leaves behind some traces of preceding frames that were erased or wiped away. Paint strokes are unexpectedly blended or shifted, grains of sand scatter and roll around, and objects imperceptibly jerk on the surface in tiny increments that will not be visible to the animator until the sequence is later projected. Moreover, working on just one continually transforming surface makes it difficult to separate between figures and backgrounds, and thus transitions between different poses frequently affect the entire composition. Figures and backgrounds appear to swell and swallow each other as their relative scales change, or entire scenes gradually morph from one to another over successive frames. Yet all of these unexpected, to some extent inevitable, artifacts of the production process provide vivid visual testimonies to the malleability of space and time: the mutually reciprocal relationship between individual parts and the whole, the porous boundaries between bodies and landscapes, and the influence of the past on the present. Unsurprisingly, all of these themes frequently appear in films animated with under-the-camera techniques.

A very different set of production methods, which do not belong to under-the-camera animation but which *also* take advantage of the camera as an image-capturing and animating device, manipulate and rework a very limited cycle of images through photography. Robert Breer's film *Blazes* (1961) is a particularly bold example of this approach. The film was made with just several dozen painted index cards that were rearranged into numerous different combinations, which were in turn re-photographed to create a rapid flow of new juxtapositions. Breer developed this method after becoming interested in optical toys, such as the **flip book** and the Mutoscope (a nineteenth-century device for animating a stack of photographs using a hand-cranked rotating mechanism, like a Rolodex of cards). Breer discovered that these simple devices could produce an astonishing variety of rhythms and effects using a very limited amount of frames: "you could sit there cranking the same cycle over and over and, through subjective changes, you would discover new images, so the piece would seem to be constantly renewing itself."[31] In several of his own films, Breer adapted the mechanics of the Mutoscope by reshuffling finite cycles of drawings and then filming the resulting sequences to generate continually changing variations.

To some extent, this approach merely adapted and expanded the standard studio practice of re-photographing fixed animation cycles to repeat certain movements again and again. Studio animators reused certain image cycles to extend a gesture or to reproduce a movement in another scene without having to recreate all of the drawings. However, studio animation still aspired to a naturalism of motion and therefore preserved the internal order of individual frames within each animated cycle. Experimental animators like Robert Breer, on the other hand, treated every single image in a series as a discrete unit with its own visual autonomy. Recovering the discrete autonomy of each frame in an animated cycle exponentially increased the possible combinations that one could achieve with very few images. Just six different drawings can be combined into 720 unique six-frame sequences; if all the different possibilities are animated "on twos," meaning each image in each combination is photographed twice, then the original half dozen drawings can potentially generate sixty seconds of film without ever repeating the same combination. This does not take into account additional variations produced by holding some images longer than others, by flipping images vertically and horizontally, or by reframing them with the camera to focus on different portions of an image.[32]

Independent animators interested in expanding the versatility of limited image cycles appropriated two other mechanical reproduction devices that were originally pioneered by mainstream animation studios: the photocopier (e.g., Photostat and Xerox) and the optical printer. The Walt Disney Studio was an enthusiastic early adopter and promoter of both types of technologies. The studio had relied on photostats to copy and distribute identical model sheets to different departments since the 1930s, invested in **optical printing** to seamlessly layer traveling mattes of drawn and live-action footage, and used xerography to transpose drawn figures onto animation cels well into the 1980s.[33] However, all of these technologies really flourished in the hands of independent animators, who embraced the textures, superimpositions, and image variations produced in the course of re-photographing or copying images repeatedly.

George Griffin's film *Head* (1975) is a playful and self-reflexive example of animating finite image cycles with xerography (fig. 4.5). Inspired in part by the work of Robert Breer, *Head* incorporates several cycles of index card drawings, which are gradually reorganized and altered to create extended sequences from limited sets. However, the film also uses Xerography to repeatedly copy the same cycle

FIGURE 4.5: (left) Still frame from George Griffin's *Head* (1976); (center) still frame from Joanna Priestley's *Rubber Stamp Film* (1983); (right) still frame from Lawrence (Larry) Jordan's *Carabosse* (1980).

of photographs (the animator's grimacing face), allowing the machine's gradual erosion of tonal gradations to transform the photographs into increasingly abstracted graphic portraits. Here the camera, conceived not as a faithful recording device but as a fallible copying device, inserts variation into an animated cycle simply by virtue of its imperfect registration of the same images over successive reproductions. This by-product of mechanical intervention, which would be considered unwanted noise or image decay in studio production, is turned into an opportunity to visually explore the broad spectrum between photographic realism and xerographic abstraction, between specific faces and general human expressions, and between a photograph and the living, aging body that it tries to preserve.

Xerographic transfer of photographed or filmed sequences onto paper had three additional benefits. First, the resulting paper copies could be torn, painted, and otherwise graphically manipulated. Animators still had to tackle large sets of individual images, but they could work directly on readymade inked backgrounds based on recorded footage. Second, a filmed sequence transferred onto paper broke up a continuous motion into discrete images, which were easier to manipulate and reorder than piles of sliced, tiny celluloid frames. Paper copies offered a more accessible method to play with the rhythm of recorded movement without remaking the same images repeatedly, allowing for what Griffin called "restructured photographic animation."[34] Third, animators could directly wreak havoc on footage of recognizable events and figures, undermining the boundaries between recorded and artificial images in ways that recalled the playful cartoons of early animation and looked forward to digital manipulation. Xerographic techniques largely disappeared in light of digital technology, but they were popular and influential among experimental animators throughout the 1970s and 1980s, eventually seeping into their commercial work and the public imagination—most famously when Candy Kugel used photocopied printouts of the first moon landing as the basis for an iconic MTV channel bumper.[35]

Optical printers (devices for selectively re-photographing film frames and compositing layers of images on film strips) provided even greater opportunities to manipulate finite image cycles. Optical printers allow a filmmaker to reorder and re-photograph frames directly, without the bulky intermediary stages of paper

cards and xeroxed transfers. Industrially produced and homemade optical printers were key to the development of postwar independent cinema in the United
States, including films based on drawn or painted images, which can be more read-
ily defined as animated works. Among these, Adam Beckett's films are most
remarkable for their astonishingly complex compositions, created with the aid
of extremely limited sequences—sometimes as limited as a single twelve-image
cycle. Many of Beckett's films evoke a tapestry of changing forms and ornamental
motifs that, when looped, create the illusion of constant forward movement (in
the way that a rotating image of a spiral produces the hypnotic effect of traveling
forward through an infinite tunnel). An optical printer is then used to further
rework sequences by selectively re-photographing parts of a tapestry at a time or
by moving incrementally across the surface of a detailed image. *Dear Janice*
(1972) is a masterpiece of this kind of intricate cyclical choreography of a limited
animated cycle. The film unfolds on the screen as a chain of words and doodles
that give the impression of a long animated letter made up of thousands of drawings, only to continually double back and reveal itself as just one single dense cycle
of images, gradually reframed with the aid of an optical printer. Other films by
Beckett add additional complexity and variation by using the optical printer to
superimpose the same cycle onto the same filmstrip again and again with slightly
offset beginning positions, forming recursive patterns.

Mechanical and optical image-reproduction devices allowed artisanal animators to build dynamic compositions using just a single canvas or limited series
of handmade images. Some animators, however, also found ways to automate the
very process of image production, making films with stock images and ready-
made forms.[36] In doing so, they could circumvent the actual process of tracing
out the same lines and color fields, placing more emphasis on arrangement and
composition. Joanna Priestley's *Rubber Stamp Film* (1983), produced with the
help of an immense collection of novelty rubber stamps, is a playful and imaginative film that takes an analog printmaking tool made for quickly reproducing
identical figures and adapts it to compose comical landscapes and surreal collage
scenes. The production of the film still required tens of thousands of stamped
index cards, years of work, and careful planning. However, the actual gestural
labor of producing animated movement consisted of inking and stamping
premade shapes, rather than manually drawing and redrawing identical forms
(fig. 4.5).

The proliferation of popular magazines, newspapers, and other mass-
distributed print objects in the postwar decades provided artists with a treasure
trove of photographs and illustrations for animation. This was a major reason why
collage animation burgeoned and diversified in this period. In *A La Mode* (1958)
by Stan VanDerBeek, newsprint reproductions of classical paintings and sculp-
tural nudes are brought together with photographs of fashion models to form surreal and witty exchanges, while frying pans, ornamental plates, tea kettles, and
butter knives (all likely pulled from advertisements) fly around like interplane-

tary invaders. The body of a swimsuit model is enlarged and rotated to suggest an erotic desert landscape; a photograph of a lavishly furnished dining room is cut and positioned to look like an anatomical X-ray of the human body; a detached leg with a heeled shoe is rotated and combined with other images to form the head and beak of a bird. *Carabosse* (1980) by Larry Jordan uses Victorian prints and illustrations, replete with etchings of refined ladies and gentlemen, floating gramophones, and botanical specimens, to create a world that seems to exist in an alternate universe (fig. 4.5). Tinted in blue hues and swimming in and out of a black horizon, the figures seem to emanate from some other metaphysical plane, in which nostalgically quaint images become an uncanny portrait of cosmic exploration. For Jordan, as for many artists interested in the collage form, working with readymade images challenged the animator to relinquish some degree of control and allow accidental juxtapositions and personal reactions to the unfolding scenes to guide the construction of the work: "I often operate on freely associated series of images, finding the trail as I go, not plotting it, though some of the films are meticulously scripted. When I astonish myself, I put it in the film. When I don't, I leave it out."[37] Taking cues from early Dada and surrealist collage art, collage animation would wrench photographs of everyday objects from their assigned utilitarian and commercial fates on the pages of print media, reanimating them into new mystical and erotic compositions.

Together, photographic collage, optical printing, and xerography were all strategies for graphically manipulating images without necessarily having to redraw and repeat thousands of discrete new frames. They offered image reproducibility with a built-in flexibility for graphic and temporal manipulation. Using these reproduction devices as animation tools blurred the boundaries between handmade and automated filmmaking approaches, and it expanded the very definition of animation in the postwar decades. Some filmmakers who did not even necessarily define themselves as "animators" nevertheless adopted animation techniques as part of a growing interest in painterly and musical approaches to cinema. For them, filmmaking was a form of composing, and the camera was an instrument for painting directly with light. To this end, they developed their own contraptions that could be used to generate dynamic compositions by simply pulling strings or shifting light beams in front of the camera. Such contraptions typically focused on objects with different light refraction properties: mirrors, projection scrims, spinning disks, mobiles, pulleys, and pendulums. Working with such three-dimensional arrangements was somewhat similar to under-the-camera animation, since small gestural interventions could noticeably alter the entire composition. Notable American artists who designed their own kinetic sculptures and mechanical light-manipulation devices included Mary Ellen Bute, Len Lye, Harry Smith, James and John Whitney, Jim Davis, and Jordan Belson.

Mary Ellen Bute (along with her partner and technical assistant Ted Nemeth) deserves particular attention for promoting the electronic **oscilloscope** as a device for automatically generating light compositions. As Bute wrote about this method in her work, the oscilloscope could be employed like a musical instrument, which would allow the artist "to manipulate light to produce visual compositions in time continuity much as a musician manipulates sound to produce music."[38] An important point in Bute's account of the oscilloscope's virtues is the device's immediate responsiveness, since it inserts continuous variation into a single image with the aid of control keys that change the image on a monitor. In the classical drawn "cartoon technique," according to Bute, "the spontaneity of the artist's concept and design becomes extremely attenuated," because the flow of work is inevitably halted in the slow production of discrete images. The oscilloscope, on the other hand, immediately registers minor technical adjustments as entirely new forms: "By turning knobs and switches on a control board I can 'draw' with a beam of light with as much freedom as with a brush. As the figures and forms are produced by light on the oscilloscope screen, they are photographed on motion picture film. . . . By changing and controlling the electrical inputs on the 'scope an infinite variety of forms can be made to move in pre-determined time rhythms, and be combined or altered *at will*."[39] Unlike most under-the-camera animation techniques, the oscilloscope also offered a more reversible process. One could return to a preceding setting, redo certain phases of movement in a different way, and try alternate variations. The process allowed for more risk and spontaneity, since any composition that was "destroyed" in the process of making changes could be recalled more easily. In many ways, the oscilloscope stood at a historical intersection between the kinetic mobiles pioneered by early abstract animators who preceded it and some of the early computer animation that would later follow.

For some independent animators, mechanical and electronic image reproduction offered a way to attain more control over their compositions, to translate what Mary Ellen Bute emphatically called the artistic *"will"* into "pre-determined rhythms." In this case, automated devices functioned like physical proxies that could generate images with greater speed and fidelity or like an orchestra playing a composer's score, creating more opportunities for precise calibrations and interventions. For other animators, however, the turn to automated imaging techniques served the opposite function—taking some measure of control away from the filmmaker and pushing the artist to respond to the unforeseen and the unexpected. In working with premade images or allowing an image to unfold in front of the camera, animators could foster a more open-ended compositional process.

Tracing Lineage

Lineage (1979), an animated essay by George Griffin, opens on a black screen enlivened by scattered white doodles drawn by the filmmaker. Griffin's voice-over states that the doodles demonstrate the kind of tradition to which his independent

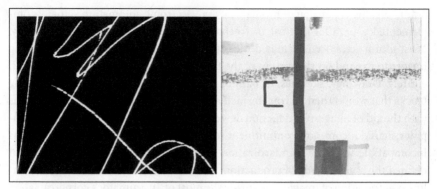

FIGURE 4.6: Still frames from George Griffin's *Lineage* (1979).

work belongs: "I would like these lines to suggest, among other things, the hand-crafted nature of animation, a vestige of manual dexterity, independent from the photographic concerns of cinema. Also as a line, it represents a connecting thread to other artists, people who make marks, and who are in turn marked by what they make." However, the very next scene in the film offers a different portrait of animation. Straightened horizontal and vertical lines of varying thickness and color stiffly move across a white surface in recurring and compounding cycles, while a voice enumerates each cycle of each line: "1, 2, 3, 4, . . . 38, 39" (fig. 4.6). The film later reveals that this second sequence is composed from a finite set of white index cards, which are recycled and re-photographed with new alterations made between each cycle. Thus, the film's titular "lineage" of independent animation is split to form at least two different lineages, each of which corresponds to a different strategy pursued by artists, whose labor consists of making thousands of marks. The first strategy commits to the rough freehand line as a foundational and versatile animation medium, embracing all of the variations, inconsistencies, and textures that define the process of solitary doodling and sketching. The second strategy adopts techniques of image automation, using devices as simple as a deck of index cards or as a complex as an optical printer to manipulate fewer, finite sets of images. In this chapter, I proposed and discussed these two production strategies as the two defining tendencies shaping the look of postwar American independent animation and bridging the works of many different artists.[40]

In *Lineage*, these two strategies are portrayed as two contradictory forces balancing an aesthetic seesaw. Throughout the chapter, I similarly framed them as distinct and different responses, each with its own underlying principles and aesthetic qualities: one stripping away sophisticated techniques in favor of a more spontaneous and gestural approach, the other minimizing gestural intervention with the aid of automation. Yet, contrary to this reductive rhetorical opposition, the two strategies are not at odds with one another. In fact, for many postwar animators, the expansion of mechanical and electronic automation actually complemented a parallel interest in freehand drawing and gestural spontaneity. Most filmmakers used various devices for copying or technically manipulating images to expand on the virtues of the freehand gesture, rather than supplant it entirely. Drawings, sketches, or painted cards would often become the building blocks that would then be transformed and reanimated into new configurations with the aid of image-reproduction devices. The two seemingly different philosophies shared a common commitment to improvisation and change, which was incompatible with the standardization of method and regulation of style that defined the studio mode of production. Both linear freehand drawing and non-linear automation of image cycles made the most of an animator's corporeal labor, and both also made physical and economical room for experimentation and potential failure.

Not long after Len Lye received his Brussels prize for *Free Radicals* and the Hubleys completed *Moonbird*, the film critic André Martin wrote that the range and diversity of new independent work heralded the end of the classical cel-animation monopoly and opened a "new era" of animation cinema "marked by the widest possible range of techniques and processes."[41] Without prescribed rules for how exactly one had to animate, the range of materials and approaches used by different filmmakers expanded: watercolors, oils, gouaches, pencils, charcoal, spray paint, sand, plasticine, water, mirrors, electric light bulbs, metal shavings, found footage, scientific and popular magazine illustrations, analog and electronic copying machines—these are just some of the materials adopted for animation in this period. In the spirit of moving away from collective standardization toward individual discovery, few filmmakers specialized in just one method or mode.

In fact, a striking feature in the work of almost all postwar independent animators is the variation of methods, genres, and production techniques in each individual's body of work—often even within the body of a single film. Sometimes a filmmaker might make three different films within the span of a decade that, if stripped of their credit sequences, could appear on the surface to have been designed by three different artists.[42] An animator's evolving ideas and interests might drive the shifts in medium and form, or a single aesthetic question could yield three very distinct answers in the shape of three different films. Postwar independent animators may have embraced working alone or in small collectives, but they rejected the value of stylistic consistency (having a "signature style") and control that often characterizes the myth of solitary authorship. The appeal of working independently was (paradoxically) the opportunity to welcome new ideas and influences, rather than to stay the same.

5

THE RISE OF COMPUTER-GENERATED IMAGERY,

1965-1989 Andrew Johnston

In the second half of the twentieth century, new technologies of computation and information processing had become commonplace at universities, government laboratories, corporate workplaces, as well as other institutions that had the resources to purchase and store these large machines. Filmmakers and animators began exploring this new technology both through the development of thematic content and the creation of new cinematic tools. While films such as *The Desk Set* (1957) spun a narrative of anxiety through a fictionalized version of the famous ENIAC computer that would replace clerical workers and other forms of labor, other films, such as the animator Jim Henson's IBM commercial *Paperwork Explosion* (1967), presented these new computers as the means through which modern managerial, financial, and information anxieties could be alleviated. These competing perceptions of information technologies and computers persist through contemporary narratives, but their appearance and intertwining with aesthetic forms and artistic techniques led to the recognition of a dramatic shift in the media landscape, signaled by a 1968 exhibit at the Museum of Modern Art entitled *The Machine as Seen at the End of the Mechanical Age*. Animators explored this new technology in a variety of production contexts, working with engineers, between computational systems, and across avant-garde and commercial film in the first decades of the development of computer-generated imagery, or CGI.

This chapter will explore the shift in animation techniques, technologies, and aesthetic productions that accompanied the rise of CGI. It will show how the laborers mentioned above, such as filmmakers, artists, programmers, and engineers, regularly worked at the same labs or studios while attempting to develop and test not only the technology of computer imaging but also the idea and goals of this new mode of animation. Though CGI is commonly associated with the creation of fantastical and plastic worlds in contemporary digital animation, the goals of most animators and programmers from its first decades centered on the registration of simple graphic elements, such as lines, shapes, and colors, as well as the impact of these forms in motion. This period, from the early 1960s through the mid-1980s, was one of intense technological change, marked by the development of information processing machines, the creation of the microchip, and the rise and dissemination of personal computers. Throughout film history, animators have routinely played with new image technologies as they have emerged, effectively recreating how cinema defines itself, or as Kristin Thompson points out, these filmmakers have helped make "cinema a perpetual novelty."[1] During this period, animators began exploring how computational technologies could be utilized to generate moving images and aesthetic effects sometimes specific to the new mechanisms. Much overlooked, this early history of CGI is marked by experimentation with the technical creation of movement, often resulting in abstract films and digital images that explore relationships between computational software and hardware.

Though the pace of technological change continued to accelerate during these first decades, there were often limitations that artists encountered when working with computers from the time, leading many to combine older animation tools and techniques with new ones. This parallel track of development—one marked by the exploration of technical and aesthetic capabilities, the other by the mixture of these new techniques with older forms of animation—resulted in a fractured history of CGI with groups of labs, artists, and engineers working independently of one another across a wide range of platforms, computer languages, and formal goals. This disunity and disintegration led Ivan Sutherland, a leader in the field and creator of the pioneering **wire-frame graphic** and image platform Sketchpad, to summarize the myriad issues facing computer graphics in a 1966 article entitled "Computer Graphics: Ten Unsolved Problems."[2] In it, he notes how broad the subject had become and how many people were already at work on each of the enumerated issues in the field. But by identifying these areas of research exploration, Sutherland was attempting to develop a shared vocabulary and research agenda that could bring a sense of cohesion and community to CGI. This same desire helped spur the development of the Special Interest Group on Computer Graphics (SICGRAPH) out of the Association for Computer Machinery (ACM) in 1967, an interest group that two years later changed its name to SIGGRAPH and began hosting their groundbreaking annual conferences on CGI in 1974. This need for dialogue and exchange amid a rapidly evolving and expanding area simultaneously reveals the difficulties inherent in writing a history of CGI during this period, whose idiosyncratic platforms, projects, and languages have far more experiments that were short-lived, unfinished, or discarded than those that led to contemporary digital animation platforms. Yet these forgotten futures of computer imaging technologies nonetheless had an effect on the shape and direction of CGI, and their traces are still visible in contemporary media landscapes. Like Sutherland, this chapter will not attempt to catalog all the various projects and technologies in the first decades of CGI's history; nor will it list all the individuals and actors who had a hand in shaping its trajectories. Instead, it will present its most common problems, sites of production, and paradigmatic work in order to introduce lines of approach and inquiry into this large arena. In many regards, the list of research items in the field of CGI that Sutherland spells out is the same one that animators work with across its history, as this mode experiments with image generation, standardization, and storage along with the aesthetic effects of these technologies. As Sutherland explains, some of CGI's problems will be resolved by research into new techniques, while others "will be with us forever."[3]

Screen Captures

In this problem-and-solution model for digital computation and animation, one of the first difficulties and areas of experimentation lay in **rendering**—the projection of computational data into a still or moving image. The difficulty was twofold: how to both generate images on computer hardware in the 1960s and how to store or transfer these images onto filmstrips. Most artists and engineers combined or braided analog and digital technologies into hybrid machines to produce animations, especially if they had experience with older computational techniques. This also resulted in more experimental work that was found in the avant-garde or that made its way into feature-length films as special effects sequences. John Whitney's analog and digital animations from the 1950s through the 1970s are exemplary of this experimentation and production context. After he and his brother, James, made their celebrated avant-garde film *Five Film Exercises* (1943–1944) using optical printing and mechanical pendulums, the brothers began working independently on various artistic projects. Each still explored the possibilities of dynamism through contrasts in visual forms,[4] but John Whitney's work pressed further into the mechanisms and techniques of animation, especially those associated with abstraction. In the early 1950s, he generated a series of **oil-wipe**

animation films, which allowed for the movement of colored oils to intersect and press against one another on glass trays but whose effects proved difficult to control relative to his past work.

After these experiments and the development of abstract sequences in UPA studio films, Whitney returned to creating animations through experiments with computational technologies. With his son, John Whitney Jr., he visited a California military depot that was selling analog computers at discounted prices after the United States military began transitioning to digital systems in the late 1950s. All electronic computers operate by manipulating electrical currents, with most measuring voltage or the direction of currents. While digital computers represent voltage through symbolic values so that determined high- and low-voltage levels for a system receive a value such as 1 or 0 that can then be easily translated into a separate system or context, analog computers from this time operate through the creation of circuits that are analogous to specific systems or conditions. Each circuit within the system continuously receives electrical voltage that must be adjusted in coordination with the others to simulate particular conditions that will be calculated by the computer. This meant that the machines were very fast at the particular calculations they were designed for, like measuring airflows or ballistic trajectories, but that changing their applications for different contexts required significant amounts of work. By 1957, Whitney built an animation mechanism out of the M5 he purchased at the depot, a World War II–era antiaircraft gun director with an analog computer specializing in ballistic tracking and predictive positioning. With the spinning gun controller eventually attached to artwork, he could calculate its movements with his computer and generate controlled articulations of lines and curves to produce evenly spaced lattices rotating in time or spirals emerging from the center of the frame in uniform progressions. This work quickly gained the attention of Hollywood special effects artists and visual designers, prompting Saul Bass to contract Whitney to make the spirographs in the opening titles of *Vertigo* (1958). Whitney later coupled the M5 with an optical printer and pioneered the **slit-scan printing** technique used by Douglas Trumbull in the "Stargate" sequence of *2001: A Space Odyssey* (1968), in addition to producing a number of animations with this machine before working on digital animation systems as an artist in residence at IBM in 1966.

Though Whitney's analog computer animations were pioneering, his frustration with the slow pace of analog programming and the inaccuracy of the rotating artwork or optical printer attached to the computer led him to seek out digital tools because of the promised precision of their screen images. But he quickly learned of the necessary compromises required in producing digital images as well. At IBM he worked with Jack Citron, a physicist who created an animation and imaging extension of the computer language Fortran for Whitney, called Graphics Additions to Fortran (GRAF). The language developed out of the simple plotting of x,y values and allowed for images to be created and drawn on an IBM

360/System and an IBM 2250 display unit attached to the mainframe. Whitney had the ability to manipulate program variables with a **light pen** and then visualize a geometric pattern or abstraction based upon the resulting equation. If he wished to record or save the algebraic function, he could print it onto a 7⅜"×3¼" paper punched card. But if he wanted to record the image, he had to connect the monitor to a camera programmed to operate in tandem with the screen's **rendering time**—the amount of time it took to translate the data into a figure on the screen. Not only was Whitney limited by the black and white resolution, but he also explains that the films he produced at IBM were not made on a real-time system. Instead, "it takes three to six seconds to produce one image . . . [and] one twenty-second sequence requires about thirty minutes computer time."[5] Furthermore, his monitor could only draw curves by placing discrete points close to one another in a discontinuous fashion or by drawing several straight lines across the screen whose endpoints intersect in what is perceived as a curve.[6] This workflow, which included the inability to see the metamorphoses of these abstractions until they were processed by a film lab and later watched on a Moviola, resulted in Whitney using the computer to generate a library of graphic elements that he later worked from on an optical printer while possibly replicating or resizing them on a film frame to produce plays with symmetry and eventually add color to the abstractions. The films made at IBM during this period, *Homage to Rameau* (1967), *Experiments in Motion Graphics* (1968), and *Permutations* (1968), bear witness to these technological negotiations in image generation and storage while also establishing a foundation for a set of aesthetic goals achievable only with digital technology. He believed that it was the best way to produce abstract visual contrasts in motion, a digital harmony whose mathematical precision provided a visual analog to musical structures.[7]

With all the problems and technological constraints Whitney and others like him faced at the time, the computational renderings made possible by the computer systems and monitors proved to be worth the effort. As Sutherland makes clear in another article from the time, "The Ultimate Display," digital computer imaging provides "a looking glass into a mathematical wonderland" by visualizing concepts not otherwise realizable.[8] Sutherland is referring to the ways in which digital displays can reveal the dynamics and forces usually invisible within the realm of particle physics, but he is more generally gesturing toward the visual rendering of algorithms, an unprecedented mathematics put into motion. Previous analog technologies, such as the cathode-ray oscilloscope, had the ability to project various acoustic or electronic wave functions by measuring such characteristics as their amplitude and frequency. Mary Ellen Bute employed this device for two animations in the 1950s, *Abstronic* (1954) and *Mood Contrasts* (1956), which contributed to her interests in synesthesia and her "seeing sound" films by allowing her to both visualize and manipulate acoustic sine waves.[9] Ben Laposky similarly experimented with this technology in the 1950s with a number of images that projected the relationship between parabolic curves. But the oscilloscope has its limitations: as an analog technology, it visualizes frequencies like sound waves coming into it, but it cannot **plug and play** variables in an equation, meaning that it could not work with complex algorithms.

That said, the oscilloscope did map its images using a **cathode-ray tube** whose **electron gun** could create lines at any point at any time on the screen, an important difference from the cathode-ray tubes used in many televisions from the time that only fired horizontal lines continuously across the entire screen as it generated images. This potential for manipulating the direction of the beam sparked Sutherland's ideas for its use in computer graphics. Sutherland's 1963 MIT PhD thesis project, Sketchpad, created a **vector graphics** system that stored image information in equations for later rendering, which allowed for dynamic image changes, less rendering time, and a reduction in data needed to store drawn paths (fig. 5.1).[10] Using mathematical calculations to plot the lines, or vectors, of an image was an important step toward being able to quickly render and manipulate pictures in digital environments. Built on a Lincoln Laboratory TX-2 computer at MIT with an oscilloscope, Sketchpad enabled an unprecedented amount of interactivity and control in computer graphics, with the input and manipulation of vector lines operating through a graphic interface controlled with a light pen. But like Whitney, Sutherland relied on older media to store images after they were produced. Also building a library of images, kept at hand on **magnetic tape**, Sutherland did outline how to animate a "winking girl" in his thesis, but the project valued the interactive production of one image over the recording, storage, and retrieval of many then necessary to produce a complex sequence.[11]

The importance of monitor types—especially **vector scan** and **raster scan displays**—for the development of computer graphics cannot be underestimated. Contemporary digital imaging systems and file formats still employ elements of vector graphics, though most monitors are not vector scan systems, which peaked in popularity in the 1960s and 1970s and were used in a few video game platforms afterward. Tektronix produced a number of these displays that took advantage of the efficiency and sharp details of lines rendered through an electron gun whose movements were programmed (as opposed to the horizontal-line-only option of most electron guns). Contemporary monitors are usually raster scan graphics systems, which employ a **bitmapped** matrix of pixels to generate a picture through a perceptual aggregate, much like a photographic halftone in newspapers. Similar to television monitors that repeatedly scan the entirety of the screen, these image systems rely on resolution and the scan rate of the gun. While they had the ability to render colors and tones in ways that vector scan monitors could not, their limitations in rendering time, resolution, and storage in the 1960s and 1970s hindered their appeal for many artists and programmers, especially since most of these early CGI platforms lacked real-time animation capabilities, an elusive goal that system designers continued to strive for by trying to optimize computational

FIGURE 5.1: Ivan Sutherland using Sketchpad on the MIT TX-2 computer in 1962.

performance. But experiments with raster scan systems nonetheless permeated labs and other spaces, especially because of their ability to map objects on a screen in relation to one another. Douglas Engelbart was one of these researchers who helped develop bitmapped screens on raster scan monitors, with screen images stored as a matrix of information about everything present on the screen at one time. This allowed for novel human-computer engagements, such as interacting with an object based on its x,y position on the screen, which is sent to the computer in the form of electronic data. Engelbart created an input device he called a "mouse" for a user to track and move objects on the screen with the new x,y coordinates.[12] These landmark achievements, along with the development of hypertext links and Engelbart's oN-Line System of computer interaction, were displayed for the public in 1968 in what was described as "The Mother of All Demos" at the Fall Joint Computer Conference.

Again, the difficulty for both Sutherland's and Engelbart's systems lay in image rendering time and its storage. Like Whitney's frustrations with screen rendering time at IBM, computers in the 1960s had limited real-time interaction and animation, in part because of the languages employed and the architecture of computer platforms. Fortran was the most popular language, especially because it was a higher-level language than many others at the time, meaning that it was abstracted from more direct communication with the physical circuitry of the computer. Because of this, Fortran could be used on a number of different machines. But the language also excelled at plotting vectors and constructing wire diagrams and images, lending itself to Whitney's abstract films developed at IBM. But memory limitations for monitors, along with an inability to plot too many abstract lines across the screen at any one time, meant that animators could not view their moving images with any kind of fluid continuity.

Two ways to store the separate images and animate them into continuous movement were photographing the screen, as Whitney did, or utilizing a **microfilm plotter**, a graphics output device that could draw directly onto film. Two important CGI pioneers, Edward Zajac and Charles Csuri, began working with plotters in the early 1960s. Zajac's film, *Simulation of a Two-Gyro Gravity-Gradient Attitude Control System* (1963), was created at Bell Labs to visualize the path of a satellite's orbit in space and was made with the intent of quickly and cost effectively rendering different object perspectives for scientists and designers (fig. 5.2). Compared to photographing screens, the plotter was a cheaper and easier means of diagramming the satellite and its control system, with Zajac even suggesting that "for technical applications, slower projection speeds (say eight or four frames per second as can be obtained on a movie editor) are often satisfactory."[13] Csuri began working with the microfilm plotter to print computer images that played with the relationship between figuration and abstraction, creating such works as *Sine Curve Man* (1967) that considered the role of technology in both the formal and cultural portrait generated.

This engagement was similar to the one A. Michael Noll researched, whose well-known computer images algorithmically mapped patterns reminiscent of mid-twentieth-century abstractions made by such artists as Piet Mondrian as a way of exploring the visual and technical dialectic between order and disorder. Noll went so far as to ascribe an amount of authorial power to his computer, publishing an article about making the images with the title "Patterns by 7090," a reference to the IBM 7090 computer he programmed to make the images that were printed on a Stromberg-Carlson 4020 microfilm plotter. As the authors of *10 PRINT* explain, Noll used eight patterns that served as the basis for an image he made for the 1965 Howard Wise gallery show entitled "Computer-Generated Pictures." He then "used existing subroutines of the printer to draw a sequence of lines to connect a series of x- and y-coordinates that he calculated and stored inside an array."[14] Some of these x,y coordinates were created through a random number generator, while others were produced through a quadratic equation, in the end creating an image that was made in collaboration with the computational platform.

Noll's and Csuri's experiments focused mostly on new interactions and collaborations with computers for the production of single images, again because of the limitations of screens and rendering time. As Zabat Patterson notes, the microfilm plotter, such as the one Noll used, grew in popularity because mainframe

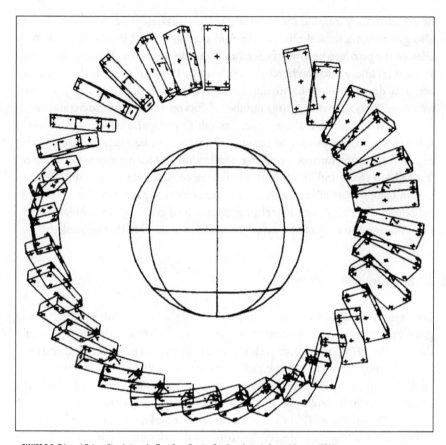

FIGURE 5.2: Edward Zajac, *Simulation of a Two-Gyro Gravity-Gradient Attitude Control System* (1963).

systems at the time could not store images in succession and because it offered a way of recording single images on paper or film to later animate them.[15] This was how Csuri used the microfilm plotter as he also began to produce films with his IBM 7094 digital mainframe. His first, *Hummingbird* (1967), works through a similar dialectic of order and disorder as Noll's images but plays with the relationship between figuration and abstraction as a line drawing of a hummingbird emerges slowly before breaking into a multiplicity of abstractions across the screen and finally reassembling itself. By focusing on vector paths and arranging moving lines to create recognizable forms, Csuri began exploring how patterns of action could be programmed through an interactive collaboration with the computer, an investigation similar to the one that occupied Whitney at IBM. In his narration to *Experiments in Motion Graphics*, Whitney explains how his images are "derived from structural configurations of the computer program," meaning that he was attempting to locate and refine the ways in which digital algorithms could control the location and paths of the lines he wanted to put on screen. As he explains, they "remind me of certain optical puzzles."[16] But like Csuri, he was also growing frustrated with screen and computational limitations that only allowed the puzzle to be slowly broken and reassembled through a mixture of various digital and analog technologies. Whitney's last film at IBM, *Permutations*, begins to develop a digital aesthetic more rooted in graphic harmonies that unfold over time by coordinating a large number of dots on-screen whose dynamic movements he likens to a visual language. Though he recognizes that this film works through visual tensions found in musical harmonies, he explains that it is also generative of a new form of visual communication rooted in computational time.[17] But as both Csuri and Whitney desired more control over time-based variables within computational practices, each sought out new platforms that could provide closer approximations to real-time interactions and graphics while also working with computer scientists and engineers to help develop that technology.

Labs and Running in Real-Time

The desire for digital real-time interactivity and graphics began to structure the goals and operations of a number of animators working in the late 1960s and through the 1970s, bridging experiments with digital image registration and their later incorporation into commercial film sequences. But real-time interactivity, which occupied the research and production of CGI at this time, also led to the creation of technical solutions that required building new platforms and research centers. The origins of CGI can many times be found in the projects of specific individuals, such as those described earlier in this chapter, but by the 1970s CGI had become a research field whose scientists and animators required more institutional support. Collaboration was necessary to solve such problems as interactivity, and viable solutions began to more frequently be associated with various universities, corporations, and research laboratories that built and developed hardware and software configurations. Such technological drives were always at the service of aesthetic ideas about animation in CGI, and the control of images in time was crucial to creating fluid animations, whether abstract or figurative on-screen. If, as Norman McLaren said about animation, "what happens *between* each frame is so much more important than what exists *on* each frame,"[18] then controlling those intervals in CGI would open the aesthetic to new possibilities.

Collaboration was in part a necessity because of the cost and size of mainframe computers in the 1960s and 1970s. Access was competitive and required applications to justify their use while also affecting how they were programmed. This usually took the form of computer usage and sharing called **batch processing**. Programmers would write code on typewriters and then, for Fortran or similar languages, store that program information on a stack of **punch cards** that would later be inserted into a computer. The cards were usually handed to a computer center reception desk and controlled by operators coordinating the run of several programs in succession, with results for each printed out and given back to the programmer.[19] Other ways of connecting to a mainframe grew in popularity later, such as **time-sharing**, which allowed computer or teletypewriter terminals to be connected simultaneously to a mainframe that would concurrently handle programming operations by processing intermittent bursts of code for each connected user.[20] Standards for time-sharing systems were developed at Dartmouth University by the same students and faculty who created the BASIC programming language in the 1960s.

Especially during this period in the history of computing, the tightly knit relationship between languages, hardware platforms, and visions of computer interaction affected the development of digital media from different institutional spaces. Bell Labs was one of the most productive and well-known sites of computational development in the 1960s, and it sponsored artists in the same way that IBM provided space and access for Whitney. At Bell, work in computer imaging was spearheaded by two engineers, Leon Harmon and Kenneth Knowlton, whose vision of CGI developed through studying **perceptual gestalts**—the moment when disparate elements in an image are recognized to be a part of a unified whole— that could be achieved with the new technology. Knowlton created a computer animation language in 1964 called BEFLIX (Bell Flicks) for the IBM 7090 and Stromberg-Carlson 4020 microfilm plotter using Fortran code understood only by that system.[21] This meant that BEFLIX was designed specifically for that IBM platform and that it would require substantial work to port it to another type of computer. Though Knowlton still concedes that an optical printer should be used edit, colorize, and "stretch" the final animation from his machine, this language operates through a representational grid that maps the surface of an image. By working with squared blocks of visual objects that when grouped together could generate whole images, a sort of CGI Lego set, BEFLIX uses a model of computer imaging reminiscent of raster scan graphics that can employ "appropriate shades of gray" for figurative elements in a defined resolution, here measured in 252 by 184 squares.[22] Patterson shows how the microfilm plotter has played a large role in the development of this language since it was the output device that helped generate some of these affordances and limitations. She also points to the other work Knowlton was made famous for in the 1960s, his *Studies in Perception I* (1966), a mural-sized computer image of a reclining nude woman generated from the printing of electronic symbols.[23] Like a Chuck Close portrait, the mural's gestalt is visible from a distance, but its reprinting in the *New York Times* in 1967 reduced its size and emphasized its triangulation of computational technology, a tradition of nude studies in art history, and pop imagery. Like the processing logic behind BEFLIX, CGI here is directed toward a construction of recognizable figurative images, leading Knowlton to create similar works in 1967, such as *Telephone*, and affecting his later work that investigates facial portraiture and perception.

The coordination of output platforms and extensions of Fortran around aesthetic goals clearly affected the creation of CGI works from this time, with Knowlton's images offering a very different experience than those created by Whitney. The films produced at Bell Labs speak to this same distinction, with both Stan VanDerBeek and Lillian Schwartz using BEFLIX and working alongside Knowlton to explore the language and platform, though with a greater focus on time-based variables than Knowlton and Harmon's experiments. Similar to Whitney, VanDerBeek was an artist in residence at Bell Labs and brought a background in experimental art and film to his exploration of CGI. Bell Labs sponsorship was part of EAT (Experiments in Art and Technology), a group founded by a number of artists and engineers, such as Robert Rauschenberg and Billy Klüver, to bridge interdisciplinary collaborations. Between 1964 and 1970, VanDerBeek produced ten animations with Knowlton in a series entitled *Poemfields*. Knowlton worked with VanDerBeek by modifying BEFLIX but continued to utilize the same representational grid described above for the language's foundation. This suited VanDerBeek's *Poemfields*, which employ a flickering grid of blocky characters that coalesce at times into words or images in a perceptually challenging manner reminiscent of other films from the time included in the category Gene Youngblood describes as expanded cinema.[24] As Knowlton suggests in his essay on BEFLIX and computer animation, VanDerBeek's films were also edited and colorized in an optical printer, revealing once again the necessity of braiding multiple technologies into the generation of computer-generated films at this moment.[25]

Like VanDerBeek, Schwartz was interested in exploring the parameters of perception and their relation to moving-image technology from the time. Arriving at Bell Labs in 1968 after meeting Harmon at the opening of *The Machine as Seen at the End of the Mechanical Age*, which she had a piece in, Schwartz started working with BEFLIX and exploring its potential. Influenced by post-Impressionist painter Georges Seurat's pointillism, she attempted to produced images whose abstractions would lead to senses of formal continuity.[26] But her frustrations with BEFLIX emerged when she encountered the limitations of what the language would allow for artists attempting to produce metamorphoses in time. She describes the working process as one rooted in blindness, where data inputted into the language would sometimes lead to surprising results after a dramatic time delay between its development, single-image visualization, and sequence in continuity.[27] That said, she completed *Pixillation* (1970) using this workflow with an updated version of BEFLIX Knowlton called EXPLOR, while also adding color to the computer images with an optical printer and incorporating sequences of hand-colored oil abstractions and stop-motion crystal growths to match the flickering grids of pixels. Continuing her study of nineteenth-century visual culture and technologies of perception, Schwartz completed *Olympiad* (1971) the following year, a film based on Eadweard Muybridge's studies of a man running. While the film contains formal qualities reminiscent of *Pixillation*, *Olympiad* grounds its investigation in the slow emergence and eventual animation of a figure against a black and then colorized background. As the wire-frame man first moves slowly and then rapidly across the screen, sometimes creating a blur across the frame, Schwartz moves between references to Muybridge and Etienne-Jules Marey's chronophotography. This film was produced more closely with Knowlton after Schwartz's first film caused him to realize that his languages were oriented more toward mathematical calculations and that "it is necessary to develop special facilities for the artists" at Bell.[28] Knowlton updated EXPLOR to give "control over the size and position of octagons" on the screen, which allowed for a continuity of motion and the nesting octagons inside larger ones to create "sense of musculature and . . . shape."[29] The animated sequence was still created on an optical printer, but the extreme sense of blindness in the production process was less severe.

Schwartz was not alone in her criticism of Knowlton's and similar computer animation platforms from the time. Of the ten unsolved problems that Sutherland identifies in the article mentioned at the beginning of this chapter, the problem of interactivity and real-time animation that Schwartz articulates was one of the most pressing for computer programmers and animators in the 1960s and early 1970s. Sutherland praises BEFLIX, especially its ability to map the force and movement of an object, but notes that it is difficult to do this outside of a theoretical space: "the hard part of using Knowlton's language is figuring out what the picture is going to look like as you write. . . . You have to make a little sketch ahead of time on graph paper. You then pick off the coordinates from the sketch and jot the coordinates down on a piece of paper to give to the computer." He argues, "I should be able to sit at the console and draw what I want."[30] This desire for real-time interaction, as well as storage and recall of images for the production animations, became a goal of a number of programmers simultaneously and led to artist and engineer collaborations such as the one between Schwartz and Knowlton. An important example of this interaction from the time can be found between the programmer and filmmaker Larry Cuba and computer scientists Tom DeFanti and Dan Sandin. Cuba was working on multiple projects in the mid-1970s in California, including a collaboration with Whitney as his programmer on *Arabesque* (1975), commercial graphics for Bob Abel, and his own abstract film *Two Space*, completed in 1979. In the midst of this productive period, Cuba was contracted by George Lucas to do the first digital special effects for a Hollywood feature film, *Star Wars* (1977). At the time, Cuba was using a similar "blind" operating model as Schwartz described, though he calls this laborious process outside of digital real-time computation "animated time" for its delays and intertwining of multiple technologies for an eventual continuity.[31] Even though Cuba had found institutional support at Information International Inc. (Triple-I) to use their powerful PDP-10 computer while working on various projects, he left California for a new lab created by Sandin and DeFanti at the University of Illinois at Chicago to create the effects for *Star Wars*, with the hopes that they had developed a real-time digital animation platform.

DeFanti had recently arrived from Ohio State University, where he was a computer science graduate student working both in that department and in the Computer Graphics Research Group funded by a National Science Foundation grant Csuri was awarded in 1968. Tired of the workflow that dominated CGI, Csuri's grant sought to develop an interactive real-time digital graphics platform, which by 1973 DeFanti helped achieve through the development of a computer language in his PhD thesis called GRAphics Symbiosis System (GRASS), an outgrowth of BASIC. This move from earlier extensions of Fortran helped produce the functionality of real-time animation in a number of ways. First, BASIC, as described above, was designed for a time-sharing environment, but the language also had a more natural syntax and could easily move across platforms while allowing for extensions to be easily incorporated into the language. This simplified coding, especially for artists unfamiliar with other languages, and it allowed for data from a variety of input devices to be controlled by any variable or parameter in the language. GRASS used an IBM vector graphics display, but DeFanti's platform added memory storage in the display to prevent images made with the scan gun from immediately fading. This hardware configuration, coupled with intuitive software with such commands as ROTATE and others for shading, merging, or scaling, allowed the digital projection of two-dimensional forms that could move and spin on the z-axis without generating scrolls of code.

DeFanti was initially hired by the Chemistry and Computer Science Departments at the University of Illinois at Chicago to digitally map molecules but with Sandin created the Circle Graphics Habitat (later called the Electronic Visualization Laboratory [EVL]) to merge digital technology and the arts utilizing the GRASS platform. Sponsoring a number of artists and programmers, the lab quickly became associated with real-time graphics through their vector system, a detailed and fluid wire-frame aesthetic showcased by the effects in *Star Wars*, the stolen data plans of the Death Star seen toward of the end of the film that map the battle station's architecture, terrain, and vulnerabilities (fig. 5.3). Cuba also produced *3/78* (1978) on the system, a film in the same tradition of abstract animation as many of Schwartz's and VanDerBeek's but whose aesthetic is indebted to GRASS, as is the look of his special effects on that system. While EVL's later reputation was built around their development of the **data glove** (a computational input device worn over the hand like a glove) and the immersive environment software and technology called Cave Automatic Virtual Environment, or CAVE, the lab's simultaneous use for artisanal and industrial applications was routine, since many filmmakers, such as Cuba and Whitney before him, moved across these production contexts in CGI, especially through growing avenues of opportunity in Hollywood special effects.

FIGURE 5.3: Larry Cuba's special-effects sequence in *Star Wars* (1977).

But such opportunities and pathways were not always easy to navigate. While theoretical ideas about computer interaction had been under development for decades, the early 1970s witnessed a wave of development in hardware and processing technology, including the microprocessor chip and the **frame buffer**. Frame buffers are devices that store rendered images in video memory for **raster graphics** systems.[32] This latter technology is still used in contemporary digital displays and also enables two-dimensional image information to be stored up and ordered in a timeline for fluid and even colorized movement. One of the early platforms to take advantage of this was at Xerox PARC (Palo Alto Research Center) on a system called SuperPaint developed by Richard Shoup, Alvy Ray Smith, Bob Flegal, and Patrick Baudelaire in 1973. Carolyn Kane attributes part of Super-Paint's rise and success to the frame buffer and development of integrated circuits, in addition to the ways SuperPaint efficiently and flexibly handled 8-bit color registrations, leading to refinements in later years to include graphical tools, brushes, and color palettes that could be navigated with a mouse.[33] The platform was used for a variety of experimental work, as well as commercial applications, helping Shoup earn an Emmy in 1983 that he shared with Xerox, even though, as Tom Sito points out, Xerox in 1974 found that SuperPaint was too expensive and began canceling the research group's equipment orders.[34] This motivated Shoup to create his own company, Aurora Systems, and many others in the group moved to different research centers or companies. While the halt of development at Xerox may seem myopic in retrospect, the decision reveals how competing priorities over visions of computational usage were many times negotiated or determined through economic rather than aesthetic priorities. Xerox explained that it was not generating enough revenue to continue refining SuperPaint, and this drove their focus on refining their black-and-white Alto personal computer with its graphical user interface.

Physical Worlds

The relationship between research and industrial applications during this period was not always defined through the type of antagonism present in the SuperPaint group at Xerox. More often than not, these interests overlapped and researchers were sponsored by governmental agencies or corporations that invested in CGI. The frame buffer that John Whitney Jr. and Gary Demos developed at Triple-I is a case in point, as was the dual corporate and research interests of many at the University of Utah in the late 1960s and early 1970s. One of the more famous spaces of innovation in CGI at the time, the Computer Science Department at the University of Utah began to flourish when Dave Evans took a position there and was then followed by his friend and collaborator Sutherland. Sutherland left a professorship at Harvard University in 1968 to establish a company dedicated to CGI, Evans & Sutherland, and to attract researchers and graduate students to the University of Utah through his reputation in the field that stemmed from Sketchpad. The department pioneered a variety of CGI technologies and foundational principles, such as **texture mapping**, object shading, and **hidden surface removal**, prompting Jacob Gaboury to locate it at the center of his study of 3D computer graphics.[35] As Gaboury shows, these techniques emerged from the consideration of problems of screen perspective, specifically investigating how to hide the two-dimensional lines that compose an image to give the illusion of depth. For example, this aesthetic with no hidden lines for 3D objects appears in Cuba's effects for *Star Wars* as the Death Star's canyon is visually mapped but is normalized through the sequence's context in the film as an architectural rendering. The difficulty lay in modeling a smooth three-dimensional space, "hiding" the rendered lines to generate solids that would appear to exist in their own space. A graduate student at Utah, Ed Catmull, helped resolve many of the issues facing this hidden surface removal, in part through, as Gaboury and others note, the allocation of information about an object's projected depth in space to a portion of memory in the display's hardware, thus isolating one particular problem of an object's projection through a rearticulation of its computational rendering. By letting the display perform an aspect of computational work, the mainframe was free to focus on other image details to enhance realistic features. Similar solutions followed that focused on lighting and color intensities, such as Henri Gourand's self-named shading technique developed in 1971, or texture mapping, which is the algorithmic interpolation of shapes and polygons over the surface of a digital object to create contrasts in depth and figure/ground distinctions.

The research problems and techniques outlined at Utah were groundbreaking for a number of reasons, but their impact shaped the history of CGI in two particular ways: (1) they modeled visual perspective in computational space, and (2) they mimicked the ways photography depicts objects and spaces. With these simultaneous operations, CGI research veered away from the creation of abstract moving images and increasingly moved toward the production of aesthetic worlds that appear contiguous with our own or approximate the laws and perspectives of that space. As lighting, texture, color, shapes, and forms were researched, they were often put to the service of what is called **physics-based animation**, which simulates how objects and environments would interact in physical space. It also introduced a workflow model for CGI that utilized raster graphics monitors and platforms but that stored information about computer objects through vector algorithms, as well as bitmapped arrays. Modeling space through polygons and initial geometries was followed by an animation of that world and finally a rendering of it that employed the graphic simulation of perspectival principles. This pipeline helped create navigable worlds, an aesthetic Evans & Sutherland capitalized on through their contract with the Defense Advanced Research Projects Agency (DARPA) to produce flight simulators for pilots. It also solidified the Utah department as the origin for this type of animation during and after Sutherland's tenure there, as a number of the researchers and students later moved into the burgeoning computer graphics industry to found such companies as Adobe, Pixar, and Atari. While abstraction was still a component for a number of these researchers, companies, and graphic products, it was now put more in conversation with perspectival realism and the constitution of CGI worlds. Tellingly, one of the most iconic objects that the Utah department generated to test the computer modeling and creation of this new space was the everyday "Utah teapot," whose curves, textures, shadows, reflections, and shape was so recognizable and ordinary that digital simulations of the form and its environment could be easily critiqued or applauded.

The "Genesis Effect" sequence in *Star Trek II: The Wrath of Khan* (1982) is an early of example of how these various CGI technologies from the time were woven together to project a physical world. Within the film's narrative, the CGI sequence functions as a simulated scientific model of how a new technology, called the Genesis Device, could create a habitable world out of a currently desolate geographic terrain. The scientific setting of the sequence provides a narrative excuse or support to the digital metamorphosis we see, or provides a sense of realism or belief that such changes digitally rendered could exist in the cinematic world that the characters populate, while also creating a structural apologia for the sequence's lack of digital perfection. Though innovative, images are still rendered through polygons whose animations are not meant to appear contiguous with the photographed space of characters watching the sequence. Like the canyon in *Star Wars*, whose architectural source in the narrative justified the presence of render lines for solid objects, the scientific sequence provides narrative justification for the abstractions, camera movements, and jagged landscapes of the Genesis Effect. The quality of the images are, in essence, narratively explained, which happens often in the history of CGI.

That said, the look and creation of the sequence were novel and sophisticated while showcasing multiple CGI techniques. Beginning with an eye scan of James Kirk, the first part of the sequence displays pixels of a retina before then moving into the z-axis through abstract patterns of lines and particle swarms meant to represent DNA and molecules. Though these two types of CGI image sequences had been created before, the third sequence introduced numerous challenges and was both the most successful and memorable part. Continuing the plays on movement into depth established in abstraction, the sequence then visualizes the Genesis Device landing on a world through swooping camera movements and pans around the planet, as well as along its surface. The filmmakers chose to use fire as a visual motif to represent the beginnings of life, which spreads on the dark planet from the point of impact as the camera moves closer to the surface before also being immersed in its red transformations (fig. 5.4). This effect of fire was created by Bill Reeves in the computer graphics group of Industrial Light & Magic, then owned by Lucasfilm, through his creation of a particle system that could track "a half-million fire particles through individual trajectories and incandescent color changes."[36] After the camera is immersed in color through these swarming particles, it descends into the new geographical terrain created by Genesis through fractal renderings of a landscape. Concerned about pixilation and smoothness, Alvy Ray Smith and others in the group, such as Catmull from Utah, combined the fractal metamorphoses with texture-mapping algorithms and motion-blurring techniques, a smoothing finish of space and time to avoid a pixilated vision of the CGI world.

Avoiding the look of computational rendering became a priority for the construction of CGI worlds that characters could navigate and exist within, even if this was only implied through establishing shots built on the computer that were edited together with live-action footage. *Tron* (1982) employs this strategy for the approximately twenty minutes of CGI animations that are complemented by visual effects created with an optical printer in much of the other footage. The film's narrative centers on a character's digitization and entrance into a computer's world that mirrors physical reality and is filled with anthropomorphized bits, programs, and an artificial intelligence Master Control Program that serves as the narrative's antagonist and bridge for both spaces. The twinning of the characters in the computational and physical worlds allows for a parallel narrative structure, but much of the action exists through points of convergence within the game arenas, where characters identified as programs compete with one another but are crosscut with players in a video game arcade moving and reacting to the action and events in the computational world. This substitution and extension into the computer provides a similar aesthetic justification to the look of the CGI found in the examples above and aligns spectators' sympathies and points of view, all while providing a brilliant marketing platform for the *Tron* video arcade game released the same year as the film.

FIGURE 5.4: The "Genesis Effect" sequence from *Star Trek II: The Wrath of Khan* (1982).

Though there were difficulties in designing shots where characters interacted in the computational world because of the optical-printing technique used, the CGI sequences in the film now had to contain conventions of perspectival realism for the spaces depicted to appear contiguous with those that the characters occupied. Sequences with the light cycles exemplify both the new problems and solutions developed by the company who created that footage, Mathematical Applications Group Inc. (MAGI). The sequence begins with an establishing shot of the arcade game unit and a camera push-in to the screen where yellow and blue lines emerge from opposing sides and begin to race toward one another while creating blocky trails of color through ninety-degree turns. As the camera gets closer to these abstractions, it cants so that the bottom of the arcade game screen is at an oblique angle before a dissolve morphs the lines into the light cycle speeders and brings the viewer into the computer's world (fig. 5.5). While the light cycle bikes required the use of some of the CGI techniques and algorithms described above, the landscape grid and realistic projection of their movement on it were the problem. MAGI could render the computer's world, but it gave a sense of flatness because of the even vector shapes projected through the image. Objects farther away contained the same lighting and rendering details as those closer to the imagined camera in the animated space, thus confusing figure/ground understandings and projections of depth. In short, everything was too even, too glossy, and too crisp in detail; though without the same **aliasing** problems as *Star Trek II*, it still looked computationally artificial. To juxtapose the arcade game abstractions and the space inside the computer so that that world could seem inhabitable by characters, two innovations were introduced. The first was **depth cueing**, where

FIGURE 5.5: Light-cycle sequence from *Tron* (1982).

a perception of depth is added to the image through sizing ratios that would indicate how objects exist relative to one another in a shot or through lighting effects, where landscapes and objects farther away are less illuminated till finally being blacked out at the vanishing point or horizon line. Both processes of depth cueing are on display in the light cycle sequence, which is why most of the CGI constructed shots in the sequence employ the same canted Dutch angle that is used in the transition from the arcade to the computer's world. With that angle, the imagined camera can better capture the white grid on the black ground used for the landscape that the bikes move on, which marks the distance the bikes travel and enables the lines to dull in color as they recede into the distance in order to better articulate a horizon line in the world. The second innovation *Tron* developed is related to the first, since it was also addressing issues of perspectival realism. But this second solution focused on the texture of objects rather than indicators of depth through size and lighting values. Noting that the CGI world in *Tron* looked too smoothly rendered, Ken Perlin developed a way to introduce texture noise in CGI objects to make them appear more realistic. Called **Perlin noise** and earning Perlin an Academy Award, this algorithm functions as a filter that introduces elements of noise into image pixels that can be controlled "to create convincing representations of clouds, fire, water, stars, marble, wood, rock, soap films and crystal."[37]

Problems still plagued the development of CGI in *Tron*, notably the fractured styles of the different computer-animated sequences due to the four companies generating them: MAGI, Triple-I, Digital Effects Inc., and Robert Abel and Associates. Though shared motifs and design languages run through each sequence,

Tron stands as a testament to how different institutions were responding to CGI problems with their own solutions crafted from the affordances of the hardware and software platforms available to each. Later films, such as *The Last Starfighter* (1984), employed a single company for the CGI sequences (Triple-I in this case), while still grappling with how to integrate CGI sequences into a fictional world populated by characters. *The Last Starfighter* uses many of the same techniques as *Tron*, especially through the ways in which it positions the narrative and action of the film around video arcade game play and the merger of the physical and computational worlds on both sides of the screen. But this three-dimensional fleshing out of a video-game world did not just aid in the justification of a CGI space. It also capitalized on the popularity of arcade and home video-game consoles that began in the 1970s with *Pong* (1972) and the release of the Atari 2600 (1977), whose rendering problems, as Nick Montfort and Ian Bogost have explained, centered on interactivity and graphics formatting for CRT television sets.[38] Most games in the late 1970s and early 1980s utilized two-dimensional image renderings, but the interest in these digital worlds sparked science fiction narrative ideas, as well as experiments in projecting digital perspectival worlds that seemed to follow the physical laws governing ours.

CGI Synergy

By the mid-1980s, computational media such as video-game consoles and personal computers had become cheaper and more widespread, with various corporations and paradigms for human-computer interactions more firmly established within the media landscape. Advertisers began working more closely with digital animators, and CGI began to wind its way into a variety of media outlets and contexts. While the most discussed Super Bowl advertisement featuring computers from that time is the Apple Inc. "1984" advertisement for the Apple Macintosh that promised that their new computer would provide tools for breaking free from the capitalist and computational dystopia dominated by IBM, another commercial from the next year's Super Bowl held more significance for the history of CGI. Robert Abel and Associates developed an advertisement called "Brilliance" for the Canned Food Information Council of a futuristic robot in space who still relied on metal for a variety of conveniences, such as canned goods. To flesh out the robot and make its movements more realistic and convincing, especially for the intended goal of using sexualized femininity to sell its product, the group developed an early motion-capture technique called **brute-force animation** that computationally transcribed the movements of dots drawn on a live model into vector paths in the computer to form a stick-figure foundation. Like rotoscoping, this was meant to grant the animation a greater sense of life and realism, though this aesthetic once again relies on a science fiction narrative context and, like *Tron* and *The Last Starfighter*, highly gendered senses of audience engagement and portrayals of technology.

Additionally, the advertisement used the workflow described above where computational objects were rendered through vectors, and bitmapped overlays that were then animated and retouched for the adherence to rules of perspectival realism. This workflow still exists, but the key problem at the time was that so many of its parts could not communicate with one another. Different algorithms for particular aspects of CGI were created by different companies, and the coordination and eventual production of the animation could be cumbersome, slow, and limited to particular platforms. While through the development of CGI numerous technical solutions emerged around specific image, time, or perspectival problems, the challenge that loomed large was one of integration. Several solutions were developed in response, but the one created by Catmull and John Lasseter became the most well known and popular. Catmull had experience working with CGI at the University of Utah and on the "Genesis Effect" sequence of *Star Trek II*, and Lasseter had worked for Disney and was inspired by the light cycle CGI sequences of *Tron*. Together, with the financial backing of Steve Jobs, they created Pixar Animation Studios and produced a short film first shown at SIG-GRAPH in 1986, *Luxo Jr.* It not only employed physics-based animation but also utilized a technology where the computational objects in the animated space could interact dynamically in real time according to physical laws. *Luxo Jr.* was a study in this rendering environment, functioning "as a test of 'self-shadowing' . . . that is, the ability of objects to shed light and shadows on themselves."[39] The film works through these CGI interactions using two anthropomorphized desk lamps who play with a rubber ball (fig. 5.6). Casting light on each other, producing reflections on the ball, directing light around the space, and generating patterns of shadow, the film successfully shows how light and color could change interactively depending upon the programmed movements of computational objects in animation. Additionally, the narrative context for the CGI in *Luxo Jr.* is an ordinary, everyday world rather than a fantastical one, while also projecting a sympathetic parent-child relationship onto the two lamps.

Luxo Jr. crafted a CGI that had greater appeal than what the aesthetic previously had, in part by employing narrative strategies Lasseter learned at Disney. The lamp became iconic and is still a part of Pixar's animated logo seen at the beginning of their feature-length films. Following the success of *Luxo Jr.*, Pixar's next short film, *Tin Toy* (1988), used a similar narrative pretext where everyday objects have a secret life revealed through CGI. But *Tin Toy* was created with a new rendering software created at Pixar, called RenderMan, designed to integrate workflow aspects of digital animation. Specifically, RenderMan standardizes the interface between different programs that communicate with one another within the standardized workflow described above. For example, if different algorithms

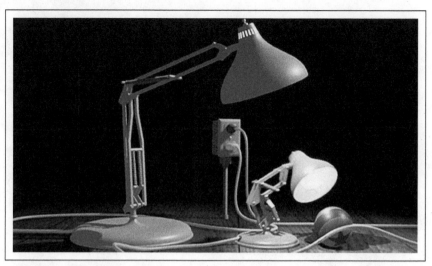

FIGURE 5.6: John Lasseter's *Luxo Jr.* (1986).

or programs are used to create the vector wire frames of an image of a ball, as well as its colors, and finally how light is cast on it and how it is textured (smooth like a beach ball or dimpled like a football), these can all work together and send information to one another if each program understands the RenderMan interface. This results in an ability to both use a larger variety of programs and CGI algorithms and protect a standardized and industrial workflow from becoming obsolete in the future. What resulted was Pixar's ability to use this digital animation engine with great efficiency, along with algorithms and techniques culled from CGI's origins. *Tin Toy* marked an industrial breakthrough in CGI and earned the first Academy Award for a digital animation, a dramatic contrast from the Academy of Motion Picture Arts and Sciences denial to consider *Tron* for an award six years earlier for special effects because they considered using CGI to be cheating. Pixar's success not only signaled a transition from an artisanal mode of digital animation production to a standardized, industrial one but also a broader cultural embrace of an aesthetic and technological mode of image production that began to move across media channels.

6

UBIQUITOUS ANIMATION, 1990–2016   Bob Rehak

Animation found itself at a significant crossroads by the close of the first decade of the twenty-first century: a period that saw digital image-creation technologies blossom from their origins in isolated research centers and experimental artists' studios to become a dominant mode of production for the movie industry and beyond. Migrating and adapting across a landscape of media convergence, animation's mutability was facilitated by another kind of convergence taking place behind the silver screen, as digital tools arose to first augment and later supplant traditional animation practice. As Esther Leslie observes, in recent years film has "merged, through CGI, with animation," through such developments as **stereoscopic filming** and high-definition image capture that collectively signal "the increasing entwinement of film and animation via the digital."[1] Reflected symptomatically in a new abundance and sophistication of reality-bending visual effects that threatened to rupture live-action cinema's grounding relationship in the real, the ubiquity of **3D animation** was in part due to a shift from proprietary software to commercial applications employed throughout the industry, driving the reinvention of the animated feature film as one established studio after another faced the choice either to restructure its labor and technical pipelines or to risk being replaced entirely by "born digital" studios and houses, built from the ground up to take advantage of the new tools that became available during the 1990s and 2000s.

Chief among these tools was the Computer Animation Production System, or CAPS, first used in *The Little Mermaid* (1989) and finally retired in 2005 after more than a decade of synthesizing 2D and 3D images across a host of Disney feature films; RenderMan, a software tool used to render the world's first fully digitally animated feature film, *Toy Story* (1995), as discussed in chapter 5 in this volume; and Autodesk Maya, introduced as a commercial product in 1998, which quickly grew to become a standard platform for creating animated 3D assets and environments in film, television, video games, and advertisements. It should be noted that not all of the significant tools that emerged during this period were digital. Starting in the 1980s, the animation photo transfer (APT) process used photography to transfer rough animation onto animation cels, adding color through the use of light-sensitive dyes in a step toward the elimination of conventional inking and painting. APT actually arose as a replacement for xerography, first utilized by Disney in 1961 as an electronic method of copying artwork onto cels rather than relying on transfer by an artist's hand. Like their digital descendants, such tools gave studios the ability to generate, at ever accelerating rates and decreasing costs, colorful and fast-moving animation populated by large numbers of moving elements mapped in consistent spatial and perspectival terms into worlds of unprecedented intricacy, dimensionality, and presence. In so doing, such systems as CAPS, RenderMan, and Maya reinvented the aesthetics and economics of animated short- and feature-length filmmaking, while their underlying base—the computer—transformed Hollywood's organization of labor by displacing onto the algorithmic engines of microprocessors, storage arrays, and server farms much of the work formerly done by human beings. The roles of individuals and the status of their artistry within the industry's labor force also shifted profoundly as animators adapted themselves to new UIs (user interfaces) that replaced pencil, paintbrush, and paper with mouse, keyboard, and monitor, and teams learned to coordinate their collaborations over great distances—often global in scale—through online conferencing, social media, and file sharing.

At the same time, however, the quarter century between 1990 and 2015 saw a resurgence of artisanal spirit in the creation of idiosyncratic tools, such as **Rotoshop**, proprietary software developed by Bob Sabiston and Flat Black Films to generate the liquid palettes and uncannily synchronized movements of "painted over" live-action in such films as Richard Linklater's *Waking Life* (2001) and *A Scanner Darkly* (2006); in the emergence of **performance-capture** technologies devoted to personal visions of animation like that of Robert Zemeckis, whose ImageMovers Digital crafted uncanny hybrids of animation and live-action in *The Polar Express* (2004), *Beowulf* (2007), and *A Christmas Carol* (2009); and in the renaissance of stop-motion animation exemplified by Laika Studios, which brought cutting-edge digital techniques, such as **support erasure** and 3D printing, to material puppet animation. The latter trends suggest that, even as contemporary animation grew to be so generalized and ubiquitous that its industrial specificity and surface aesthetics bordered on becoming simply a default mode of film production for the digital era, in other ways animation asserted its status as a unique way of doing creative work and manufacturing screen realities by explicitly associating its methods and makers with traditions of an artisanal, analog past.

To a great degree, this proliferation of content was due to transformations in the typical animation workflow wrought by digital technology. Digital cameras and systems for data storage and playback enabled animators to work much more quickly, replaying moves in real time and correcting errors on the fly, instead of having to wait for film to be developed as in the photochemical era (or rendered, as in the transitional period between analog and digital filmmaking). Digital sound mixing and editing similarly became more flexible. On a managerial level, programs for coordinating the planning, execution, and assembly of animated content, from storyboards and **sequence pre-visualization** to **digital compositing** of elements and the final polish and cleanup through the use of **digital intermediates** (DI) all accelerated production, enabling more content to be produced in shorter time spans. This was true even of the artisanal modes that emerged in the 2000s, which invisibly augmented their "handmade" aesthetic with digital techniques. And it was true of companies that continued to produce "traditional" animation alongside their embrace of digital rendering.

Pixar and Disney: The Little Fish That Swallowed the Big Fish

At the end of the closing credits of *Finding Nemo* (2003), there is a small, funny coda involving two of the film's minor characters: a nervous little fish, menaced by a toothy, monstrous anglerfish, turns the tables on its aggressor and swallows the larger fish whole. A quick reading might interpret this as a visual parable of the relationship between giant Disney and pipsqueak Pixar, which first emerged as a denigrated offshoot of a visual-effects house but went on to mount the most commercially successful and aesthetically influential films of the digital-animation era—eventually taking over the industry and forcing the more established studio to follow suit by abandoning its **2D animation** raison d'être (fig. 6.1). In this narrative, the last twenty-five years of animated feature filmmaking might be seen as an economic and ideological contest between Disney, exemplar of old-school ink-and-paint artistry, and Pixar, brash newcomer of the digital era. With their every frame rendered by computer, Pixar's films took the upstart studio from obscurity to blockbuster success nearly overnight, establishing digital animation as the new norm and inspiring numerous other studios to follow suit. Over the same time span, Disney eventually shuttered their traditional animation facilities and began

FIGURE 6.1: *Toy Story* (1995), the first animated feature film produced entirely with digital imaging.

to focus primarily on digital features, starting with *Chicken Little* in 2005 and continuing through *Meet the Robinsons* (2007), *Bolt* (2008), *Tangled* (2010), *Wreck-It Ralph* (2012), *Frozen* (2013), *Big Hero 6* (2014), and *Zootopia* (2016)—each a larger success than the one before. Perhaps most tellingly in terms of this David-and-Goliath narrative, Disney's acquisition of Pixar for $7.4 billion in 2006 installed Pixar founders Ed Catmull and John Lasseter as heads of Disney Animation Studios, seemingly signaling the collapse of traditional animation as a dominant mode alongside the computer's ascendancy as an all-purpose production tool.

Such a narrative ironically harkens to the way in which even the most commercially and popularly intended animation has always carried a whiff of the avant-garde in its exploding of live-action cinema's limitations. Further, this saga of succession in which the digital "conquers" the analog is reinforced by our collective desire to embrace the new—and the readiness of the motion-picture industry to market that newness back to us in the pleasing form of the state of the art. But the Pixar-versus-Disney scenario is in fact too easy and felicitous, especially when reduced simply to box-office performance. It neglects at least two crucial factors that characterized the period: first, a complex interdependence of the studios as they progressed through different configurations of ownership, creative management, and distribution agreements; and second, a hybridity of digital and analog techniques at the production level that undermined, both then and now, any straightforward distinction between traditional and digital animation practices.

At the end of the 1980s, traditionally animated feature films made up a relatively minor percentage of the box office. The most successful example, *The Little*

Mermaid, married the classic Disney formula to the Broadway musical through the songwriting involvement of Howard Ashman and Alan Menken. Earning $84 million during its initial release, it was the thirteenth most profitable film of the year. More significantly, it was the only animated feature to make it into the year's top forty moneymakers; the next most profitable animated feature, *Peter Pan*, was a rerelease of the 1953 original. Nevertheless, *The Little Mermaid* ended a lengthy lull in Disney's fortunes; the previous decade had been especially uneven for the studio, with only *The Fox and the Hound* (1981) and *The Great Mouse Detective* (1986) registering as moderate critical and commercial successes, *Oliver & Company* (1988) profitable but critically derided, and *The Black Cauldron* (1985) a major failure that marked, for many, the nadir of a company that had been foundering in the wake of its beloved founder's death in 1966.

In their mode of production, there was little to distinguish Disney's output during this period from the decades prior. The dominant animation of this time largely hewed to the look of traditional animation long associated with the "illusion of life" aesthetic: (apparently) hand-drawn and -painted cels presented in resolute two-dimensionality, their sense of depth achieved through variations on the multiplane camera technique pioneered in the early 1930s by Ub Iwerks but polished to a house style in such Disney productions as *Snow White and the Seven Dwarfs* (1937) and *Fantasia* (1940). Behind the scenes, however, late-analog and early-digital tools were being invoked ever more centrally, streamlining the production process at the industrial level while introducing a beguiling new dimensionality and geometrical complexity to the frame. The studio was still using the xerographic system, introduced in 1959 during production of *101 Dalmatians*, to transfer animators' drawings onto acetate. This method reduced the need for manual inking while enabling figures to be used in multiple instances (such as ninety-nine puppies) within the frame. An alternative to xerography arrived with the animation photo transfer process. APT was another method for copying artwork onto cels using high-contrast lithographic film and light-sensitive dyes that produced fields of color automatically. Xerography and APT were pre-digital solutions to problems faced both on the level of labor, with the ever-present need to reduce the number of individuals needed to shepherd animation from rough to finished form, and on the level of aesthetics, where they enabled greater control over larger numbers of screen elements.

As Hannah Frank explains, economic pressures motivated the incorporation of xerography into Disney's traditional animation pipelines; substituting machine for human labor cut costs and speeded production, enabling studios to produce animated features more quickly.[2] Even as limitations on resolution resulted in thicker, less delicate lines and stark outlines around characters and objects in motion, the mechanized transfer of key-frame art to finished cel (and the subsequent elimination of the labor force of in-betweeners, mostly women) did much to preserve, at least in the animators' eyes, an indexical connection between their

FIGURE 6.2: The Big Ben sequence in *The Great Mouse Detective* (1986).

artistry and the final result. But as an early application of cutting and pasting and a precursor of digitality's object orientation, xerography enabled screen elements to be multiplied and recombined far more easily than would have been possible had everything been drawn by hand; the dozens of dogs in any given frame of *Dalmatians* are one example. Thus, although the first generation of machine-assisted animation followed the 2D format of traditional cel animation, it prefigured the crowded, busy mise-en-scène that would dominate animation in the digital era. *The Black Cauldron* also featured an early use of CGI, or computer-generated imagery, to create atmospheric elements, such as bubbles and an orb of light, along with props, such as the titular cauldron. One notable example of the latter was a chase sequence in *The Great Mouse Detective*, in production concurrently with *Black Cauldron*, set inside the interlocking gearwheels of Big Ben. This brief cinematic exploration of a software-generated environment, its wire-frame graphics calculated by computer before being traced onto transparent cels, moves by the rules of a clean, frictionless geometry that is almost jarring in contrast to the hand-drawn animal characters who navigate its treacherous spaces (fig. 6.2). It resembles sequences in science-fiction films of the same period—such as *Tron* (1982) and *The Last Starfighter* (1984)—that intercut live-action and digitally generated settings.

But a complete digital mimesis of live-action film—discernible in a newly dynamic movement of animation's virtual camera, fluidly dimensional environments, and seemingly solid objects whose own movements followed consistent (if idiosyncratic) physical laws—arrived in 1991's *Beauty and the Beast* during a musical number in which Belle and the Beast dance a waltz (fig. 6.3). Opening with traditionally animated tableaux showing the two characters descending staircases

FIGURE 6.3: Digital and analog animation meet in *Beauty and the Beast* (1991).

and dining together, the sequence soon breaks from its largely static aesthetic as Belle rises from the table to take the Beast's hand and lead him into the ballroom. As Mrs. Potts (Angela Lansbury) sings the film's signature tune, "Beauty and the Beast (Tale as Old as Time)," the camera moves along the z-axis in a smooth tracking shot, following the pair into the opulent space. Pillars ring the room, a finely filigreed chandelier hangs overhead, and stars dot a deep blue sky visible beyond the tall windows—all of these elements shifting in realistic parallax as the point of view tracks and spins. As the song crescendos, the camera surges upward to study a painted mural on the ceiling and then descends as though on a crane, circling the chandelier and dropping back to eye level with the characters, all in an unbroken shot unmistakably intended to showcase a new way of presenting space and action in animation.

The ballroom sequence was created with the help of Disney's Computerized Animation Production System (CAPS), a network of specialized scanners, servers, and proprietary software comprising a fully digital ink-and-paint process. Because every element, from background artwork to the cels depicting individual characters, could be scanned into the computer and assembled there before being rendered and output to film, CAPS largely freed animation from material constraints, such as the number of layers that could be combined in one image or the size of artwork across which the camera could move. That artwork, moreover, could be digital in origin: envisioned from the start as a CG construct, the ballroom's architecture, colors, and textures were all generated using the RenderMan interface, Pixar's proprietary software (as discussed in chapter 5). Although put to only limited use in *Beauty and the Beast* and *The Little Mermaid*, CAPS formed the central pipeline for Disney's next feature, *The Rescuers Down Under* (1990), and all of the studio's work that followed, shifting Disney's animation output to a digital base even as its ability to merge 2D and 3D elements was only occasionally highlighted. (The stampede sequence in *The Lion King*, to cite another example, multiplied the number of charging animals on-screen beyond anything that could be created by hand in a reasonable amount of time.)

Further complicating the apparent opposition between analog Disney and digital Pixar is the fact that all of Pixar's films, starting with *Toy Story*, have been distributed under the Disney banner, albeit with varying degrees of involvement by the venerable studio. This strategy, which has generally worked to the advantage of both companies, reflects a behind-the-scenes sharing of personnel and technologies dating back to Pixar's earliest days as a shadowy adjunct not just to Disney but to another important player in high-tech blockbuster filmmaking, George Lucas's LucasFilm and its special- and visual-effects house, Industrial Light & Magic (ILM). Founded in 1975 to provide optical and mechanical effects for the first *Star Wars* (1977), ILM began developing a computer-graphics team as early as 1979. *Star Wars* had employed only one short segment of digital animation, the wire-frame fly-through of the Death Star trench shown in a briefing to rebel pilots before the final battle (as detailed in chapter 5); for *Return of the Jedi* (1983), a similar visual was used at a rhyming juncture in the narrative to prepare rebel forces for an assault on the moon Endor. Under Ed Catmull, who studied at the University of Utah's computer-graphics program and later worked at the New York Institute of Technology, ILM's fledgling CG wing also provided one of the most celebrated digital sequences of the era, the Genesis simulation in *Star Trek II: The Wrath of Khan* (1982).

As explored by Andrew Johnston in chapter 5, the Genesis sequence reflected Ed Catmull's desire to produce photorealistic imagery through the digital creation of textures and **interactive lighting**, a process to which the RenderMan interface was essential. Distinct from 3D modeling programs, in which objects are created as geometric solids, RenderMan was designed to take such objects and place them in virtual environments where a user-directed "camera" can explore them freely, maintaining perspectival relationships no matter how complex the relative movement; in the process, the software would also wrap realistic surface textures around all visible surfaces. In a digital-animation pipeline, rendering follows the modeling, animation, and lighting stages to generate each finished frame—an essential moment in realizing the artist's initial vision as a final image. RenderMan's status as an industry standard for the production of visual effects in live-action film reflects its origins at ILM; but its importance to animation was the result of Pixar and especially John Lasseter, a graduate of the California Institute of the Arts who came to work at ILM in early 1984.

Co-founded by Walt Disney in 1961, CalArts trains students in the style and techniques of classical animation, in particular the "twelve principles"—squash and stretch, anticipation, exaggeration, and so on—canonized by Ollie Johnston and Frank Thomas, two of the "Nine Old Men," a group of artists responsible for most of the Disney studio's output from *Snow White and the Seven Dwarfs* (1937) onward. Channeling this approach through his own "affinity for bringing inanimate objects to life and giving them personalities of their own," Lasseter found himself at odds with ILM's mission, set by Lucas, of pursuing digital animation as a subset of visual effects.[3] Between 1984 and 1986, Lasseter headed up a series of shorts from LucasFilm's Computer Division, including *The Adventures of Andre and Wally B.* (1984), *Luxo Jr.* (1986), and *Red's Dream* (1987), which received acclaim before audiences at the computer-graphics conference SIGGRAPH as instances of digital animation with a heartbeat: charming stories increasingly focused on picayune household objects, such as lamps and toys, that came to life in quiet moments of dream and play. This marriage of simple storytelling values to high-tech digital imaging would endure for the next twenty-five years as Pixar's highly successful brand, seeing the company through its string of hits from *Toy Story* (1995) to *Finding Dory* (2016).

New Studios

Meanwhile, new animation studios began to appear in the 1990s, starting with DreamWorks Animation, which merged several animation companies that had come of age in the 1980s, such as Pacific Data Images (PDI)—one of the first computer-graphics creators—and Amblimation, part of Spielberg's Amblin Entertainment (1981), which worked in the more traditional ink-and-paint format. DreamWorks' *The Prince of Egypt* (1998) stages in particularly interesting ways the evolving symbiosis between conventional and digital animation as the end of the century neared. Certainly the film arrived amid much fanfare: the first animated feature to be released by the fledgling studio startup DreamWorks SKG—those initials reflecting its creation in 1994 as the brainchild of Steven Spielberg, Jeffrey Katzenberg, and David Geffen—*Prince of Egypt* was ambitious both at the level of its story, an adaptation of the saga of Moses, and of its production, a $70 million experiment in merging hand-drawn 2D animation with a plethora of digital tools.

Although concentrated in the movie's most spectacular sequences, such as the voice of God speaking through a burning bush and the parting of the Red Sea discussed below, these tools worked throughout the film to portray the world of ancient Egypt at a level of physical detail unavailable to previous animation regimes. These included the use of so-called 2D CGI to produce digital images existing only in the plane of the screen, such as lighting and shadowing effects; glows and halos; fog, dust, and smoke; and any background art that doesn't need to shift perspectively in relation to camera movement. In *Prince of Egypt*, shots of slaves staggering over the sand and kicking up clouds of dust while the hot sun

FIGURE 6.4: The parting of the Red Sea in *The Prince of Egypt* (1988).

casts long shadows from their legs would be an example of this form of digital imaging, which carries on a long tradition of environmental animation in the analog era, in which artists painstakingly copied the appearance and movement of natural phenomena, such as frost patterns on the surface of water in the sugar plum fairies' dance in *Fantasia* (1940). Although generated by the same underlying technology, this is distinct from the better-known 3D CGI, in which models created in the computer are placed into scenes where their ability to be rotated and viewed from any perspective lends the animated mise-en-scène a more perceptually realistic depth and dynamism. Both 2D and 3D digital tools come together in such sequences as the chariot race, wherein the carriages driven by Moses (Val Kilmer) and Rameses (Ralph Fiennes) careen and crash into each other as 3D objects while the arena walls behind them, blurred by speed, scroll past as flat 2D textures.

But it is in the Red Sea parting that digital and conventional animation mingle most vividly (fig. 6.4). Occurring at the film's climax, the sequence begins with Moses leading the Israelites out of Egypt, pursued by Rameses and his army. A whirlwind of fire, created as a 3D digital object, blocks the army's path as Moses stabs his staff into the shore, releasing a wave of energy that causes the waters to recede. As the surging, splashing waves draw back, a valley forms, through which the Israelites begin to advance. Rendered in long shots, the lines of people form ant-like chains, lending perspective to the exposed seabed; the smaller forms are simple digital models with individually customized gaits, while figures in the foreground are drawn and inked in the traditional style of 2D cel animation. A medium shot shows the line of people progressing past, shadowed shapes of whales occasionally visible behind the walls of water. Finally, as an enraged Rameses commands his troops to chase down the escaping diasporans, the tides crash inward, again relying on algorithmically generated water forms for realism and 2D digital animation for exaggerated accents of mist and spray. To create these showcases of computer technology, the production utilized Silicon Graphics workstations and servers and a suite of both commercial and proprietary software tools, including Alias/Wavefront and Animo, later subsumed into the animation application ToonBoom. In a shift from the relative subtlety with which CAPS-produced animation appeared in such cases as *The Little Mermaid*, the computer's role in making *The Prince of Egypt* was foregrounded in the film's publicity, which cast the production as a turning point in the evolution of the medium; for example, Greg Estes at Silicon Graphics remarked, "As a feature film targeted at adult audiences, *The Prince of Egypt* signals a true coming of age for animation."[4]

Earning multiple awards and grossing more than $218 million, *The Prince of Egypt* became the most successful non-Disney animated film—a record it held for only two years, before losing it to *Chicken Run* (2000), a stop-motion-animated movie created by the British Aardman Animation and released by DreamWorks. The next release from DreamWorks Animation, *Shrek* (2001), was the studio's first fully digital feature and an enormous financial success, earning $485 million against a $60 million production cost. With its caricature-based character design and remix approach to sending up fairy tales, *Shrek* established a brand of jokey, densely referential storytelling distinct from the approaches of Disney and Pixar (see below). Perhaps most importantly, *Shrek* demonstrated the franchise potential of digital animation, launching string of feature film sequels along with a spinoff feature, *Puss in Boots* (2011), plus numerous extensions in other media, including television specials, video games, and comic books. Neither was this DreamWorks Animation's only successful franchise; following *Shrek*, the studio launched the series *Madagascar*, *Kung Fu Panda*, and *How to Train Your Dragon*.

Nickelodeon Movies, responsible for the other nominee for Best Animated Feature in 2001, *Jimmy Neutron: Boy Genius*, was also notable for its transmedial reach. Originating not in film but cable television, Nickelodeon Movies was born in 1995 as a merger between the Nickelodeon Channel and Twentieth Century Fox to turn Nickelodeon's trio of original animated TV series *The Ren & Stimpy Show* (1991–1995), *Doug* (1991–1994), and *The Rugrats* (1991–2004) into movies. By the 2000s, it had been joined by other U.S. studios, such as Warner Brothers Animation, Sony Pictures Animation, Tim Burton Productions, and Laika, along with Britain's Aardman, Japan's Studio Ghibli, France's Les Armateurs, and Ireland's Cartoon Saloon, as producers of feature films and animated content for television, video games, and advertising—making animation a ubiquitous presence not just in movie theaters but across a galaxy of screens.

This radical expansion of animated content, both in scope and quantity, would have been impossible without the development of such software tools as Maya. Growing out of a 3D graphics program used in the 1980s, Maya is an application suite possessing an open architecture, which makes it highly customizable for use on individual projects while facilitating its general deployment across the industry. Distinct from RenderMan, with which it is often paired as part of an animation workflow, Maya enables its users to define 3D digital "assets," such as characters and props, and place them into virtual workspaces known as "scenes." Subcomponents of Maya generate fluid, cloth, and fur simulations, as well as particle effects to create atmospheric phenomena, such as fog, smoke, and sparks. Since its introduction in 1998, Maya has become not just a media but a transmedia engine. Given the software's flexibility and the variety of customizations it allows, it might seem difficult to summarize one overall aesthetic marking the software's use across so many manifestations; yet the kind of materials it can produce translates into an increasingly common visual vocabulary shared by animation, live-action films using extensive visual effects, television, and video games. Dynamic and interactive lighting, volumetric depth, unbroken camera movement, and the consistent representation of objects in space combine to create a dimensionality which, more than anything else, has supplanted the look of traditional animation. Similarly, Maya's shift to database storage of assets and sharing of files across global information networks has obviated many of the technologies that underlie traditional animation. Character model sheets and other reference tools that once helped to ensure a uniform-looking result from the many hands of an animation studio are in Maya handled by software.

Maya has now become a standard tool across both the animation and visual-effects industries, and, indeed, this shared base emphasizes the ways in which animation and special effects overlap far more than their labels would suggest. In the analog era, animated elements made brief appearances in live-action films, often to suggest environmental phenomena, such as lightning bolts rippling across a night sky in *Dracula* (1931), or science-fictional ones, such as the crackling, sporadically visible Id monster in *Forbidden Planet* (1956). As described in reference to *The Prince of Egypt* above, digital animation was put to similar use in otherwise traditionally animated films to contribute environmental effects, such as dust, water, sparks, and smoke. But the wholesale adoption of Maya irrevocably tipped a balance between animation and live-action, making it possible for animated characters and environments to blend with photographically captured ones. This development is impossible to separate from the rise of transmedial properties whose manifestations encompass multiple media, from video games to television and cinema. One example of Maya's central role in creating a blended animated–live-action screen world while facilitating transmedia expansion is *Warcraft* (2016). An adaptation of a long-running video-game series, which itself spawned an enormously popular virtual realm (2004's massively multiplayer online role-playing game, or MMORPG, *World of Warcraft*), *Warcraft* uses environments and characters created in Maya by Industrial Light & Magic to portray the world of Azeroth with its many fantastical species. These characters, the product of **performance**

capture similar to that discussed below in relation to Robert Zemeckis's films, were true to the designs of the video game, as were the film's largely digital "locations."

The Artisanal (Re)Turn

But if the digitally reinvented children's feature enabled by new digital tools has come to dominate the contemporary box office alongside screen worlds built from digitally animated visual effects, a countervailing trend saw the reappearance of traditional animation—at the level of aesthetics, if not underlying technique. As if in dialectical counterpoint to the rapid rise to dominance of digital, dimensional animation, "artisanal" animation explicitly marking itself as belonging to an older, handmade school of craft began to show up at several points along the contin-uum. Robert Rodriguez's *Spy Kids 2: The Island of Lost Dreams* (2002), for example, takes place on an island off the coast of Madagascar, which the mad scientist Romero (Steve Buscemi) has populated both with miniaturized versions of real animals and mutant creatures, such as the Spork, a breed of flying pig. Segments of the film devoted to the mutants, along with such sequences as a battle with skeletons, pay homage to the work of Ray Harryhausen by emulating the appearance and movement of stop-motion animation and in particular Harry-hausen's patented Dynamation method. In *Jason and the Argonauts* (1963), such sequences as a swordfight with an army of skeletons were achieved by the frame-by-frame adjustment of puppets rigged with metal armatures against a rear-projected backdrop on which previously captured footage was projected, allowing live-action elements to integrate with animated ones. Although such sequences in *Spy Kids 2* as the monster attack on the beach were realized digitally, their impression of physicality—and direct homage to a renowned auteur—cheekily showcased the production's mashup of analog and digital aesthetics, further reflected in the "hybrid" natures of the mutant monsters.

A more sustained invocation of the charms of old-school animation could be found in the output of Laika Studios. Formed in the early 2000s, Laika grew out of the animation shop run by Will Vinton, another well-known auteur whose work from the 1970s to the 1990s produced such memorable screen creations as the singing California Raisins featured in a series of commercials. Vinton's studio con-tributed stop-motion sequences to such productions as Bette Midler's concert film *Divine Madness* (1980) and the Michael Jackson–Francis Ford Coppola col-laboration *Captain Eo* (1986), along with several fast-food brand mascots, such as the Domino's Pizza "Noid." Purchased by Nike founder Phil Knight in 2002, Vin-ton's former operation became known in its new capacity through director Henry Selick, who worked there from 2003 to 2009, a period that also saw the stu-dio rechristened as Laika in 2005. Under the direction of Selick, whose stop-motion film *The Nightmare before Christmas* (1993) was both a popular and cult favorite, Laika worked on another Tim Burton production, *Corpse Bride* (2005), and released *Coraline* in 2009; following Selick's departure, the studio went on to create *ParaNorman* (2012) and *The Boxtrolls* (2014).

Coraline was an unusual production in many respects, starting with the fact that it was filmed stereoscopically, using two cameras to capture each frame for later exhibition in 3D venues. Metaphorically reflecting this double nature, the process of making the movie was rooted both in an emphatic materiality and the high-tech ephemera of coded data and digital devices. The first aspect is evident from the physical infrastructure of the stage where animation took place, an Oregon warehouse containing more than a hundred settings and thousands of detailed puppets and props with hand-knitted costumes. These were combined with digital technologies, including 3D-printed facial sections for each puppet—lower and upper faces in hundreds of variations for thousands of combinatorial possibilities. As teams of animators worked to position the puppets in the frame-by-frame increments typical of stop-motion cinematography, facial sections were applied to create the characters' expressions, the seams between the pieces later digitally painted out. In addition, certain environmental elements, such as smoke, fire, and liquids (e.g., gravy), were created and composited digitally but were designed to give the appearance of having been achieved through physical means.

That year (2009) also saw the release of another film executed in determinedly old-school stop-motion animation, *Fantastic Mr. Fox*. Roald Dahl's 1970 novel was adapted by Wes Anderson, known for meshing whimsical subject matter with intricate production design and a theatrically presentational rather than realist mise-en-scène. Anderson initially developed the project with Henry Selick, who had previously worked on the director's *The Life Aquatic with Steve Zissou* (2004), contributing shots of deep-sea creatures, dueling crabs, and diving submersibles to that fantasia on the theme of Jacques Cousteau. Selick left *Mr. Fox* during preproduction to work on *Coraline*, but his imprint remained on Anderson's movie in the form of its open embrace of stop-motion materiality. Filmed with twelve-inch-tall puppets dressed in hand-knitted clothes modeled on the director's own style, the animal characters of *Mr. Fox* bristled with fur—which combined dyed goats' hair with fake fur harvested from toys—that Anderson wanted to bristle and twitch with a look directly inspired by the stop-motion craft of decades past, such as Ladislaw Starewich's *Roman de Renard* (1930). Wishing to avoid the overly smooth animation style of recent stop-motion animated films, such as *Corpse Bride*, Anderson "instead wanted viewers to notice and embrace the medium of stop-motion itself, which had enchanted him as a child, especially in holiday shorts such as *Rudolph the Red-Nosed Reindeer*" (a Rankin/Bass television special first broadcast in 1964). Anderson further affirmed his love of "herky-jerkiness" by dictating that *Mr. Fox* be animated on twos, doubling each frame of film and in effect decreasing the resolution of characters' movement.[5] The director's hipster-ish commitment to stop-motion suggests that this mode of animation has taken on new appeal in an era when the analog has gained rhetorical weight and cultural capital in relation to the digital.

Arising as it did in dialectical answer to digital image making and the hype surrounding it, the artisanal turn of the 2000s was not without its own share of proud self-awareness. Much of this took the form of celebratory coverage in the press, praising the hard work of physical animation in implicit contrast to the apparent ease and automation of state-of-the-art CGI; Christopher Jobson, for example, writes, "One of the most gratifying aspects of watching stop-motion films is the knowledge that every bit of motion seen on screen is created by human hands, frame by frame, millimeter by millimeter."[6] But at other times, perhaps encouraged by the proliferating availability of behind-the-scenes materials through online video-streaming services, such as YouTube and Vimeo, the subtext of labor occasionally slipped into the foreground of the text, as in the last few minutes of Laika's *The Boxtrolls* (2014). Two of the film's characters, Mr. Trout (Nick Frost) and Mr. Pickles (Richard Ayoade), stand on a street corner, engaging in idle discussion of free will and determination (fig. 6.5). As the dialogue turns to existential speculations about the motive force behind our behavior, the camera pulls back, slowly revealing that the town is in fact an elaborate tabletop set, with a cycloramic sky painting behind it and studio lights on tripods all around. As the pullback continues, the figure of animator Travis Knight becomes faintly visible, captured in the process of manipulating the puppets of Trout and Pickles. Knight's ghostly cameo re-performs a trope dating back to silent-era animation in which, as Donald Crafton notes, the hand of the animating artist appears in literal and figurative ways within the film text.[7] Combined with the disclosure of the mise-en-scène's constructedness and the winking double entendre of the philosophical debate taking place on-screen, the revelatory pullback (itself a feat of meticulous, frame-by-frame planning) updates the gesture identified by Crafton, making of its very materiality a defiant riposte to the smooth erasures of the digital era.

Yet, as Andrea Comiskey observes, the continued viability of stop-motion animation in feature films is imbricated in complex ways with the rise of digital animation. Starting with the twin release in 1993 of *Jurassic Park* and *The Nightmare before Christmas*, stop-motion features "have flowered at the same time that CGI has both rendered stop motion obsolete as a visual-effects medium and usurped cel animation as the dominant mode of feature-length animation production." Of this counterintuitive arrangement she writes, "On the one hand, digital technologies have provided a new set of craft tools that have helped puppet animators solve many of the most daunting challenges posed by stop-motion production (especially at feature length). But on the other hand, the digital serves as a computerized 'other' against which stop-motion is frequently positioned, thereby affirming the medium's cultural and economic value—and indeed its ontological status—as a material, tactile and *handmade* medium."[8] Comiskey tracks this

FIGURE 6.5: Characters in *The Boxtrolls* (2014) comment on their own constructedness.

"handmade imperative" across a body of films, including the Selick productions already discussed, along with the British Aardman Animation features *Chicken Run* (2000), *Wallace & Gromit: The Curse of the Were-Rabbit* (2005), and *The Pirates! Band of Misfits* (2012) (released in the United Kingdom as *The Pirates! In an Adventure with Scientists!*). To this list we could add such recent releases as Laika's *ParaNorman*, as well as *The Secret of Kells* (2009) and *The Secret of the Sea* (2014). The latter two films, from the Irish animation studio Cartoon Saloon, were created largely with traditional cel animation.

Stretching the parameters of animation in another direction, some animated films in this era used live-action as a basis for rotoscope-style animation, effectively painting each frame over a photographic reference. Two Richard Linklater productions, *Waking Life* (2001) and *A Scanner Darkly* (2006), used a proprietary software package called Rotoshop, developed by Bob Sabiston in the 1990s, to accomplish this; another, Ari Folman's *Waltz with Bashir* (2008), employed a combination of traditional animation and digital cutouts in Adobe Flash. Unlike the performance-captured movies of the same period, which carefully counterweighted the plasmatic potential of their new form of animation with their referential base and firmly entrenched cultural heritage to produce screen worlds that behaved in predictable, recognizable, and—at least in the hopes of their makers—non-alienating ways, the three rotoscope-style films made much of their ability to distort, ornament, and editorially comment on their own presentation, establishing in effect an additional channel of "voice" to both reinforce and destabilize the meanings ostensibly presented in their narratives.

Waking Life, a philosophical meditation on dreams and the nature of existence, was filmed by Linklater as a series of semi-improvised conversations held by the unnamed protagonist (Wiley Wiggins) with a series of street characters and think-ers. In much the same fashion as the director's *Slacker* (1991), the result was a branching, peripatetic flow of ideas whose steam-of-consciousness meander lent itself to the fluid, ever-changing shapes and colors of the animated imagery. *Waking Life*'s patchwork narrative, however, is amplified by its visual structure, achieved with the help of multiple animators whom Linklater assigned to animate separate sequences. If the live-action footage establishes one sort of continuity across the body of the film, and Rotoshop another, these gestures toward homo-geneity are disrupted by the intentional heterogeneity of the contrasting choices made by different animators. Cut from a slightly more traditional narrative cloth and industrially positioned less as an independent than a studio film, *A Scanner Darkly*—adapted from a 1977 novel by Philip K. Dick—correspondingly draws upon a more consistent style in Rotoshopping its characters and settings, down-playing flux in favor of the narrative and spatial clarity prized in classical Holly-wood storytelling.

Caroline Ruddell analyzes both of Linklater's movies through the lens of the Rotoshop software they employed, arguing that their meanings must be framed in relation to their underlying technology, as expressed in their treatment of the line. Resisting any simple determinism, Ruddell suggests that the "blurred lines" in each film must be understood in complex and subtle ways; both movies play with the notion of identity as perpetually in flux, befitting the sliding and mutat-ing color fields of Rotoshopped animation, but also comment on changing rela-tionships between independent and blockbuster film and the tension between narrative and spectacle that has shaped debates around special effects from the early **cinema of attractions** to the contemporary reception of digital performers, such as Gollum in the *Lord of the Rings* films. As Ruddell notes, Rotoshop is a descendent of the hand-drawn rotoscope, an animation technique dating back to the work of Max Fleischer in the 1910s, which even then was promoted as high-tech novelty (see chapter 1).[9] By continually spectacularizing the relationship between live-action reference and painterly overlay, the current use of Rotoshop preserves this spark of the avant-garde in ways that break with other forms of digi-tally produced illusion: "Rotoscoped material allows and revels in this 'seeing under' and encourages viewers to see both under and between, whereas certain (albeit not all) other forms of digital (and pre-digital) effects in some way attempt to hide their derivation, or the fact that they are effects at all."[10]

Waking Life demonstrates this double movement of the rotoscoped/Roto-shopped aesthetic in such scenes as the dialogue between the protagonist and the "self-destructive man" played by J. C. Shakespeare (fig. 6.6). As the two men stroll down the street and the self-destructive man opines about an inescapably rigged political system in which human agency and choice is rendered meaningless, the background swims abstractly, with such elements as fences, windows, and water meters shivering like Scrabble pieces spilled across a desktop—flaunting in their

FIGURE 6.6: Rotoshopped dreams in *Waking Life* (2001).

un-mooredness a freedom from the lack of registration that would otherwise keep every element in tight alignment. The generally monochrome palette is broken by the bright red of a can, which the self-destructive man fills with gasoline and then pours over himself, sitting cross-legged on the ground. He lights a match and drops it into himself, bursting into flame; within a few seconds, his charred and stiffened body falls to one side. Meanwhile, pedestrians and bicyclists pass by obliviously. In live-action reference footage available on the DVD, the man merely dumps water on himself, pantomiming the match lighting and performing the fall. The orange flames and billowing smoke of his self-immolation exist wholly within the digitally painted animation, but because Rotoshopping renders the preceding material at once so banal and so heightened, the uncanniness of the handoff draws attention to itself as a point of spectatorial fascination.

The films of Robert Zemeckis and his production company ImageMovers during this same period went even further into the realm of blending live-action and animation but hewed to a more traditional narrative aesthetic even as they demonstrated animation's protean and galvanizing presence in the first decades of an emergent digital cinema. Known since the late 1970s for his ability to fuse comedy and action genres with high-tech special effects, in blockbusters such as *Back to the Future*, "mature" SF cinema in *Contact* (1997), and more idiosyncratic but still popular and critically well-received films such as *Cast Away* (2000) and *Flight* (2012), Zemeckis stands among a group of directors known for their innovative use of visual effects in crowd-pleasing blockbusters, figures Chuck Tryon calls "technoauteurs": George Lucas, Steven Spielberg, Peter Jackson, James Cameron, David Fincher.[11] In terms of their shared desire to push technological development in the film industry while maintaining fidelity to the box-office-friendly genre and franchise structures within which they tend to work, this group—composed of white men born between 1947 and 1961—has been a driving force in the last twenty-five years of expensive and technologically audacious filmmaking while easing audiences through that period of change, often in narratives built around the problem of balancing the technological and the human. Fitting, then, that Zemeckis's output in the 2000s was a sustained push to jump-start a new mode of filmmaking poised in the middle space between live-action and animated cinema. His *Who Framed Roger Rabbit* (1988) presented a world in which animated cartoons fully interpenetrated our reality, drawing on a nostalgic archive of beloved animation and, equally publicly, a cutting-edge fusion of painted cel animation and optical compositing—the latter a technology already on the verge of obsolescence due to the emergence of digital compositing whose aesthetics have been described by Lisa Purse.[12]

As much as that film spectacularized hybridity, Zemeckis's more recent productions have tried to sublimate it, answering the challenge of technological flux with entertaining films built around beloved standards. Instead of the animation archive that *Roger Rabbit* references, *The Polar Express* (2004) adapts a children's book, *Beowulf* (2007) an ur-myth, and *A Christmas Carol* (2009), a fixture of sentimental literature (fig. 6.7). In addition to the promise of a cultural pedigree, a "built-in audience" generalized beyond fandom's subcultures, all three films brandished their adapted nature on their sleeve, reinforced in the marketing as a dual performance of fidelity and experimentalism. Zemeckis's articulation of this pairing centered on performance-capture technology and its capacity to capture a spark of life specific to animation: the digital's larger struggle to prove itself real and not a hyped but ultimately disappointing simulacrum.

His first performance-captured film, *The Polar Express*, was adapted from a 1985 children's book by Chris Van Allsburg. "Captured" rather than shot on a stage called a **performance volume**, the actors wore special outfits equipped with tracking devices to record kinesthetic data both at the broad level of their body position and limb movement and the finer level of facial expression. Plugging these data into software that generated three-dimensional environments, Zemeckis's goal was to let the performances drive the animated screen world. The fundamental mutability of the captured data—which operate according the duplicative, copy-and-paste logic of digital code—enabled "real" bodies to be divorced from and married to screen bodies in unusual ways, for example, allowing Tom Hanks to play multiple roles, including the young protagonist known as the Hero Boy, the boy's father, the train conductor, and, in the film's sumptuous climax, Santa Claus. Another affordance of the performance-capture process was the blending of multiple actors into one on-screen body, as when Josh Hutcherson provided additional motion-capture information that was merged into Hanks's data.

For a sequence in which the Hero Boy meets a hobo traveling atop the *Polar Express* and then rides on the hobo's shoulders as he skis across the train cars,

FIGURE 6.7: Digital doubles summon the ghost of cinema future in *A Christmas Carol* (2009).

shooting took the form of multiple passes, each capturing the performance of a different character. Hanks played both parts on a motion-capture stage dressed with props and furniture made out of chain-link fence, the perforated structure of which enabled cameras to capture positional data based on small markers dotting the actor's body.[13] The Hero Boy's performance was assembled from data recorded from a child actor on the shoulders of a stuntman, spliced with another motion-capture "take" of Hanks's performance as the boy. These separate passes took place on sets scaled to fit the boy size of the screen characters so that when Hanks performed as the Hero Boy, he did so on an oversized set. Zemeckis then introduced movements of his virtual camera to maximize the sequence's visual impact.[14] In the final stage, all of these data were combined and sent to Render-Man to generate the finished images, reflecting a tight interplay between live-action reference and digital animation.

These recombinatory possibilities stand in contrast to the emphasis placed within the marketing publicity on the authentic nature of the movie's performances, which sought to establish a reliable, one-to-one relationship between real actors and screen bodies. Rather than seeing these as opposed or incoherent forces within the messaging around the movie, however, it is more useful to view them as inherently related to the intended appeal of Zemeckis's performance-capture initiative; rather than resolving the discrepancy between live-action and its illusionistic double, *The Polar Express* delights in straddling the line. The film does not, in other words, want to cross the **uncanny valley**—the term, developed in robotics, for the problematic nature of simulations that come close but fall just short of the real thing—but to dwell in it. While this might have been the production's intent, tepid critical response to *The Polar Express* and its two follow-up films coalesced around the notion that all of them failed at their attempt to duplicate live-action cinema—in short, reading Zemeckis's performance-captured films by the logic of live-action rather than of animation, which throughout its history had happily occupied the uncanny middle space summarized in the concept of an "illusion of life" in which both keywords are required to generate the oscillatory, strange-attractor affect of the properly *unheimlich*.

The profit ratio for each successive Zemeckis production was shrinking however: *Polar Express* made $162 million against a $165 million production expense, *Beowulf* $82 million against a $150 million cost, and *A Christmas Carol* $139 million against $200 million. And by 2010, it had become clear that while Zemeckis's auteurist brand might guarantee something close to breaking even, the larger aesthetic and technological imperative behind his trilogy could not carry over to similar productions not directly helmed by him. Directed by *Roger Rabbit* animator and storyboard artist Simon Wells, the 2011 feature *Mars Needs Moms*, adapted from a graphic novel by Berkeley Breathed, carried a production cost typical of performance-capture 3D films, $150 million, but made only $21 million in domestic release, making it one of the biggest box-office failures in history. Lambasted not just for the undead look of its characters but its dark tone and disturbing character designs, *Mars Needs Moms* was the end of the line for ImageMovers Digital, whose closing was announced even before the film was released. Absorbed back into ImageMovers, the short-lived team up with Disney died with several projected features on its slate, including a remake of the Beatles' animated film *Yellow Submarine* (George Dunning, 1968), a sequel to *Roger Rabbit*, and an adaptation of *The Nutcracker*—abandoned relics of an optimistic decade in which the ambitious pursuit of a new fusion between animation and live-action promised to forge a fresh cinematic ontology.

Convergent and Democratic Animation

Although no fewer than ten films released in 2009 received nominations for Best Picture, most media coverage of the 82nd Academy Awards centered on the rivalry between front-runners *The Hurt Locker* and *Avatar*. Directed respectively by Kathryn Bigelow and her ex-husband, James Cameron, the two movies—beyond their focus on military culture—differed profoundly: one was a hard-edged and grittily realistic study of a bomb-disposal squad in the Iraq War, the other an opulent science-fiction saga about the clash between humans and blue-skinned aliens living in the star system of Alpha Centauri. But behind this contest of genres and genders (which *The Hurt Locker* ended up winning) roiled another set of tensions having to do with a fundamental shift in the nature of cinema itself. Pointing out *Avatar*'s heavy reliance on computer-generated imagery to create its characters and environments, some commentators questioned the grounds for classifying Cameron's movie as live-action in the first place: "Why is the CG in *Avatar* considered visual effects while the CG employed for a Pixar or Dreamworks film [is] simply considered animation?" Brad Brevet asked. "If *Avatar* is up for Oscar's Best

Visual Effects award, shouldn't *Up* and *Monsters vs. Aliens* be as well? . . . Perhaps the real question is When is CGI no longer considered visual effects and when is it considered animation?"[15]

As the latter examples suggest, even partly animated screen bodies, from earthly animals to aliens, superheroes, robots, and wizards, enjoy an unusual degree of mobility across media screens, making them an inescapable component not just of commodified visual culture but the franchise structures that generate and regulate that environment. While efforts to capture and generate simulacra of real people, as in the varieties of "posthumous performance" used to resurrect dead actors,[16] may headline rapturous accounts of industry technology even as they prompt alarmist reactions to the replacement of human beings by cinematic cyborgs, a far more common and populous class of screen body is those whose animated nature is, as it were, worn on the sleeve. The cel-animated characters in the musical band The Archies, after all, were created by Don Kirshner in 1968 as an early form of what Matt Stahl terms virtual labor: "performative labor that *appears* to be performed by an individual but that is actually the result of a division of labor incorporating creative and technical workers, intellectual property, and high-tech equipment."[17] Tying these cartoon bodies of the 1960s to contemporary synthespians, such as Gollum in *The Lord of the Rings*, Stahl charts the ways in which a technically oriented discourse of actors as animated properties works on an ideological level to hide the ways in which capitalist systems, such as movie and TV studies, dehumanize performers' labor, turning it into just another commodity. Stahl's politically pointed analysis might well be extended in the hyper-mediated intertextuality of transmedia storytelling,[18] proliferation of para-textual tie-ins,[19] and franchise management in the era of media convergence,[20] whose cultivation of intellectual properties across a network of screens and streams depends—particularly within the invented realms of fantastic media—on the controlled replication and deployment of animated bodies. In these bodies, animation merges the potent, instantly recognizable iconography of design with the total compliance of corporately owned and technologically produced forms that can appear in multiple incarnations across a host of narrative and interactive environments.

Take, for example, the various members of the Avengers: Iron Man, Captain America, Hulk, Thor, Hawkeye, and Black Widow. Anchors of the highly successful Marvel Cinematic Universe (MCU), these characters have been most recently brought to life in a series of feature films, some focused on individuals and others on the team together. Within those films, human performers, such as Mark Ruffalo and Robert Downey Jr., are augmented by digital visual effects and animation to grant them everything from their distinctive looks (Hulk's beastly green body, Iron Man's armor) to their superpowers. But their greater "powers" involve transmedia travel, for all of these characters were not only born in another medium—comic books and graphic novels—but now circulate among a variety of media homes and formats, including television series, video games, and collectible card games. Rendered in the fine detail of cinematography in the feature films, the superheroes scale easily to "lower resolution" environments, such as Disney XD's *Avengers Assemble* (2013–present). In all of these cases, the ubiquity of animation as both a production tool and discursive "idea" about bodies and identities on-screen helps to bridge and connect disparate media and storytelling practices.

Another area of animation's spread across media platforms can be seen in the rise of machinima, or animation using video-game engines. A movement traceable to the explosion of personal computing and home gaming in the 1980s, early forms of machinima involved edited play throughs of networked "deathmatches" in such games as iD's *Doom* (1993) and *Quake* (1996), whose graphic engines—collections of algorithms for rendering navigable, volumetric environments in real time—had semi-open architectures and user interfaces making them accessible to players and not just professional coders. Three decades later, machinima has evolved into a rich universe of homebrew animation in a variety of formats and genres, from comedic parody to deadly serious documentary, fan films, and performance art. The top-down deployment of corporately owned animated bodies and the grassroots, unauthorized production of machinima come together in media forms that range beyond the flat screen and into material shapes, using 3D printing to replicate animated bodies as physical maquettes. These liminal bodies, half on-screen and half on the desktop, are the selling point of such game series as Skylanders (2011) and Disney Infinity (2013), in which virtual avatars are reborn in plastic outfitted with **near-field communication** (NFC) technologies and docking stations that unlock new levels within games for consoles, such as the Xbox One, PlayStation 4, and Nintendo Wii University. Itself a practice with a lengthy prehistory in the hobby of plastic model kits, garage and vinyl kits, and scratch building,[21] 3D-printed bodies take their place amid the figurines and armies of tabletop fantasy role-playing games and war gaming to mark the far boundaries of the medium.

Such examples suggest that animation in the digital age has become an omnipresent force in contemporary and emergent media not only because of the way key software packages have evolved to augment and supplant traditional labor practices and pipelines employed by studios but because of the democratization of animation wrought by such tools. Ubiquitous computing devices and network access have spread processing power and wireless connectivity to vast numbers of people. As these platforms proliferate, applications refine their user interfaces to streamline the process of creating and "spreading" media, whether through the sharing of corporately produced animation or through user-generated content.[22] Fans express their transformative takes on their favorite media by making and sharing GIFs—short, moving loops—on Tumblr, while YouTube and Vimeo provide fledgling animators a portal for showcasing their work and receiving critiques.

Adobe's Animate, which grew out of its groundbreaking 1990s software Flash, can work in a number of file formats to create content for the web, television, and video games, putting production power in the hands of ordinary users. In the same vein, Pixar made a free version of RenderMan available in 2015, stipulating only that any use of the software does not generate profits, protecting personal projects, educational use, and experimentation and research. Thus, although they mark the apex of technological sophistication under the hood, digital tools paradoxically open up the production of animation to a much broader audience, no longer divided into independent artists and tinkerers on the one hand and well-heeled studios on the other. Even as animation continues to dominate both traditionally styled cartoon features and live-action visual effects, as a creative practice it has colonized the screens of an entire mediascape.

ACADEMY AWARDS FOR ANIMATION

1931/32	SHORT SUBJECT (Cartoon), Walt Disney, Producer	*Flowers and Trees*
1932/33	SHORT SUBJECT (Cartoon), Walt Disney, Producer	*The Three Little Pigs*
1934	SHORT SUBJECT (Cartoon), Walt Disney, Producer	*The Tortoise and the Hare*
1935	SHORT SUBJECT (Cartoon), Walt Disney, Producer	*Three Orphan Kittens*
1936	SHORT SUBJECT (Cartoon), Walt Disney, Producer	*The Country Cousin*
1937	SHORT SUBJECT (Cartoon), Walt Disney, Producer	*The Old Mill*
1938	SHORT SUBJECT (Cartoon), Walt Disney, Producer	*Ferdinand the Bull*
	SPECIAL ACHIEVEMENT AWARD, Walt Disney	*Snow White and the Seven Dwarfs*
1939	SHORT SUBJECT (Cartoon), Walt Disney, Producer	*The Ugly Duckling*
1940	SHORT SUBJECT (Cartoon), Metro-Goldwyn-Mayer	*The Milky Way*

1941	SHORT SUBJECT (Cartoon), Walt Disney, Producer	*Lend a Paw*
1942	SHORT SUBJECT (Cartoon), Walt Disney, Producer	*Der Fuehrer's Face*
1943	SHORT SUBJECT (Cartoon), Frederick Quimby, Producer	*Yankee Doodle Mouse*
1944	SHORT SUBJECT (Cartoon), Frederick C. Quimby, Producer	*Mouse Trouble*
1945	SHORT SUBJECT (Cartoon), Frederick Quimby, Producer	*Quiet Please!*
1946	SHORT SUBJECT (Cartoon), Frederick Quimby, Producer	*The Cat Concerto*
1947	SHORT SUBJECT (Cartoon), Edward Selzer, Producer	*Tweetie Pie*
1948	SHORT SUBJECT (Cartoon), Fred Quimby, Producer	*The Little Orphan*
1949	SHORT SUBJECT (Cartoon), Edward Selzer, Producer	*For Scent-Imental Reasons*
1950	SHORT SUBJECT (Cartoon), Stephen Bosustow, Producer	*Gerald McBoing Boing*
1951	SHORT SUBJECT (Cartoon), Fred Quimby, Producer	*The Two Mouseketeers*
1952	SHORT SUBJECT (Cartoon), Fred Quimby, Producer	*Johann Mouse*
1953	SHORT SUBJECT (Cartoon), Walt Disney, Producer	*Toot, Whistle, Plunk and Boom*
1954	SHORT SUBJECT (Cartoon), Stephen Bosustow, Producer	*When Magoo Flew*
1955	SHORT SUBJECT (Cartoon), Edward Selzer, Producer	*Speedy Gonzales*
1956	SHORT SUBJECT (Cartoon), Stephen Bosustow, Producer	*Magoo's Puddle Jumper*
1957	SHORT SUBJECT (Cartoon), Edward Selzer, Producer	*Birds Anonymous*
1958	SHORT SUBJECT (Cartoon), John W. Burton, Producer	*Knighty Knight Bugs*
1959	SHORT SUBJECT (Cartoon), John Hubley, Producer	*Moonbird*
1960	SHORT SUBJECT (Cartoon), William L. Snyder, Producer	*Munro*
1961	SHORT SUBJECT (Cartoon), Zagreb Film	*Ersatz (The Substitute)*
1962	SHORT SUBJECT (Cartoon), John Hubley and Faith Hubley, Producers	*The Hole*

1963	SHORT SUBJECT (Cartoon), Ernest Pintoff, Producer	*The Critic*
1964	SHORT SUBJECT (Cartoon), David H. DePatie and Friz Freleng, Producers	*The Pink Phink*
1965	SHORT SUBJECT (Cartoon), Chuck Jones and Les Goldman, Producers	*The Dot and the Line*
1966	SHORT SUBJECT (Cartoon), John Hubley and Faith Hubley, Producers	*Herb Alpert and the Tijuana Brass Double Feature*
1967	SHORT SUBJECT (Cartoon), Fred Wolf, Producer	*The Box*
1968	SHORT SUBJECT (Cartoon), Walt Disney, Producer	*Winnie the Pooh and the Blustery Day*
1969	SHORT SUBJECT (Cartoon), Ward Kimball, Producer	*It's Tough to Be a Bird*
1970	SHORT SUBJECT (Cartoon), Nick Bosustow, Producer	*Is It Always Right to Be Right?*
1971	SHORT SUBJECT (Animated), Ted Petok, Producer	*The Crunch Bird*
1972	SHORT SUBJECT (Animated), Richard Williams, Producer	*A Christmas Carol*
1973	SHORT SUBJECT (Animated), Frank Mouris, Producer	*Frank Film*
1974	SHORT FILM (Animated), Will Vinton and Bob Gardiner, Producers	*Closed Mondays*
1975	SHORT FILM (Animated), Bob Godfrey, Producer	*Great*
1976	SHORT FILM (Animated), Suzanne Baker, Producer	*Leisure*
1977	SHORT FILM (Animated), Co Hoedeman, Producer	*The Sand Castle*
1978	SHORT FILM (Animated), Eunice Macaulay and John Weldon, Producers	*Special Delivery*
1979	SHORT FILM (Animated), Derek Lamb, Producer	*Every Child*
1980	SHORT FILM (Animated), Ferenc Rofusz, Producer	*The Fly*
1981	SHORT FILM (Animated), Frédéric Back, Producer	*Crac*
1982	SHORT FILM (Animated), Zbigniew Rybczynski, Producer	*Tango*

1983	SHORT FILM (Animated), Jimmy Picker, Producer	*Sundae in New York*
1984	SHORT FILM (Animated), Jon Minnis, Producer	*Charade*
1985	SHORT FILM (Animated), Cilia Van Dijk, Producer	*Anna & Bella*
1986	SHORT FILM (Animated), Linda Van Tulden and Willem Thijssen, Producers	*A Greek Tragedy*
1987	SHORT FILM (Animated), Frédéric Back, Producer	*The Man Who Planted Trees*
1988	SHORT FILM (Animated), John Lasseter, William Reeves	*Tin Toy*
1988	SPECIAL ACHIEVEMENT AWARD, Richard Williams	*Who Framed Roger Rabbit*
1989	SHORT FILM (Animated), Christoph Lauenstein, Wolfgang Lauenstein	*Balance*
1990	SHORT FILM (Animated), Nick Park	*Creature Comforts*
1991	SHORT FILM (Animated), Daniel Greaves	*Manipulation*
1992	SHORT FILM (Animated), Joan C. Gratz	*Mona Lisa Descending a Staircase*
1993	SHORT FILM (Animated), Nick Park	*The Wrong Trousers*
1994	SHORT FILM (Animated), Alison Snowden, David Fine	*Bob's Birthday*
1995	SHORT FILM (Animated), Nick Park	*A Close Shave*
1995	SPECIAL ACHIEVEMENT AWARD, John Lasseter	*Toy Story*
1996	SHORT FILM (Animated), Tyron Montgomery, Thomas Stellmach	*Quest*
1997	SHORT FILM (Animated), Jan Pinkava	*Geri's Game*
1998	SHORT FILM (Animated), Chris Wedge	*Bunny*
1999	SHORT FILM (Animated), Alexander Petrov	*The Old Man and the Sea*
2000	SHORT FILM (Animated), Michael Dudok de Wit	*Father and Daughter*
2001	SHORT FILM (Animated), Ralph Eggleston	*For the Birds*
	ANIMATED FEATURE FILM, Aron Warner	*Shrek*

2002   SHORT FILM (Animated), Eric Armstrong   *The ChubbChubbs!*
       ANIMATED FEATURE FILM, Hayao Miyazaki   *Spirited Away*

2003   SHORT FILM (Animated), Adam Elliot   *Harvie Krumpet*
       ANIMATED FEATURE FILM, Andrew Stanton   *Finding Nemo*

2004   SHORT FILM (Animated), Chris Landreth   *Ryan*
       ANIMATED FEATURE FILM, Brad Bird   *The Incredibles*

2005   SHORT FILM (Animated), John Canemaker and Peggy Stern   *The Moon and the Son: An Imagined Conversation*
       ANIMATED FEATURE FILM, Nick Park and Steve Box   *Wallace & Gromit: The Curse of the Were-Rabbit*

2006   SHORT FILM (Animated), Torill Kove   *The Danish Poet*
       ANIMATED FEATURE FILM, George Miller   *Happy Feet*

2007   SHORT FILM (Animated), Suzie Templeton and Hugh Welchman   *Peter & the Wolf*
       ANIMATED FEATURE FILM, Brad Bird   *Ratatouille*

2008   SHORT FILM (Animated), Kunio Kato   *La Maison en Petits Cubes*
       ANIMATED FEATURE FILM, Andrew Stanton   *WALL-E*

2009   SHORT FILM (Animated), Nicolas Schmerkin   *Logorama*
       ANIMATED FEATURE FILM, Pete Docter   *Up*

2010   SHORT FILM (Animated), Shaun Tan and Andrew Ruhemann   *The Lost Thing*
       ANIMATED FEATURE FILM, Lee Unkrich   *Toy Story 3*

2011   SHORT FILM (Animated), William Joyce and Brandon Oldenburg   *The Fantastic Flying Books of Mr. Morris Lessmore*
       ANIMATED FEATURE FILM, Gore Verbinski   *Rango*

2012   SHORT FILM (Animated), John Kahrs   *Paperman*
       ANIMATED FEATURE FILM, Mark Andrews and Brenda Chapman   *Brave*

2013   SHORT FILM (Animated), Laurent Witz and Alexandre Espigares   *Mr. Hublot*
       ANIMATED FEATURE FILM, Chris Buck, Jennifer Lee,   *Frozen*
          and Peter Del Vecho

2014   SHORT FILM (Animated), Patrick Osborne and Kristina Reed   *Feast*
       ANIMATED FEATURE FILM, Don Hall, Chris Williams, and   *Big Hero 6*
          Roy Conli

2015   SHORT FILM (Animated), Gabriel Osorio and Pato Escala   *Bear Story*
       ANIMATED FEATURE FILM, Pete Docter and Jonas Rivera   *Inside Out*

2016   SHORT FILM (Animated), Alan Barillaro and Marc Sondheimer   *Piper*
       ANIMATED FEATURE FILM, Byron Howard, Rich Moore,   *Zootopia*
           and Clark Spencer

2017   SHORT FILM (Animated), Glen Keane and Kobe Bryant   *Dear Basketball*
        ANIMATED FEATURE FILM, Darla K. Anderson and   *Coco*
           Lee Unkrich

NOTES

Introduction

1 Terms in boldface are defined in the glossary.

2 Mark Langer, "The Disney-Fleischer Dilemma: Product Differentiation and Technological Innovation," *Screen* 33, no. 4 (Winter 1992): 343–360.

3 Walt Disney to Don Graham, interoffice communication, Walt Disney Productions, December 23, 1935 (p. 2), Box 3, Folder 74 (Graham, Don), Accretions 2003, John Canemaker Animation Collection, Fales Library and Special Collections, Elmer Holmes Bobst Library, New York University, New York.

4 John Hubley and Zachary Schwartz, "Animation Learns a New Language," *Hollywood Quarterly* 1, no. 4 (July 1946): 360–363; John Hubley, "Beyond Pigs and Bunnies: The New Animator's Art," *American Scholar* 44, No. 2 (Spring 1975): 213–223. See also Dan Bashara, "Cartoon Vision: UPA, Precisionism and American Modernism," *Animation: An Interdisciplinary Journal* 10, no. 2 (2015): 82–101; and Daniel Bashara, *Cartoon Vision: UPA Animation and Postwar Aesthetics* (Berkeley: University of California Press, 2019).

5 Kristin Thompson, "Implications of the Cel Animation Technique," in *The Cinematic Apparatus*, ed. Teresa de Lauretis and Stephen Heath, 106–120 (New York: St. Martin's Press, 1980).

6 Nicholas Sammond, *Babes in Tomorrowland: Walt Disney and the Making of the American Child, 1930-1960* (Durham, N.C.: Duke University Press, 2005).

1 The Silent Screen, 1895-1928

1 Philippe Gauthier, "A Trick Question: Are Early Animated Drawings a Film Genre or a Special Effect?," *Animation: An Interdisciplinary Journal* 6, no. 2 (2011): 163–175.

2 Donald Crafton, *Before Mickey: The Animated Film, 1898–1928* (Chicago: University of Chicago Press, 1982/1993), 26.

3 For a recent summary of the long discussion on this topic, see Drew Morton, "Sketching under the Influence? Winsor McCay and the Question of Aesthetic Convergence between Comic Strips and Film," *Animation: An Interdisciplinary Journal* 5, no. 3 (2010): 295–312.

4 Crafton, *Before Mickey*, 36–37.

5 Crafton, *Before Mickey*, 44.

6 Donald Crafton, "Animation Iconography: The Hand of the Artist," *Quarterly Review of Film Studies* 4, no. 1 (Fall 1979): 409–428.

7 Crafton, *Before Mickey*, 48.

8 Colin Williamson, *Hidden in Plain Sight: An Archaeology of Magic and the Cinema* (New Brunswick, N.J.: Rutgers University Press, 2015).

9 Donald Crafton, *Emile Cohl, Caricature, and Film* (Princeton, N.J.: Princeton University Press, 1990), 116–121.

10 Crafton, *Before Mickey*, 61.

11 Crafton, *Before Mickey*, 59.

12 Crafton, *Emile Cohl*, 121.

13 Crafton, *Before Mickey*, 61.

14 Pixilation is the animation of humans—using live actors as frame-by-frame subjects, as in Norman McLaren's *Neighbors* (1952). In *Little Nemo*, McCay's hand is the subject of time-lapse photography or frame-by-frame animation.

15 Crafton, *Emile Cohl*, 150–151.

16 Crafton, *Before Mickey*, 89–90.

17 Crafton, *Emile Cohl*, see filmography in the appendix.

18 *Moving Picture World* 15, no. 7 (February 15, 1913): 695. See also Crafton, *Before Mickey*, 81; Crafton, *Emile Cohl*, 161–163.

19 Crafton, *Before Mickey*, 84.

20 Crafton, *Before Mickey*, 86; Crafton, *Emile Cohl*, 174.

21 Crafton, *Before Mickey*, 83.

22 Crafton, *Emile Cohl*, 175.

23 Crafton, *Before Mickey*, 180–182.

24 John Canemaker, *Winsor McCay: His Life and Art*, rev. and exp. ed. (New York: Harry N. Abrams, 2005), 169, 175.

25 David Nathan and Donald Crafton, "The Making and Re-making of Winsor McCay's *Gertie* (1914)," *Animation: An Interdisciplinary Journal* 8, no. 1 (2013): 23–46, here 31.

26 Nathan and Crafton, "Making and Re-making," 33–34.

27 Nathan and Crafton, "Making and Re-making," 32.

28 Donald Crafton, *Shadow of a Mouse: Performance, Belief, and World-Making in Animation* (Berkeley: University of California Press, 2013).

29 Crafton, *Before Mickey*, 100–101.

30 On Fitzsimmons, see Canemaker, *Winsor McCay*, 169–175; on number of drawings, see Nathan and Crafton, "Making and Re-making," 40.

31 Winsor McCay, "How I Originated Motion Picture Cartoons," *Cartoon and Movie Magazine* 31 (April 1927): 11–15, here 15; qtd. in Canemaker, *Winsor McCay*, 169.

32 Nathan and Crafton, "Making and Re-making," 30.

33 Winsor McCay, "Animated Art," in *Illustrating and Cartooning: Animation*, comp. and ed. Chas. L. Bartholomew and Joseph Almars (Minneapolis, Minn.: Federal Schools, 1923), Box 17 Folder 181 (Winsor McCay: Article: Animated Art), Series I, Subseries B, Canemaker Collection, Bobst Library, New York University. This correspondence course was originally published in 1919.

34 Nathan and Crafton, "Making and Re-making," 28.

35 Crafton, *Emile Cohl*, 149.

36 Crafton, *Emile Cohl*, 74.

37 Canemaker, *Winsor McCay*, 169–175; Nathan and Crafton, "Making and Re-making," 27.

38 Crafton, *Before Mickey*, 9.

39 Crafton, *Before Mickey*, 194.

40 Canemaker, *Winsor McCay*, 172.

41 Canemaker, *Winsor McCay*, 174.

42 Canemaker, *Winsor McCay*, 172.

43 Mark Langer, "John Randolph Bray: Animation Pioneer," in *American Silent Film: Discovering Marginalized Voices*, ed. Gregg Bachmann and Thomas J. Slater, 94–114 (Carbondale: Southern Illinois University Press, 2002), here 98.

44 "History of the Animated Motion Picture," undated typescript courtesy of Bray Studio, New York; Box 5, Folder 16 (Bray, J. R.,) Series I, Subseries B, Canemaker Collection, Bobst Library, New York University.

45 Langer, "John Randolph Bray," 98. On the director-unit system, see Janet Staiger, "The Director System: Management in the First Years" and "The Director-Unit System: Management of Multiple-Unit Companies after 1909," in David Bordwell, Janet Staiger, and Kristin Thompson, *The Classical Hollywood Cinema: Film Style and Mode of Production to 1960*, 113–128 (New York: Columbia University Press, 1985).

46 Patent no. 1,107,193 in John Randolph Bray and Earl Hurd, "Bray-Hurd: The Key Animation Patents," *Film History* 2, no. 3 (September–October 1988): 229–266.

47 Patent no. 1,143,542 in Bray and Hurd, "Key Animation Patents," 245–249.

48 Crafton, *Before Mickey*, 148; Langer, "John Randolph Bray," 99.

49 Patent no. 1,179,068 in Bray and Hurd, "Key Animation Patents," 251–255. First mention of the "Bray-Hurd Process Company" is in "Bray Wins Interference," *Moving Picture World*, January 19, 1918, 348: "Recently the Bray-Hurd Process Company was formed to control the patents of J. R. Bray and Earl Hurd," which perhaps implies that their licensing company was formed in 1917.

50 Langer, "John Randolph Bray," 104.

51 Crafton, *Emile Cohl*, 179.

52 Harvey Deneroff, *Interview with John Randolph Bray*, January 12 and 19, 1972, American Film Institute Oral History Project, II2B 22, qtd. in Langer, "John Randolph Bray," 100.

53 For the social background to this "Taylorization" of the industry—so called because it reflected a larger trend in corporate management during this period, inspired by Frederick Winslow Taylor's "scientific management" system of organizing and incentivizing workers—see Crafton, *Before Mickey*, 162–167.

54 Kristin Thompson, "Implications of the Cel Animation Technique," in *The Cinematic Apparatus*, ed. Teresa de Lauretis and Stephen Heath, 106–120 (New York: St. Martin's Press, 1980).

55 Dick Huemer, "Animation Pioneer Portraits," *Cartoonist PROfiles* 1, no. 3 (Summer 1969): 14–18, here 15.

56 Crafton, *Before Mickey*, 167.

57 For Walt Disney Studio's principles of animation, see Frank Thomas and Ollie Johnston, *Disney Animation: The Illusion of Life* (New York: Abbeville Press, 1984).

58 The story of Bray fleecing McCay has a happy end, sort of: apparently McCay took Bray to court and won participation in the profits of the Bray-Hurd Process Company, receiving royalties as late as 1932. Canemaker, *Winsor McCay*, 174.

59 Crafton, *Before Mickey*, 157.

60 Crafton, *Before Mickey*, 194; see also Langer, "John Randolph Bray," 255n16.

61 David S. Hulfish, "Recent Patents in Motography," *Motography* 15, no. 1 (January 1, 1916): 19–20.

62 Neil Harris, *Humbug: The Art of P. T. Barnum* (Boston: Little, Brown, 1973), 79.

63 "The Cartoon Comedy, Last Mystery of the Movies," *Philadelphia Evening Ledger*, October 30, 1915, Amusement Section, 1.

64 "Animated Cartoons in the Making," *Scientific American* 116, no. 16 (October 14, 1916): 354; Eustace L. Adams, "The Secret of the Animated Cartoon," *Popular Science Monthly* 87, no. 4 (October 1915): 443–444; Homer Croy, "Making the Movie Cartoon Move," *Everybody's Magazine* 37 (September 1917): 355–360; Homer Croy, "A Five Thousand Dollar Job Goes Begging," *Illustrated World* 27 (March 1917): 108–109.

65 See, for example, C. Francis Jenkins and Oscar B. Depue, *Handbook for Motion Picture and Stereopticon Operators* (Washington, D.C.: Knega Company, 1908), 92; Colin N. Bennett, *The Handbook of Kinematography* (London: Kinematograph Weekly, 1911); Frederick A. Talbot, *Moving Pictures: How They Are Made and Worked* (Philadelphia: J. B. Lippincott Company, 1912); Epes Winthrop Sargent, *The Technique of the Photoplay* (New York: Moving Picture World, 1913); Robert E. Welsh, *ABC of Motion Pictures* (New York: Harper and Brothers, 1916).

66 "Uncle Harry Explains Animated Cartoons," *Washington Times*, October 30, 1916, Home edition, 4.

67 McCay, "Animated Art."

68 Allan Harding, "They All Thought Him Crazy, but They Don't Think So Now," *American Magazine* 99, no. 1 (January 1925): 30–32, 126–129.

69 Crafton, *Before Mickey*, 184.

70 John R. McCrory, *How to Draw for the Movies; or, The Process of Cartoon Animation* (Kansas City, Mo.: Feature Publishing Bureau, 1918). Similar examples include Homer Croy, *How Motion Pictures Are Made* (New York: Harper and Brothers, 1918); Bert Green, "The Making of Animated Cartoons," *Motion Picture Magazine* 17, no. 4 (May 1919): 51–52, 104. A more technical, fulsome explanation from the period can be found in Carl Louis Gregory, ed., *A Condensed Course in Motion Picture Photography* (New York: New York Institute of Photography, 1920), 257–266.

71 E. G. Lutz, *Animated Cartoons: How They Are Made, Their Origin and Development* (New York: Charles Scribner's Sons, 1920).

72 Russell Merritt and J. B. Kaufman, *Walt in Wonderland: The Silent Films of Walt Disney*, rev. English-language ed. (Pordenone, Italy: Giornate del Cinema Muto; Baltimore, Md.: Distributed by Johns Hopkins University Press, 1993), 39.

73 Lutz, *Animated Cartoons*, 58.

74 Lutz, *Animated Cartoons*, 59.

75 Notices in *Moving Picture World* 32, no. 4 (April 28, 1917): 684; *Moving Picture World* 32, no. 8 (May 26, 1917): 1273; "Animated Drawings," *Moving Picture World* 32, no. 13 (June 30, 1917): 2078.

76 See Jam Handy, "Marvels of Animated Diagrams and Their Ever Widening Uses," *Reel and Slide* 2, no. 2 (February 1919): 12; Jerome Langenbruch, "The Animated Drawing in Popular Science," *Educational Film Magazine* 2 (October 1919): 12. See also Langer, "John Randolph Bray," 103; "History of the Animated Motion Picture," undated typescript courtesy of Bray Studio, Canemaker Collection.

77 Crafton, *Before Mickey*, 157–162.

78 Charles Frederick Carter, "Speeding Military Training with Films," *Educational Film Magazine* 1, no. 1 (January 1919): 14–15.

79 Charles Frederick Carter, "What Makes a Gas Engine Go?" *Photoplay* 15, no. 6 (May 1919): 45–46, 108.

80 Kristian Moen, "Imagination and Natural Movement: The Bray Studios and the 'Invention' of Animated Film," *Film History* 27, no. 4 (2015): 130–150, here 143–145.

81 Mark Langer, "Introduction to the Fleischer Rotoscope Patent," *Animation Journal* (Spring 1993): 66–73.

82 Merritt and Kaufman, *Walt in Wonderland*, 64–65.

83 Mark Langer, "Polyphony and Heterogeneity in Early Fleischer Films: Comic Strips, Vaudeville, and the New York Style," in *Funny Pictures: Animation and Comedy in Studio-Era Hollywood*, ed. Daniel Goldmark and Charlie Keil, 29–50 (Berkeley: University of California Press, 2011), here 30.

84 Langer, "Polyphony and Heterogeneity," 31.

85 Leslie Cabarga, *The Fleischer Story*, rev. ed. (New York: DaCapo Press, 1988), 34; John Canemaker, *Felix: The Twisted Tale of the World's Most Famous Cat* (New York: Pantheon Books, 1991), 104; Merritt and Kaufman, *Walt in Wonderland*, 85.

86 Langer, "Polyphony and Heterogeneity," 46.

87 Merritt and Kaufman, *Walt in Wonderland*, 98.

88 Canemaker, *Felix*, 104.

89 Canemaker, *Felix*, 106.

90 Merritt and Kaufman, *Walt in Wonderland*, 22.

91 Rob King, *The Fun Factory: The Keystone Film Company and the Emergence of Mass Culture* (Berkeley: University of California Press, 2009); see also Henri Bergson, *Laughter*, ed. Wylie Sypher (Garden City, N.Y.: Doubleday Anchor, 1956).

92 Merritt and Kaufman, *Walt in Wonderland*, 28.

93 Merritt and Kaufman, *Walt in Wonderland*, 29.

2 Classical Hollywood, 1928–1946

1 "Academy Awards Database," http://awardsdatabase.oscars.org/search/results.

2 Douglas Gomery, *The Hollywood Studio System* (New York: St. Martin's Press, 1986), 11–12.

3 Tino Balio, ed., *Grand Design: Hollywood as a Modern Business Enterprise, 1930–1939*, vol. 5 of *History of American Cinema*, rev. ed. (Berkeley: University of California Press, 1996), 73–75.

4 Michael Barrier, *Hollywood Cartoons: American Animation in Its Golden Age* (New York: Oxford University Press, 1999), 34, 168.

5 Leonard Maltin, *Of Mice and Magic: A History of American Animated Cartoons*, rev. ed. (New York: New American Library, 1987), 133.

6 Ian T. Macauley, "Mighty Mouse (and Others)," *New York Times*, February 7, 1982, WC1.

7 Joe Adamson, *The Walter Lantz Story, with Woody Woodpecker and Friends* (New York: Putnam's, 1985), 36–53.

8 Adamson, *Walter Lantz Story*, 99.

9 Danny Peary, "Reminiscing with Walter Lantz," in *The American Animated Cartoon*, ed. Danny Peary and Gerald Peary, 195–196 (New York: Dutton, 1980).

10 Michael Barrier, *Hollywood Cartoons*, 22–24.

11 Richard Fleischer, *Out of the Inkwell* (Lexington: University of Kentucky Press, 2005), 50–53.

12 Fleischer, *Out of the Inkwell*, 45–48; Barrier, *Hollywood Cartoons*, 25–26.

13 Gomery, *Hollywood Studio System*, 35–40.

14 Mark Langer, "Polyphony and Heterogeneity in Early Fleischer Films: Comic Strips, Vaudeville, and the New York Style," in *Funny Pictures: Animation and Comedy in Studio-Era Hollywood*, ed. Daniel Goldmark and Charlie Keil, 29–50 (Berkeley: University of California Press, 2011); Nicholas Sammond, *Birth of an Industry: Blackface Minstrelsy and the Rise of American Animation* (Durham, N.C.: Duke University Press, 2015).

15 Barrier, *Hollywood Cartoons*, 157–160.

16 Barrier, *Hollywood Cartoons*, 323–365.

17 "Warner Bros. Cartoon Characters List," The Big Cartoon Database, https://www.bcdb.com/cartoons/Warner_Bros./Characters/.

18 Barrier, *Hollywood Cartoons*, 165–168, 188–192, 287–91, 296–301, 403–410.

19 Barrier, *Hollywood Cartoons*, 35–55.

20 Barrier, *Hollywood Cartoons*, 60–62.

21 Gomery, *Hollywood Studio System*, 143.

22 "Shorts No Longer Just 'Filler,'" *Film Daily*, April 28, 1936, 28.

23 Giannalberto Bendazzi, *Cartoons: One Hundred Years of Cinema Animation* (London: John Libbey; Bloomington: Indiana University Press, 1994), 84.

24 Maltin, *Of Mice and Magic*, 125.

25 The discussion of the process of production at Terrytoons here draws on Dorothy Tilka Stone, "Constructing the Animated Cartoon," *New York Times*, December 6, 1931, X7; Theodore Strauss, "Mr. Terry and the Animal Kingdom," *New York Times*, July 7, 1940, sec. 9, p. 3. The documentary *Makin' 'Em Move* (1938) presents a humorous dramatization of these processes.

26 Barrier, *Hollywood Cartoons*, 35.

27 Joe Adamson, "Working for the Fleischers: An Interview with Dick Huemer," *Funnyworld* 16 (Winter 1974–1975): 23.

28 "Complicated Work of Making Film Cartoons," *New York Times*, December 28, 1930.

29 Clarke Wales, "Out of the Inkwell," *Boston Globe*, March 28, 1937, 8.

30 Shamus Culhane, *Talking Animals and Other People* (New York: St. Martin's Press, 1986), 149.

31 "The Big Bad Wolf," *Fortune*, November 1934, 93.

32 Culhane, *Talking Animals*, 95.

33 Walter Lantz, "Synchronizing Sound Cartoons," *American Cinematographer* 16, no. 2 (February 1935): 82.

34 Lantz, "Synchronizing Sound Cartoons," 76, 82–83.

35 Steve Schneider, *That's All Folks! The Art of Warner Bros. Animation* (New York: Henry Holt, 1988), 22.

36 Carl Fallberg, "Animated Cartoon Production Today: Part II—Production Preparation," *American Cinematographer* 23, no. 5 (May 1942): 202–203.

37 Culhane, *Talking Animals*, 40.

38 Timothy R. White, "From Disney to Warner Bros.: The Critical Shift," *Film Criticism* 16, no. 3 (Spring 1992): 3016.

39 Joseph Barbera, *My Life in 'Toons* (Atlanta: Turner Publishing, 1994), 46–47.

40 Carl Fallberg, "Animated Cartoon Production Today: Part III—Animation," *American Cinematographer* 23, no. 6 (June 1942): 282–285.

41 Culhane, *Talking Animals*, 113–114.

42 Carl Fallberg, "Animated Cartoon Production Today: Part V—Painting, Photographing, and Re-recording," *American Cinematographer* 23, no. 8 (August 1942): 344–346.

43 Richard Neupert, "Colour, Lines and Nudes: Teaching Disney's Animators," *Film History* 11 (1999): 77–84.

44 Culhane, *Talking Animals*, 40–41.

45 The process by which the Lantz studio recorded sound is shown in *Cartoonland Mysteries* (1936), no. 18 in the series *Going Places with Lowell Thomas* at https://www.youtube.com /watch?v=yDzXFZvLWqA.

46 Walt Disney, "Growing Pains," *Journal of the Society of Motion Picture Engineers* 36 (January 1941): 31 and Frederick James Smith, "Out of the Inkwell," *Los Angeles Times*, December 10, 1939, K4.

47 Smith, "Out of the Inkwell," K4.

48 William E. Garity and J. L. Ledeen, "The New Walt Disney Studio," *Journal of the Society of Motion Picture Engineers* 36 (January 1941): 7–8.

49 Culhane, *Talking Animals*, 58.

50 Harvey Deneroff, "'We Can't Get Much Spinach': The Organization and Implementation of the Fleischer Strike," *Film History* 1, no. 1 (1987): 2.

51 Norman M. Klein, *Seven Minutes: The Life and Death of the American Animated Cartoon* (London: Verso, 1993), 104.

52 Douglas Gomery, *The Hollywood Studio System: A History* (London: British Film Institute, 2005), 185–193.

53 Tom Sito, *Drawing the Line: The Untold Story of the Animation Unions from Bosko to Bart Simpson* (Lexington: University of Kentucky Press, 2006), 7–152.

54 For an extensive discussion of the Fleischer strike, see Deneroff, "'We Can't Get Much Spinach,'" 1–14.

55 Bendazzi, *Cartoons*, 83.

56 For a comprehensive look at Disney animation in this period, see Frank Thomas and Ollie Johnston, *Disney Animation: The Illusion of Life* (New York: Abbeville Press, 1984).

57 Bendazzi, *Cartoons*, 84.

58 "Hollywood Has 'Double Trouble,'" *New York Times*, July 7, 1940, sec. 9, p. 3.

59 Edward R. Beach, "Double Features in Motion Picture Exhibition," *Harvard Business Review* 10 (July 1932): 505–507.

60 "Shorts Merchandizers Hope Anew," *Variety*, January 13, 1937, 2.

61 "Spread of Duals Ditches Shorts," *Variety*, January 13, 1937, 5.

62 "Double Features Cut Out Shorts," *Variety*, November 5, 1930, 11.

63 "Shorts' Prospects Bright, Says Lantz," *Film Daily*, September 23, 1938, 10.

64 "Double Features Cut Out Shorts," 11.

65 "Spread of Duals Ditches Shorts," *Variety*, January 13, 1937, 5, 21.

66 "Deplore Shorts Getting Exhib Nix," *Variety*, April 23, 1940, 20.

67 "Spread of Duals Ditches Shorts," 21.

68 Richard de Cordova, "The Mickey in Macy's Window: Childhood, Consumerism, and Disney Animation," in *Disney Discourse: Producing the Magic Kingdom*, ed. Eric Smoodin, 203–213 (New York: Routledge, 1994).

69 See, for example, "Scrappy Cartoons Plugged by Tie-Ups," *Film Daily*, April 28, 1936, 34; "80 Radio Stations" and "Novel Accessories," *Film Daily*, September 16, 1936, 24.

70 "150,000 Grocers," *Film Daily*, September 16, 1936, 24.

71 Popeye ad, *Film Daily*, April 28, 1936, 8.

72 "100 Manufacturers in Disney Tie-Ups," *Film Daily*, September 23, 1938, 10.

73 "Short Subject Producers Pioneered in Color to Offset Double Features," *Film Daily*, April 28, 1936, 21.

74 "Cartoons Step Forward," *Variety*, October 30, 1939, 87.

75 John Culhane, "*Snow White* at 50: Undimmed Magic," *New York Times*, July 12, 1987.

76 "'Wind' Rides Atlanta," *Motion Picture Herald*, December 16, 1939, 23.

77 Barrier, *Hollywood Cartoons*, 292–296, 301–306.

78 Mae D. Huettig, *Economic Control of the Motion Picture Industry* (Philadelphia: University of Pennsylvania Press, 1944), 121.

79 "Warners to Hold Special Tradeshows for Shorts," *Film Daily*, July 30, 1941, 1, 7; "Morgan Finds Exhibitors Ready," *Film Daily*, May 12, 1941, 1, 2; Bosley Crowther, "Two-Reeler's Comeback," *New York Times*, October 26, 1941.

80 "Record Early Shorts Selling," *Motion Picture Herald*, March 22, 1941, 30.

81 John Stuart Jr., "That 'New Order' Brings a New Day for the Short Subject," *Motion Picture Herald*, August 9, 1941, 16.

82 Stuart Jr., "That 'New Order,'" 16; "Studios' Push behind Shorts," *Hollywood Reporter*, July 11, 1941, 1, 4.

83 "Shorts—the Exhibitor Speaks Out," *Film Daily*, June 1, 1939, 9.

84 Stuart Jr., "That 'New Order,'" 16.

85 Paramount ads, *Film Daily*, April 30, 1941, 6–9.

86 Phil M. Daly, "Along the Rialto," *Film Daily*, May 1, 1941, 4.

87 Stuart Jr., "That 'New Order,'" 16; "Record Early Shorts Selling," *Motion Picture Herald*, March 22, 1941, 30.

88 "Paramount Sets Shorts," *Film Daily*, April 30, 1941, 9.

89 Daly, "Along the Rialto," 3; "Significant Slant on Shorts," *Film Daily*, June 1, 1939, 14.

90 Fred Stanley, "Off the Hollywood Wire," *New York Times*, August 12, 1945, sec. 2, p. 1.

91 "Cartoon Producers Band for Closer Organization," *Hollywood Reporter*, September 30, 1943, 3.

92 Philip K. Scheuer, "Town Called Hollywood," *Los Angeles Times*, July 26, 1942, C3.

93 "Walt Disney: Great Teacher," *Fortune*, August 26, 1942, 90–95.

94 Scheuer, "Town Called Hollywood," C3.

95 John Baxter, *Disney during World War II* (Glendale, Calif.: Disney Editions, 2014), 1.

96 Carl Nater, "Walt Disney Studio—a War Plant," *Journal of the Society of Motion Picture Engineers* 42, no. 3 (March 1944): 170–176.

97 "Ingenuity and Efficiency Speed Up Cartoon Prod'n," *Hollywood Reporter*, October 20, 1942, 6.

98 Jack Kinney, *Walt Disney and Other Assorted Characters* (New York: Harmony Books, 1988), 122.

99 "Breakdown of Cartoon Prod. Basis of Lantz Incentive Plan," *Hollywood Reporter*, September 1, 1944, 3.

100 "Ingenuity and Efficiency," 6.

101 "New Lantz Cartoon Device Cuts Labor Outlay in Half," *Hollywood Reporter*, November 3, 1943, 6.

102 "Ingenuity and Efficiency," 6.

103 Nater, "Walt Disney Studio," 174–175.

104 Nater, "Walt Disney Studio," 171.

105 Hugh Harmon, *Commandments for Health* (U.S. Navy, 1945), https://www.youtube.com/watch?v=grZyVGBZlcU&list=PLIn8Ziqz_266GVmIZSDP24-JhoLGmjZEB.

106 *The Enemy Bacteria* (Walter Lantz, 1945), https://www.youtube.com/watch?v=twXKyi8tidY.

107 For an annotated list of such films, see Michael S. Shull and David E. Wilt, *Doing Their Bit: Wartime American Animated Short Films 1939–1945*, 2nd ed. (Jefferson, N.C.: McFarland, 2004).

108 *Ration Bored* (Walter Lantz/Universal, 1943), https://www.youtube.com/watch?v=bo2At1iYtEY.

109 *Scrap for Victory* (Terrytoons, 1943), https://www.youtube.com/watch?v=VEAxe9u4ZZg.

110 For a more extensive discussion on this period, see J. B. Kaufman, *South of the Border with Disney* (New York: Walt Disney Family Foundation Press, 2009).

111 See, for example, Julianne Burton-Carvajal, "'Surprise Package': Looking Southward with Disney," in *Disney Discourse: Producing the Magic Kingdom*, ed. Eric Smoodin, 131–147 (New York: Routledge, 1994).

112 "Current Gov't Emphasis on Value of Good Shorts," *Variety*, November 4, 1942, 5, 38.

113 "Shorts Taking Play from Duals," *Motion Picture Herald*, June 30, 1945, 13; "Exhibitors Use Shorts to Supplant Dual Bills," *Motion Picture Herald*, October 23, 1943, 17.

114 "Music and Color Highlight New Season," *Motion Picture Herald*, August 4, 1945, 29.

115 "Shorts Taking Play," 13.

116 "Swing to Single Bills," *Hollywood Reporter*, December 20, 1946, 1, 8.

117 "Shorts Improve Status," *Motion Picture Herald*, September 2, 1944, 13. Also see "Color and Music Dominate," *Motion Picture Herald*, June 3, 1944, 13.

118 "Music and Color," 29; "WB Promotes Shorts to Hilt," *Film Daily*, February 7, 1951, 16.

119 "Short Subject Biz," *Film Daily*, January 11, 1945, 10; "Increased Releasing of Shorts No Barb at Duals," *Variety*, September 25, 1946, 27.

120 "Famous Studio Enlarges Its Cartoon Activities," *Film Daily*, September 20, 1944, 1, 6; "MGM Adding 100 Cartoonists," *Hollywood Reporter*, May 14, 1946, 1, 11.

121 "Film Shortage Hits Shorts Releases," *Motion Picture Herald*, May 12, 1945, 14; "More Shorts More Regularly Are Promised," *Motion Picture Herald*, September 29, 1945, 22.

122 "Majors Ask Shorts Rental Rise to Match Cost Spiral," *Motion Picture Herald*, November 9, 1946, p. 13; Joseph W. Taylor, "Cartoon Crisis," *Wall Street Journal*, January 20, 1947, pp. 1, 4.

123 "Stuffed Duck," *Time*, August 12, 1946, p. 86.

124 "Heavier Costs May Force Disney," *Variety*, November 6, 1946, p. 9.

125 "Majors Ask Shorts Rental Rise," *Motion Picture Herald*, November 9, 1946, p. 13.

126 "Cartoon Industry Threatened," *Film Daily*, August 26, 1946, pp. 1, 8.

127 W. R. Wilkerson, "Trade Winds," *Hollywood Reporter*, April 18, 1947, p. 1.

128 "Paradise Lost?" *Time*, January 19, 1948, p. 87.

129 "Cartoon-Making Kicked Around," *Variety*, May 28, 1947, p. 6.

130 "Lantz Seeks Cost," *Film Daily*, February 19, 1948, pp. 1, 4.

3 Limited Animation, 1947–1989

1 Charles and Mirella Jona Affron, *Best Years: Going to the Movies, 1945–1946* (New Brunswick, N.J.: Rutgers University Press, 2009), 4.

2 Maureen Furniss, *Art in Motion: Animation Aesthetics*, rev. ed. (New Barnet, United Kingdom: John Libbey, 2009), 133.

3 John Hubley and Zachary Schwartz, "Animation Learns a New Language," *Hollywood Quarterly* 1, no. 4 (July 1946): 362.

4 Tralfaz, "NBC Comics, Part 1," March 10, 2012, http://tralfaz.blogspot.com/2012/03/nbc-comics-part-1.html.

5 Greg Ehrbar, "Winky Dink, Howdy Doody, and You!," July 8, 2014, http://cartoonresearch.com/index.php/winky-dink-howdy-doody-and-you/; Billy Ingram and You, "Winky-Dink and You," http://tvparty.com/requested2.html.

6 Keith Scott, *The Moose Who Roared: The Story of Jay Ward, Bill Scott, a Flying Squirrel, and a Talking Moose* (New York: Thomas Dunne Books, 2000), 16–17.

7 Quoted in Gary H. Grossman, *Saturday Morning TV: Thirty Years of the Shows You Waited All Week to Watch* (New York: Arlington House, 1987), 343. Ironically, the one piece of animation that would appear in every episode—the opening credits of Crusader Rabbit galloping toward the camera astride a horse—would be the only fully animated sequence in the entire series. Later animated series would follow *Crusader*'s lead.

8 Scott, *Moose Who Roared*, 17.

9 Quoted in Charles Solomon, *Enchanted Drawings: The History of Animation*, rev. ed. (New York: Wings Books, 1994), 230.

10 Gene Deitch, "Chapter 15: The Terry-Fying Challenge," from *How to Succeed in Animation*, Animation World Network, http://www.awn.com/genedeitch.

11 Dan Bashara, "Cartoon Vision: UPA, Precisionism and American Modernism," *Animation: An Interdisciplinary Journal* 10, no. 2 (2015): 96.

12 John Hubley, "Beyond Pigs and Bunnies: The New Animator's Art," *American Scholar* 44, no. 2 (Spring 1975): 219–220.

13 Bashara, "Cartoon Vision," 83.

14 Leonard Maltin, *Of Mice and Magic: A History of American Animated Cartoons*, revised and updated (New York: Plume, 1987), 331.

15 Michael Frierson, "The Carry Over Dissolve in UPA Animation," *Animation Journal* 10 (2002): 56–57.

16 The year *Gerald McBoing Boing* won the Academy Award, no Disney film had been nominated; it was only the second time that had happened since the category's inception in 1932.

17 Michael Barrier, *Hollywood Cartoons: American Animation in Its Golden Age* (New York: Oxford University Press, 1999), 523; Maltin, 332.

18 Adam Abraham, *When Magoo Flew: The Rise and Fall of Animation Studio UPA* (Middletown, Conn.: Wesleyan University Press, 2012), 213.

19 The only film to post a profit from this group was *The Teahouse of the August Moon*. See Peter Lev, *The Fifties: Transforming the Screen 1950–59* (Berkeley: University of California Press, 2003), 198.

20 Bill Hanna with Tom Ito, *A Cast of Friends* (Dallas: Taylor Publishing Company, 1996), 8, emphasis in original.

21 This television deal did not include UPA cartoons, which Columbia distributed from 1948 to 1959.

22 Jeff Lenburg, *William Hanna and Joseph Barbera: The Sultans of Saturday Morning* (New York: Chelsea House, 2011), 74. Each cartoon had roughly two and a half minutes of animation if titles were deleted and the scene setter was reused from the previous cartoon.

23 In fact, while under contract at MGM in the mid-1950s, Bill Hanna and animator Mike Lah had actually produced *Crusader Rabbit* cartoons for Ward by forming an independent studio called Shield Productions with investment by radio syndication firm RCA. Shield Productions made eleven color episodes until ceasing production when they were made aware that Bonsall, not Ward, actually owned *Crusader Rabbit*; Bonsall subsequently produced his own series through TV Spots. See Scott, *Moose Who Roared*, 26–30.

24 Quoted in Cecil Smith, "Cartoon Capers Win Adult Friends," *Los Angeles Times*, September 4, 1960, H4.

25 Jerry Eisenberg, personal interview, May 17, 2016.

26 Quoted in Norman M. Klein, *7 Minutes: The Life and Death of the American Animated Cartoon* (London: Verso, 1993), 244.

27 Hanna, *A Cast of Friends*, 84.

28 Iwao Takamoto with Michael Mallory, *Iwao Takamoto: My Life with a Thousand Characters* (Jackson: University Press of Mississippi, 2009), 90.

29 From "Cartoon Tracks: The Art of Hanna-Barbera Sound," on disc 2 of *The Yogi Bear Show: The Complete Series* DVD collection.

30 Barry Hansen and Earl Kress, "An Interview with Hoyt Curtin," in *The Cartoon Music Book*, ed. Daniel Goldmark and Yuval Taylor, 169 (Chicago: A Capella Books, 2002). Originally appeared in *Hanna Barbera's Pic-A-Nic Basket of Cartoon Classics* (Rhino RD-72290, 1996).

31 Barry Hansen, "Yabba-Dabba Duets and Musical Meeces," *Hanna Barbera's Pic-A-Nic Basket of Cartoon Classics* (Rhino RD-72290, 1996).

32 Yowp, "Capitol Hi-Q—Cartoon Music for Huck and Yogi," Yowp: Stuff About Early Hanna-Barbera Cartoons, December 25, 2009, http://yowpyowp.blogspot.com/2009/12/capitol-hi -q-cartoon-music-for-huck-and.html.

33 Daniel Goldmark, "Drawing a New Narrative for Cartoon Music," in *The Oxford Handbook of Film Music Studies*, ed. David Neumeyer, 238 (New York: Oxford University Press, 2014), emphasis in original.

34 Hanna, *A Cast of Friends*, 115.

35 Joe Barbera, *My Life in 'Toons: From Flatbush to Bedrock in under a Century* (Atlanta: Turner, 1994), 136.

36 Thomas J. Fleming, "TV's Most Unexpected Hit," *Saturday Evening Post*, December 2, 1961. However, Joe Barbera says in his autobiography that *The Flintstones* cost $52,000 per episode in 1963. See Barbera, *My Life in 'Toons*, 163.

37 Ted Sennett, *The Art of Hanna-Barbera: Fifty Years of Creativity* (New York: Viking Studio Books, 1989), 84.

38 John Kricfalusi, "Animation: John K on Flintstones Animators," AnimationResources.org, http://animationresources.org/biography-john-k-on-flintstones-animators/.

39 Lenburg, *William Hanna and Joseph Barbera*, 108.

40 Doug Wildey interview in *Amazing Heroes* 95 (May 1986). Can be accessed at http://www.classicjq.com/info/AmazingHeroes95.aspx.

41 Lenburg, *William Hanna and Joseph Barbera*, 109.

42 Rocky and Bullwinkle originally were created for an unsold series by Ward and Alex Anderson called *The Frostbite Falls Review* in 1950.

43 Darrell Van Citters, *The Art of Jay Ward Productions* (Los Angeles: Oxbury Press, 2013), 11, emphasis in original.

44 Quoted in Scott, *Moose Who Roared*, 94–95, emphasis in original.

45 Quoted in Scott, *Moose Who Roared*, 95.

46 Quoted in Van Citters, *Art of Jay Ward*, 54.

47 Tom Sito, *Drawing the Line: The Untold Story of the Animation Unions from Bosko to Bart Simpson* (Lexington: University of Kentucky Press, 2006), 251–252.

48 Van Citters, *Art of Jay Ward*, 52–54. Bill Scott offers a different number for the cost of *Rocky and His Friends* for the first season. He states that "Hanna-Barbera was making its shows for a production cost of $21,000 per half hour, or two and half times more than the *Rocky* show budget." Scott, *Moose Who Roared*, 84.

49 Scott, *Moose Who Roared*, 86–104. Actually, *Fractured Fairy Tales* has better animation, layouts, and graphics than the other segments as several episodes were made in Hollywood by Ward or subcontracted to TV Spots. See Scott, *Moose Who Roared*, 117–122.

50 Scott, *Moose Who Roared*, 131.

51 Hal Erickson, *Television Cartoon Shows: An Illustrated Encyclopedia, 1949–2003, Volume 2*, 2nd ed. (Jefferson, N.C.: McFarland & Company, 2005), 529. Walt Disney used xerography for *101 Dalmatians* (Geronimi, Reitherman, and Luske, 1961) after first testing it on a few scenes in *Sleeping Beauty* (Geronimi, 1959) and then using it in the short *Goliath II* (Reitherman, 1960).

52 Quoted in Adam McGovern, "Marvel Man," *Jack Kirby Collector* 41 (Fall 2004): 43.

53 Erickson, *Television Cartoon Shows*, 326.

54 John Canemaker, *Felix: The Twisted Tale of the World's Most Famous Cat* (New York: Pantheon, 1991), 150.

55 Gene Deitch, "Chapter 22: Spinach & Bricks," from *How to Succeed in Animation*, Animation World Network, http://www.awn.com/genedeitch.

56 Gene Deitch, "Chapter 18: Prague, A Change of Life," from *How to Succeed in Animation*, Animation World Network, http://www.awn.com/genedeitch, emphasis in original.

57 Quoted from "Tom and Jerry . . . and Gene," in *Tom and Jerry: The Gene Deitch Collection*, DVD (Twentieth Century Fox, 2015).

58 Jason Mittell, *Genre and Television: From Cop Shows to Cartoons in American Culture* (New York: Routledge, 2004), 74. Mittell's chapter on cartoons also appears in abbreviated from in "The Great Saturday Morning Exile: Scheduling Cartoons on Television's Periphery in the

1960s," in *Prime Time Animation: Television Animation and American Culture*, ed. Carol A. Stabile and Mark Harrison (London: Routledge, 2003), 33–54.

59 Mittell, *Genre and Television*, 74, emphasis in original.

60 Barbera, *My Life in 'Toons*, 167.

61 Cy Schneider, *Children's Television* (Lincolnwood, Ill.: NTC Business Books, 1987), 62.

62 Lou Scheimer with Andy Mangels, *Lou Scheimer: Creating the Filmation Generation* (Raleigh, N.C.: TwoMorrows Publishing, 2012), 47.

63 Hanna, *A Cast of Friends*, 187.

64 Scheimer, *Lou Scheimer*, 47, 59, 161.

65 Solomon, *Enchanted Drawings*, 241.

66 Scheimer, *Lou Scheimer*, 45–46. For the difficulty in drawing humans versus animals, see among others, Grossman, *Saturday Morning TV*, 363; Torene Svitil, *So You Want to Work in Animation and Special Effects* (Berkeley Heights, N.J.: Enslow, 2008), 38–40.

67 Scheimer says the one big difference was that "Robin's costume got a black 'R' on a yellow circle, instead of the other way around." Scheimer, *Lou Scheimer*, 139. Also see *The Dark Knight Revisited*, documentary, *The New Adventures of Batman*, DVD; Scheimer

68 See Scheimer, *Lou Scheimer*, 46; "Animation Maverick: The Lou Scheimer Story," *DC Comics Super Heroes: The Filmation Adventures*, DVD.

69 *Filmation Layout Manual*, 1985, p. 7, emphasis in original.

70 See Greg Erhbar, "A Very Merry Spin," http://www.cartoonresearch.com/index.php/a-very-brady-animation-spin/. Accessed August 2, 2016.

71 Scheimer, *Lou Scheimer*, 53.

72 Sito, *Drawing the Line*, 254–256.

73 See Hanna, *A Cast of Friends*, 196–201; Scheimer, *Lou Scheimer*, 60.

74 Sito, *Drawing the Line*, 226.

75 Quoted in Grossman, *Saturday Morning TV*, 347.

76 Grossman, *Saturday Morning TV*, 361.

77 Sito, *Drawing the Line*, 224–225; Gerald Baldwin, *From Mr. Magoo to Papa Smurf: A Memoir* (Austin: Neighborhood Publishers, 2015), 155.

78 Scheimer, *Lou Scheimer*, 145.

79 Jim Colucci, "Interview with Arthur Rankin, Jr.," *Archive of American Television*, http://www.emmytvlegends.org/interviews/people/arthur-rankin-jr#.

80 A lot of information in this paragraph comes from various pages of Charles Solomon, *The Art and Making of Peanuts Animation: Celebrating Fifty Years of Television Specials* (San Francisco: Chronicle Books, 2012). Melendez says that he put $20,000 more into *A Charlie Brown Christmas*.

81 Quoted in Charles M. Schulz, *A Charlie Brown Christmas: The Making of a Tradition* (New York: HarperResource, 2000), 58.

82 Quoted in Solomon, *Art and Making of Peanuts*, 27.

83 Quoted in Solomon, *Art and Making of Peanuts*, 17.

84 Marc Steinberg, *Anime's Media Mix: Franchising Toys and Characters in Japan* (Minneapolis: University of Minnesota Press, 2012), 7–13.

85 Steinberg, *Anime's Media Mix*, 15–16.

86 Steinberg, *Anime's Media Mix*, 17.

87 Amanda Lotz, *The Television Will Be Revolutionized*, second edition (New York: New York University Press, 2014), 23.

88 John Kricfalusi, "Filmation's Golden Age," February 9, 2010, www.johnkstuff.blogspot.com.

4 Independent Animators and the Artisanal Mode, 1947–1989

1 For example, see Paul Wells's contrast between the absence of the artist in "orthodox animation" and the presence of the artist in "experimental animation," in his *Understanding Animation* (New York: Routledge, 1998), 36–46; Birgitta Hosea, "Drawing Animation," *Animation: An Interdisciplinary Journal* 5, no. 3 (November 2010): 353–367; Ruth Hayes, "The Animated Body and Its Material Nature," in *Animating the Unconscious*, ed. Jayne Pilling, 208–218 (New York: Columbia University Press, 2012).

2 Donald Crafton notes the motif of "the hand of the artist" in *Before Mickey: The Animated Film 1898–1928* (Chicago: University of Chicago Press, 1982), 5–12.

3 See Donald Crafton's more recent study *Shadow of a Mouse: Performance, Belief, and World-Making in Animation* (Berkeley: University of California Press, 2012).

4 Pioneering historians of this tradition include William B. Moritz, P. Adams Sitney, Robert Russett, and Cecile Starr. Moritz tends to refer to these artists' work as "non-objective" or "non-figurative" animation; Sitney discusses this tradition of animation within a larger context of "absolute film" and "graphic cinema," while Russett and Starr describe it as "experimental animation," which is the most frequently used term in scholarship to date. See William Moritz, "Non-Objective Film: The Second Generation," in *Film as Film: Formal Experiment in Film, 1910–1975*, ed. David Curtis and Richard Francis, 59–71 (London: Arts Council of Britain, 1979); P. Adams Sitney, *Visionary Film: The American Avant-Garde, 1943–2000*, 3rd ed. (London: Oxford University Press, 2002); Robert Russett and Cecile Starr's seminal *Experimental Animation: An Illustrated Anthology* (New York: Van Nostrand Reinhold, 1976).

5 The Women in Animation (WIA) organization collates and distributes the most recent statistics on this issue.

6 Oskar Fischinger, "My Statements Are in My Work," first printed in a program catalog for the *Art in Cinema* film exhibition at the San Francisco Art Museum, 1947. Republished in digital format by the Center for Visual Music at http://www.oskarfischinger.org /MyStatements.htm (Emphasis in the original).

7 Fischinger, "My Statements."

8 Len Lye and Gretchen Weinberg, "Interview with Len Lye," *Film Culture* 29 (Summer 1963): 44.

9 For exemplary popular discourse on Walt Disney from that period, see the December 27, 1954, issue of *Time* magazine, featuring Walt Disney on the front cover and a profile of Disney ("Father Goose") that extols his managerial genius.

10 Pat McGilligan and Faith Hubley, "Faith Hubley: An Interview," *Film Quarterly* 42, no. 2 (Winter 1988–1989): 12.

11 McGilligan and Hubley, "Faith Hubley," 11.

12 The actual animation of *Moonbird* was completed by two additional artists, Robert Cannon and Ed Smith, but the initial concept and the visual language of the film were determined by the Hubleys, who also financed the project themselves.

13 Examples of animators and experimental filmmakers who became influential teachers include Jules Engel (first director of the experimental animation program at CalArts), David Hilberman (San Francisco State University), Preston Blair (author of seminal animation

guides), John Hubley (Harvard University), Larry Jordan (San Francisco Art Institute), Stan VanDerBeek (University of Maryland), Robert Breer (Cooper Union), and Stan Brakhage (University of Colorado Boulder).

14 See Breer's remarks in an interview with Scott MacDonald, "Robert Breer," in *A Critical Cinema 2: Interviews with Independent Filmmakers*, 15–50 (Berkeley: University of California Press, 1992). In particular, Breer discusses the impossibility of precisely copying the same hand-drawn lines from frame to frame and the inevitability of a "breathing presence" in drawn animation (21).

15 Breer recalls feeling disappointed when he became experienced enough to be able to predict how his sequences would look on film before projecting them. See "An Interview with Robert Breer Conducted by Jonas Mekas and P. Adams Sitney on May 13, 1971 in New York City," *Film Culture* 56–57 (1973): 39–55.

16 McGilligan and Hubley, "Faith Hubley," 12–13.

17 From the televised segment "Lynn Smith: Method" in *Animating Women* (1996), dir. Sybil DelGaudio, produced by Side-Kicks Productions for Independent Television Service (ITVS).

18 George Griffin, "The Anxious Pencil," 1. Published online at http://www.geogrif.com/pdf /anxiouspencil4.pdf.

19 A decade later the famous studio animator Chuck Jones would write: "Occasionally, an artist should look at his tools and ask himself what he cannot do without—the essentials—what he must have to pursue his form of expression in animation. In animation, as different from other art forms, he must have only three things: a pencil, a number of sheets of paper and a light source. With these things he can animate, without them he cannot." Chuck Jones, "Animation Is a Gift Word," *AFI Report* 5, no. 2 (1974). Republished online at https:// animationresources.org/theory-chuck-jones-animation-is-a-gift-word.

20 Ralph Bakshi, "Theory: Advice from Ralph Bakshi," published by Animation Resources at http://animationresources.org/advice-bakshi-on-surviving-tough-times.

21 On the importance of metamorphosis in the history animation, see Tom Gunning, "The Transforming Image: The Roots of Animation in Metamorphosis and Motion" in *Pervasive Animation*, ed. Suzanne Buchan, 52–70 (London: Routledge Press, 2013).

22 Most pioneering early animation was made using under-the-camera (or before-the-camera) techniques, including work by pioneers like Emile Cohl, Walter Ruttmann, and Vladislav Starevich. Object or puppet animation is not typically considered an under-the-camera technique, but it shares the same principles and is also a popular independent animation mode.

23 A particularly interesting challenge to conceptual boundaries between animation and live-action cinematography is the animation technique called pixilation, in which a scene with human characters is treated as a stop-motion studio, with static snapshots of action captured frame by frame to produce the illusion of impossible movements (such as humans floating in the air in Norman McLaren's *Neighbours* [1952]).

24 Classical studio animation also relies on this strategy to some extent, particularly in multi-plane animation, which separates figure from background and maintains some layers between frames. However, under-the-camera animation takes this approach much further, extending it to all parts of the image.

25 The compilation was not planned as a single film. Because of the early timing of these experiments and Crockwell's relative isolation in upstate New York, it is difficult to ascertain whether he was inspired by similar techniques developed in Europe in the 1920s (by such artists as Walter Ruttmann and Oskar Fischinger) or whether Crockwell arrived at these techniques independently.

26 Quoted in Giannalberto Bendazzi, *Cartoons: One Hundred Years of Cinema Animation* (Bloomington: Indiana University Press, 1994), 100. Similar descriptions of animation as

an art of four-dimensional choreography were written by such animators as Alexandre Alex-eieff, Len Lye, and Hans Richter.

27 This is just one way of interpreting the description of a "four-dimensional" form, because the concept of the fourth dimension holds different scientific and metaphysical meanings.

28 Sand animation had been explored before Caroline Leaf by filmmakers in other countries, though Leaf may not have been aware of those experiments.

29 Midhat Ajanovic, "An Interview with Caroline Leaf" (June 2002), republished online at http://www.ajan.se/index.php?option=com_content&view=article&id=46%3Aan-interview-with-caroline-leaf-in-english&catid=26%3Ainterviews&Itemid=43.

30 See Corrie Francis Parks, *Fluid Frames: Experimental Animation with Sand, Clay, Paint, and Pixels* (New York: Focal Press, 2016).

31 MacDonald, "Robert Breer," 30.

32 The variability of finite animation cycles are foregrounded in films like Kathy Rose's *The Doodlers* (1975) and Paul Glabicki's *Five Improvisations* (1979).

33 For a historical overview of the Walt Disney Studio's development of copying and reproduction technology for the purposes of animation, particularly during the transition to xerography, see Chris Pallant, *Demystifying Disney: A History of Disney Feature Animation* (London: Bloomsbury, 2011).

34 George Griffin, "Cartoon, Anti-Cartoon," in *The American Animated Cartoon: A Critical Anthology*, ed. Gerald Peary and Danny Peary, 7 (New York: E. P. Dutton, 1980). Republished online at http://www.geogrif.com/pdf/anti-cartoonOrig.pdf.

35 Candy Kugel, "The Creation of an Icon: MTV," *Animation World Magazine* 2, no. 10 (January 1998), http://www.awn.com/mag/issue2.10/2.10pages/2.10mtv.html.

36 Of course, archives of premade poses and layers have also been utilized in studio animation, particularly in limited animation.

37 Quoted from a statement posted on the artist's website at http://lawrencecjordan.com/Films.html.

38 In Mary Ellen Bute, "Abstronics," *Film in Review* 5, no. 6 (June–July 1954), republished online by the Center for Visual Music and available online at the Center for Visual Music Library's Bute Research papers under http://www.centerforvisualmusic.org/Bute.htm.

39 Bute, "Abstronics."

40 Although these production modes and aesthetic approaches can be located in animated works from other national contexts, they do not follow the same periodization or hold the same "independent" status (for instance, in national contexts where individual animation artists enjoyed more support from state-funded institutions or nations that did not have a robust "studio" mode against which to make comparative claims.)

41 André Martin, "Animated Cinema: The Way Forward," *Sight and Sound* 28, no. 2 (1959): 80.

42 The series of films by Harry Smith typically grouped under the title *Early Abstractions* (1939–1956) are exemplary in their wide range of techniques, from direct animation painted on celluloid to filmed mirror contraptions and found-image collage animation.

5 The Rise of Computer-Generated Imagery, 1965–1989

1 Kristin Thompson, "Implications of the Cel Animation Technique," in *The Cinematic Apparatus*, ed. Teresa de Lauretis and Stephen Heath, 111 (London: Palgrave Macmillan, 1980).

2   Ivan E. Sutherland, "Computer Graphics: Ten Unsolved Problems," *Datamation* 12, no. 5 (May 1966): 22–27. Wire-frame graphics is a visualization technique used in the creation of three-dimensional figures.

3   Sutherland, "Computer Graphics," 26.

4   John and James Whitney, "Audio-Visual Music and Program Notes" (1946), in *Digital Harmony: On the Complementarity of Music and Visual Art* (Peterborough, N.H.: Byte Books/McGraw-Hill, 1980), 147.

5   John Whitney, "Narration to Experiments in Motion Graphics," Whitney Files, Academy of Motion Pictures Arts and Sciences.

6   J. Citron and John H. Whitney, "Camp—Computer Assisted Movie Production," in *American Federation of Information Processing Societies (AFIPS), 1968 Proceedings of the Fall Joint Computer Conference* 33, no. 2 (Washington, D.C.: AFIPS and Thompson Book Company, 1968): 1299–1305.

7   For more on Whitney's aesthetic aims, see his collection of essays in *Digital Harmony: On the Complementarity of Music and Visual Art*, as well as John Whitney, "Motion-Control: An Overview," *American Cinematographer* 62, no. 12 (December 1981): 1223.

8   Ivan Sutherland, "The Ultimate Display," in *Proceedings of International Federation for Information Processing Congress* (Washington, D.C.: Spartan, 1965), 506.

9   See Mary Ellen Bute, "New Film Music for New Films," *Film Music*, 12, no. 4 (March–April 1953): 15–18; Mary Ellen Bute, "Abstronics: An Experimental Filmmaker Photographs the Esthetics of the Oscillograph," *Films in Review* 5, no. 6 (June–July 1954): 263–266.

10 Ivan Edward Sutherland, "Sketchpad: A Man-Machine Graphical Communication System" (PhD diss., MIT, 1963).

11 Sutherland, "Sketchpad," 130, 132.

12 See Douglas C. Engelbart, X-y position indicator for a display system, U.S. patent 3,541,541, filed June 21, 1967, and issued November 17, 1970; Paul E. Ceruzzi, *A History of Modern Computing* (Cambridge, Mass.: MIT Press, 1998), 260.

13 E. E. Zajac, "Computer-Made Perspective Movies as a Scientific and Communication Tool," *Communications of the ACM* 7, no. 3 (March 1964): 170.

14 Nick Montfort, Patsy Baudoin, John Bell, Ian Bogost, Jeremy Douglass, Mark C. Marino, Michael Mateas, Casey Reas, Mark Sample, and Noah Vawter, *10 PRINT CHR$(205.5+ RND(1));: GOTO 10* (Cambridge, Mass.: MIT Press, 2013), 136.

15 Zabat Patterson, *Peripheral Vision: Bell Labs, the S-C 4020, and the Origins of Computer Art* (Cambridge, Mass.: MIT Press, 2015), xiv, 7.

16 John Whitney, narration to *Experiments in Motion Graphics*.

17 John Whitney, "Computer Art for the Video Picture Wall" (1971), in *Digital Harmony: On the Complementarity of Music and Visual Art* (Peterborough, N.H.: Byte Books/McGraw-Hill, 1980), 196–197; Roy Prendergast interview with John Whitney, "Film Music" (1977), in *Digital Harmony: On the Complementarity of Music and Visual Art* (Peterborough, N.H.: Byte Books/McGraw-Hill, 1980), 218.

18 Norman McLaren, "The Definition of Animation: A Letter from Norman McLaren," *Animation Journal* 3, no. 2 (Spring 1995): 62, emphasis in original.

19 Martin Campbell-Kelly and William Aspray, *Computer: A History of the Information Machine* (New York: BasicBooks, 1996), 208.

20 Montfort et al., *10 PRINT*, 163–167.

21 Kenneth C. Knowlton, "A Computer Technique for Producing Animated Movies," in *AFIPS '64 (Spring) Proceedings of the April 21–23, 1964 Spring Joint Computer Conference* (New York: ACM, 1964), 67–87.

22   Knowlton, "Computer Technique," 69, 67.

23   Patterson, *Peripheral Vision*, 45–63.

24   See Gene Youngblood, *Expanded Cinema* (New York: Dutton, 1970); Stan VanDerBeek, "New Talent: The Computer," *Art in America*, January 1970, 86.

25   For additional context about this technological mix, see Kenneth C. Knowlton, "Computer-Generated Movies, Designs and Diagrams," in "Design and the Computer," ed. Peter Seitz, *Design Quarterly* 66/67 (1966): 58–63.

26   Lillian F. Schwartz with Laurens R. Schwartz, *The Computer Artist's Handbook: Concepts, Techniques and Applications* (New York: Norton, 1992), 5.

27   Schwartz, *Computer Artist's Handbook*, 32.

28   Schwartz, *Computer Artist's Handbook*, 151.

29   Schwartz, *Computer Artist's Handbook*, 166, 169.

30   Sutherland, "Computer Graphics," 25.

31   Larry Cuba, interview by Andrew R. Johnston, July 27, 2010.

32   Campbell-Kelly and Aspray, *Computer*, 231–232.

33   Carolyn Kane, *Chromatic Algorithms: Synthetic Color, Computer Art, and Aesthetics after Code* (Chicago: University of Chicago Press, 2014), 161–162.

34   Tom Sito, *Moving Innovation: A History of Computer Animation* (Cambridge, Mass.: MIT Press, 2013), 87.

35   Jacob Gaboury, *Image Object* (Cambridge, Mass.: MIT Press, forthcoming); Jacob Gaboury, "Hidden Surface Problems: On the Digital Image as Material Object," *Journal of Visual Culture* 14, no. 1 (2015): 40–60.

36   Alvy Ray Smith, "Special Effects for *Star Trek II*: The Genesis Demo, Instant Evolution with Computer Graphics," *American Cinematographer* 63, no. 10 (October 1982): 1050.

37   Ken Perlin, "An Image Synthesizer," in *SIGGRAPH '85 Proceedings of the 12th Annual Conference on Computer Graphics and Interactive Techniques* (New York: ACM, 1985), 285.

38   Nick Montfort and Ian Bogost, *Racing the Beam: The Atari Video Computer System* (Cambridge, Mass.: MIT Press, 2009).

39   David Price, *The Pixar Touch* (New York: Alfred A. Knopf, 2008), 90.

6   Ubiquitous Animation, 1990–2016

1   Esther Leslie, "Animation and History," in *Animating Film Theory*, ed. Karen Beckman, 25–36 (Durham, N.C.: Duke University Press, 2014).

2   Hannah Frank, "Looking at Cartoons: The Art, Labor, and Technology of American Cel Animation" (PhD diss., University of Chicago, August 2016).

3   David A. Price, *The Pixar Touch: The Making of a Company* (New York: Vintage, 2009), 54.

4   HPCWire.com, "DreamWorks SKG Looks to SGI for Viz Tech for *Prince of Egypt*," January 15, 1999, https://www.hpcwire.com/1999/01/15/dreamworks-skg-looks-sgi-viz-tech -prince-egypt.

5   Julian Sancton, "How the Puppets from *Fantastic Mr. Fox* Were Made [Slide Show]," *Vanity Fair* online, November 13, 2009, http://www.vanityfair.com/hollywood/2009/11/how-the -puppets-from-fantastic-mr-fox-were-made-slideshow.

6   Christopher Jobson, "End-Credits Timelapse in *Boxtrolls* Brilliantly Reveals the Hidden Labor of Stop Motion Animation," *Colossal*, December 29, 2014, http://www.thisiscolossal .com/2014/12/boxtrolls-animation-behind-the-scenes.

7 Donald Crafton, *Before Mickey: The Animated Film 1898–1928* (Chicago: University of Chicago Press, 1993).

8 Andrea Comiskey, "(Stop) Motion Control: Special Effects in Contemporary Puppet Animation," in *Special Effects: New Histories, Theories, Contexts*, ed. Dan North, Bob Rehak, and Michael S. Duffy, 45 (London: BFI/Palgrave Macmillan, 2015), emphasis in original.

9 Caroline Ruddell, "'Don't Box Me In': Blurred Lines in *Waking Life* and *A Scanner Darkly*," *Animation: An Interdisciplinary Journal* 7, no. 1 (2011): 7–23, here 8.

10 Ruddell, "'Don't Box Me In,'" 12.

11 Chuck Tryon, "Digital 3D, Technological Auteurism and the Rhetoric of Cinematic Revolution," in *Special Effects: New Histories, Theories, Contexts*, ed. Dan North, Bob Rehak, and Michael S. Duffy, 183–195 (London: BFI/Palgrave Macmillan, 2015).

12 Lisa Purse, *Digital Imaging in Popular Cinema* (Edinburgh: Edinburgh University Press, 2013).

13 Ron Magid, "All Aboard," *American Cinematographer* 85, no. 11 (2004): 64–66, 68, 70–75, here 68.

14 Magid, "All Aboard," 71.

15 Brad Brevet, "Should *Avatar* Be Considered for Best Animated Oscar?" Comingsoon.net, December 14, 2009, http://www.comingsoon.net/movies/news/539758-should-avatar-be -considered-for-best-animated-oscar.

16 Lisa Bode, "No Longer Themselves? Framing Digitally Enabled Posthumous 'Performance,'" *Cinema Journal* 49, no. 4 (2010): 46–70.

17 Matt Stahl, "The Synthespian's Animated Prehistory: *The Monkees*, *The Archies*, Don Kirshner, and the Politics of 'Virtual Labor,'" *Television and New Media* 12, no. 1 (2011): 3–22, here 4.

18 Henry Jenkins, *Convergence Culture: Where Old and New Media Collide* (New York: New York University Press, 2006).

19 Jonathan Gray, *Show Sold Separately: Promos, Spoilers, and Other Media Paratexts* (New York: New York University Press, 2010).

20 Derek Johnson, *Media Franchising: Creative License and Collaboration in the Culture Industries* (New York: New York University Press, 2013).

21 Bob Rehak, "Materializing Monsters: Aurora Models, Garage Kits and the Object Practices of Horror Fandom," *Journal of Fandom Studies* 1, no. 1 (2013): 27–45.

22 Henry Jenkins, Sam Ford, and Joshua Green, eds. *Spreadable Media: Creating Value and Meaning in a Networked Culture* (New York: New York University Press, 2013).

GLOSSARY

2D ANIMATION   Animation that uses drawings, **cels**, **cutouts**, or other flat images.

3D ANIMATION   Animation that uses objects with volume, such as puppets, but now referring to computer animation that makes extensive use of texture and **depth cues** to depict objects in such a way as to suggest volume.

ABOVE THE LINE   Those crew members—such as the writers, directors, actors, and producers—responsible for the creative direction of the film; in a budget outline, they are typically entered above a line separating them from the more technical crew, collectively designated as **below the line**.

ALIASING   The presence of pixels in **computer-generated imagery** due to low resolution; the existence of visible polygons that **CGI** uses to construct three-dimensional surfaces.

ANALYTICAL EDITING   A style of editing that beings with a master **shot** showing the whole space of the scene and then cuts into the space, leading the viewer through it while preserving a sense of continuity and flow.

ANIMATION DIRECTOR   The lead figure in **industrial animation** and the person in charge of coordinating every phase of production on the studio assembly line: the tempo and pacing of the film, the layout, backgrounds, sounds, color, and editing.

ANIMATION DISC   A circular metal disc that fits into the **animation table**, usually over the **light box**. The disc operates like a turntable, allowing the animator to rotate the drawing surface for a better angle.

ANIMATION PHOTO TRANSFER (APT)   A descendant of **xerography**, APT copies artwork onto **cels** using high-contrast lithographic film and light-sensitive dyes that produce fields of color automatically. (This is in contrast to xerography, which only copies lines in black.)

ANIMATION STAND   A device used by animators to transfer their drawings to film. The drawings are placed one at a time on a flat platform—often covered by a glass plate to hold it steady—while the camera is positioned above, shooting straight downward. The drawings are then photographed in sequence, creating a filmstrip that contains the resulting images for projection. Also known as a **camera stand**.

ANIMATION TABLE   The desk at which an animator draws the individual frames of the animated film. It contains a **light box**, which backlights drawings and allows them to be traced, two or more **pegs** to keep drawings aligned, and sometimes an **animation disc**, which allows the animator to rotate the drawing surface for a better angle. Also known as an animation desk.

ANIME   A form of limited animation, taking stylistic cues from manga (comics), developed by Japanese animation studios; to save labor and money, animators sought to minimize the number of drawings needed by lengthening their on-screen duration. Hence it is a form of **limited animation**.

ARTISANAL ANIMATION   A method or mode of animation that relies on an individual, crafts-centered approach to the product; one person primarily makes the film from beginning to end, mastering all of the tasks required to produce a finished film.

ASIFA   The International Animated Film Association (Association International du Film D'Animation); a nonprofit organization founded in 1960 to support the production and exhibition of animated film.

B-FILM   A lower-budget commercial movie, often independently produced and marketed for its broaching of taboo content, adult material, or more niche subject matter.

BAR SHEET   A shot-by-shot outline of the action in a cartoon, with a column for the bars of music that will accompany each action and shot.

BATCH PROCESSING   An economical form of data processing in the 1960s and 1970s in which computer programmers wrote code on typewriters and then submitted them to operators who would run several programs in succession, printing out the results and returning them to the programmers.

BELOW THE LINE   Crew members—such as gaffers, camera operators, and assistants—on a film production responsible for tasks that do not entail decision making about the creative vision of the film; those responsible for that vision are designated collectively as **above the line**.

BIG FIVE, THE   The five top-tier major studios in the classical Hollywood era, comprising Twentieth Century-Fox, Loew's/Metro-Goldwyn-Mayer, Warner Bros., Paramount, and RKO (see also the **Little Three**). Their **vertical integration**—control of production, distribution, and exhibition—came under legal scrutiny in the 1940s, resulting in the oligopoly-breaking **Paramount Decision of 1948**.

BIPACK OR BIPACKING   Loading two reels of film in the same camera so that they are exposed together. This method was used to create special effects in the camera as an alternative to **optical printing**, as in Disney's Alice in Cartoonland series.

BITMAP   See **raster graphics**.

BLIND BIDDING   The studio practice of selling films to theaters without allowing theater owners to see them first. Outlawed in the **Paramount Decision of 1948**.

BLOCK BOOKING   The studio practice of selling multiple films to theaters as an inseparable unit; typically, this was a way for Hollywood studios to sell less appealing films by attaching them to a more desirable film of higher quality or profitability. Outlawed in the **Paramount Decision of 1948**.

BOILING An effect of tracing images on paper and animating the series; even when directly tracing the previous image using semitransparent paper, such as **rice paper**, tiny imperfections in the animator's handiwork create tiny differences in the drawn lines. The result, when projected, is slightly unstable outlines that appear to vibrate, shimmer, or "boil." Less likely to appear with more stable media, such as **cels**, and better **registration** techniques.

BRUTE-FORCE ANIMATION An early **motion-capture** technique that computationally transcribes the movements of dots drawn on a live model into vector paths in the computer to form a stick figure; the goal is to grant animation a greater sense of life and realism. Compare to **Rotoscope**.

CAMERA STAND See **animation stand**.

CAMERALESS ANIMATION See **direct animation**.

CAPS See **Computer Animation Production System**.

CATHODE-RAY TUBE A display technology built with a vacuum tube that houses an **electron gun** and phosphorescent screen; the gun fires electron beams onto the screen to create scanned images. This technology was used for television sets from the 1930s through the early twenty-first century.

CEL A sheet of transparent celluloid on which backgrounds or figures are drawn or painted. Because of celluloid's transparency, one sheet containing a character can be overlaid atop another sheet containing a background, eliminating the need to redraw backgrounds for every frame.

CEL REVERSAL Turning the completed **cel** over and photographing the reverse side to depict the opposite angle. A labor-saving technique common in **limited animation**.

CEL WASHING Washing the ink and paint off **cels** so that they can be reused. "Cel washer" was a starting position in many early animation studios.

CGI See **computer-generated imagery**.

CHALK TALK See **lightning sketch**.

CINEMA OF ATTRACTIONS A term coined by Tom Gunning and André Gaudreault to describe a dynamic of early cinema in which filmmakers purposefully broke the illusion of the fictional world to draw the audience's attention to spectacle and thereby to the novel power of the film camera.

CLAY ANIMATION A form of **stop-motion animation** in which clay is reshaped frame by frame to create the illusion of moving figures in a three-dimensional world.

COCKLING The wrinkling of a sheet of paper caused by liquid—in early drawn animation, the ink used to solidify outlines of figures would wrinkle the **rice paper**, for example.

COLLABORATIVE ANIMATION A method or mode of animation based on a non-hierarchical organization of multiple people; two or more individuals share labor, technical knowledge, and creative vision more or less equally. Labor is not strictly defined; each member of the team can do any job required.

COLLAGE ANIMATION A form of **stop-motion animation** that combines newspaper, magazines, photographs, and other forms of illustration to create an animated world.

COLOR KEY An element of the animation planning process in which a color scheme is developed for both the background and the foreground figures to ensure that a character's movement across the background will not create any moments of clashing or merging of colors.

COMPUTER ANIMATION PRODUCTION SYSTEM (CAPS) A network of specialized scanners, servers, and proprietary software comprising a fully digital ink-and-paint process, developed by Disney and Pixar in the late 1980s. CAPS freed animators from material constraints, such as the number of layers that could be combined in one image or the size of artwork across which the camera could move.

COMPUTER-GENERATED IMAGERY (CGI) The use of computer graphics software to produce figures and environments for media; digital data are **rendered** to create imagery.

CONSENT DECREE OF 1940   A government decision requiring studios to offer blocks of no more than five feature films, to allow exhibitors to see them in advance, and to sell short films separately from features. This gave exhibitors more power in setting their own schedules and also improved the status of animation studios, whose cartoon shorts received increased publicity and marketing attention.

CROSSCUTTING   An editing technique that alternates between two separate lines of action in two different places, giving the impression that they are occurring simultaneously.

CUTOUT   A flat image, such as an image from a magazine, cut out and animated in **stop-motion**.

CYCLING   A labor-saving technique common in animation in which a rhythmic action, such as walking or running, is repeated in a loop. For such repetitive motions, the animator draws only one iteration of the sequence; these drawings are then photographed again to create a looped, regular movement in the finished film.

DATA GLOVE   A computational input device worn over the hand like a glove that operates through the movements of the fingers or hand.

DEPTH CUEING   A computer animation technique in which depth is added to the image through sizing ratios that indicate how objects exist relative to one another in a shot or through lighting effects whereby landscape and objects farther away are less illuminated until finally being blacked out at the vanishing point or horizon line.

DIGITAL COMPOSITING   The use of digital technology to combine visual elements from separate sources into one image; for example, creating a background by combining elements of various scenery shots and then inserting a figure into the scene, creating one seamless image. Compare **matte** shot or **optical printing**, a form of analog compositing.

DIGITAL INTERMEDIATES   Computer processes that act as a polishing stage between the completion of a film and its distribution. This includes such processes as color grading, color correcting, and mastering.

DIRECT ANIMATION   A method of animation in which images are made directly on film stock, for example by painting directly on celluloid, scratching film emulsion, pasting small objects to the celluloid surface, or exposing the film to filtered lights. This form of animation is sometimes also called **cameraless animation**, even though a camera is still typically used to photograph and print the manipulated film stock.

DIRECTOR-UNIT SYSTEM   A system of **industrial animation** in which a director oversees one or several different teams, each staffed by different animators working on different aspects of one or several projects. This allows animation studios to meet the increased production requirements of industrial distribution and exhibition; the finishing dates of the projects are staggered to ensure a constant stream of films.

DRAWN ANIMATION   Animation in which every frame of the film is drawn by hand with a pencil or pen or other drawing medium. This differs from **stop-motion animation**, computer animation, and other forms of animation that achieve the illusion of motion through other techniques. Also known as traditional animation, classical animation, and **cel** animation.

ELECTRON GUN   A device that fires electrons at a **cathode-ray tube** to produce an image in early television sets and monitors.

EXPOSURE SHEET   A set of instructions that studio animation departments send to the photography department along with their drawings. These instructions establish the proper order and timing of photographic exposures to prevent misplaced images or errors of tempo in the finished film.

EXTREMES   The "peak" poses of a movement, also known as "key poses." These poses guide the trajectory of character movement; they are usually drawn by the head animator and are then sent to **in-betweeners** to be supplemented with intermediate drawings. See also **key framing**.

FLIP BOOK   A series of drawings on separate sheets of paper in which each drawing is incrementally different from the previous one. These drawings are bound sequentially into book form; the viewer then rapidly flips through the pages by thumb, creating the illusion of the drawn figure's movement. See also **Mutoscope**.

FRAME   A single image on a filmstrip; projected in quick succession, a series of frames presents cinema's illusion of movement. Typically, twenty-four frames equals one second of projected cinematic movement.

FRAME BUFFER   A device in computer animation that stores **rendered** images in video memory for **raster** graphics systems. It enables two-dimensional image information to be stored up and ordered in a timeline for fluid and even colorized movement.

FULL ANIMATION   A style of drawn animation that aspires to fluid movement by using one drawing (or at most two) per **frame** of film (that is, twenty-four drawings per second).

GAG   A moment of humor or a visual joke; gags were often the story beats of theatrical cartoons, providing the narrative structure of the film.

"HAND OF THE ARTIST"   A common trope especially of silent-era animation: cartoons would often begin with a depiction of the artist's hand drawing the cartoon figure; Out of the Inkwell cartoons by the Fleischer Studio are typical examples. See also **self-figuration**.

HIDDEN SURFACE REMOVAL   The practice of hiding the two-dimensional lines comprising a digital image to give the illusion of depth; the goal is to create a smooth, seemingly three-dimensional space populated by solids that seem to exist in their own space.

HOLDS   A labor- and time-saving technique: the drawn image is exposed as a still image (without movement) for a few extra frames, often at the beginning or ending of a shot.

IN-BETWEENER   A central figure in the **key framing** method of animation. Once the head animator draws the key poses of a movement, this assistant animator fills in the remaining transitional drawings. This frees the head animator to provide the template for the movement without having to perform every step of the process. Needless to say, this assistant must learn to draw the character exactly as the head animator.

INDUSTRIAL ANIMATION   A method or mode of animation characterized by a hierarchical organization of labor divided into strictly defined specialties, as in an assembly line. One person (usually a director) oversees many workers, each doing only the job they are assigned. A large labor force turns out films at a rapid pace for large-scale distribution and exhibition.

INK AND PAINT   The department in studio-era animation responsible for tracing, **inking**, **opaquing**, and coloring the **cels** for photography. Also used colloquially to refer to traditional cel animation.

INKING   Retracing an animator's pencil sketches with ink to create a firm, solid outline. The job may also include filling in any elements of the scene that needed to be dark in the finished film (or that job may be further specialized into an opaquer; see **opaquing**). In the studio era, this job was an apprentice position for an aspiring animator.

INTERACTIVE LIGHTING   The use of lighting effects in computer animation to mimic the presence of a specific light source in a scene. This is particularly important in the use of **digital compositing**, when scene elements drawn from various sources are intended to respond to a light source in a realistic way.

IRIS   An editing technique that uses a circular mask to end a scene or to focus on an element in a scene by gradually closing until the entire screen is black (an "iris out") or that begins a scene by gradually opening to reveal the image (an "iris in").

KEY FRAMING   A method of **drawn animation** in which the animator draws the first and last poses of a figure's movement, splits the trajectory of that movement in half, and then draws the pose directly in the middle. He or she then repeats that split, cutting each segment in half again and again. Significant drawings along the arc of movement, such as the first, the last, and the middle point, are called **extremes**, "key frames," or "key poses." Also known as pose-to-pose animation. Invented by Winsor McCay, who called it his "split system."

LAYOUT   A comprehensive line drawing of the setting in which an animated film will take place. This is then colored or painted to produce the finished background.

LAYOUT ARTIST   The artist responsible for determining the overall composition of scenes and the size and position of characters within the space of action. He or she might also develop a distinctive color palette for the scene.

LIGHT BOX   A translucent pane of glass or Plexiglas installed in the surface of an **animation table**, behind which is a light source. This backlit surface allows the animator to trace images on **cels** or **rice paper** to ensure consistency when drawing a background or the stages of a movement.

LIGHT PEN   A computational input device shaped like a pen that operates on a **cathode-ray tube** display to manipulate visual objects directly or to select information in a computational interface.

LIGHTNING SKETCH   A vaudeville stage act featuring a quick-draw artist who, usually with crayon or chalk, rapidly sketches a face or an object and then transforms it into other objects in a series of quick, carefully choreographed strokes. Also known as a **chalk talk**.

LIMITED ANIMATION   A style of animation that cuts corners due to budgetary pressures and/or simplifies the animation process due to artistic inclination. Unlike **full animation**, it often uses fewer than twenty-four images per second of film (see **shooting on twos**), repeats images to save labor (see **cycling**), and animates only a part of the image, such as a character's mouth or hand. The style is linked with both cheap television animation and modern theatrical cartoons; either way, it dominated the animation scene in the 1950s–1980s and is associated with television animation. Also known as **planned animation**.

LITTLE THREE, THE   The three second-tier major studios in the classical Hollywood era, comprising Columbia, United Artists, and Universal. Unlike the **Big Five**, the Little Three did not own their own theater chains.

LIVE-ACTION   Motion pictures that are photographed in real time, as opposed to the frame-by-frame exposures of animation.

MACHINIMA   A method of animation that uses video-game engines to create homemade animation well beyond the world of the game itself, including comedic parody, documentary, fan films, and performance art.

MAGNETIC TAPE   A medium for storing digital information.

MAINFRAME COMPUTER   A large computer, especially in the early period of computing, that could support many workstations and bulk processing jobs.

MATCH ON ACTION   An editing technique in which two different angles of the same action are spliced together at the same moment in the action, giving the impression of a continuous action across two shots.

MATTE   A "matte shot" is the result of an **optical printing** process in which different areas of the image are photographed separately and combined into one image; usually the shape of one area to be combined is blackened so that its photographic equivalent can be superimposed neatly. See also **traveling matte**.

METAMORPHOSIS   The transformation of one object into another object; an important feature of animation from its beginnings onward.

METRONOME   A device that marks time at regular intervals: an arm swings back and forth like a pendulum, sounding a tick at each interval. Animators used it to time music to images.

MICROFILM PLOTTER   A computer graphics output device that can draw directly onto film or paper.

MODE OF PRODUCTION   The way in which labor is divided and resources, such as tools and technologies, are distributed in order to accomplish the work required. There are three main modes of production in animation history: **artisanal**, **industrial**, and **collaborative**.

MODEL SHEET   A set of drawings on a single sheet that establish the basic features of a character, including facial expressions and various angles. It helps to ensure continuity of style and character in **industrial animation**, when different artists might be drawing the same character for different films.

MOTION CAPTURE   Recording human movement in such a way that its essential features can be translated into digital data and used as the basis of character movement in **computer-generated imagery**. See also **performance capture**.

MOVIOLA   A small, motorized projection device used by editors to see individual frames of a film while they are editing; it also allows the user to run the film forward and backward, at the desired speed, to choose the optimal moment to cut a shot. In animation, it would be used to check the fluidity of movement. Compare to the non-motorized **Mutoscope** or **flipbook**.

MULTIPLANE CAMERA   An expansion of the **animation table** involving multiple layers of **cels**, each of which can be moved independently of each other between each photographic exposure of the film camera. This enables a **depth cue** called parallax: objects closer to the foreground seem to move more quickly, while objects closer to the background seem to move more slowly. A Disney invention that gave the impression of depth and dimensionality to their cartoons.

MUTOSCOPE   An early motion-picture device in which a series of photographic images are attached to a circular core. By turning a hand crank, the viewer spins the core and the pictures rapidly flip past, creating the illusion of a moving image. A technological descendant of the **flip book**. In early animation, it was used to check the movement of a series of drawings. Compare to **Moviola**.

NEAR-FIELD COMMUNICATION   A communications technology in which two electronic devices, placed within a few centimeters of each other, can communicate.

NEEDLE-DROPS   Licensed music that could be purchased and inserted into the soundtrack of a cartoon, rather than being composed specifically to complement the image; popularly used in television animation.

OBJECT ANIMATION   Animation that, unlike **drawn animation**, is made using three-dimensional objects, such as dolls, puppets, or clay. But in theory, any object can be manipulated to create the illusion of movement via **stop-motion animation**.

OIL-WIPE ANIMATION   A method of animation in which colored oils are distributed on a glass plate and allowed to intersect and press against one another.

OPAQUING   Filling in outlines of characters or objects with opaque ink or paint; part of **cel** animation. Opaquers were often apprentice animators in **industrial animation** of the studio era.

OPTICAL PRINTING   A filmmaking technique involving an optical printer, a device that links a film projector with a film camera. An optical printer allows the filmmaker to selectively re-photograph film frames and to layer images, thereby reproducing film images, either whole or in part, onto other film frames. Optical printing allows for the manipulation of color, scale, and other attributes of the film image.

OSCILLOSCOPE   An electronic device that translates abstract inputs (voltage, sound, vibration, amplitude, frequency) into light patterns on a **cathode-ray** screen; experimental animators used these devices to "draw" with light and to create visual forms from innovative inputs, such as music and gesture. See also **visual music**.

PACKAGE FILMS   A means of saving time and money in the industrial Hollywood system, especially in the 1940s and 1950s. Animation studios would repackage preexisting theatrical shorts into a feature-length "film," often with newly drawn or recorded interstitial material linking them together.

PAN   A cinematographic technique in which the camera remains in one place and swivels right or left, scanning the scene.

PARAMOUNT DECISION OF 1948   A Supreme Court decision declaring the five major Hollywood studios (see the **Big Five**) in violation of antitrust law; the decision mandated the end of **vertical integration**, as well as its attendant practices, including **blind bidding** and **block booking**. This decision is also seen as a blow to animation studios, which gradually contracted and shut down as the major studios struggled financially under the ruling.

PENCIL TEST   A rough, perfunctory draft of an animated scene, photographed and projected to test for humor and movement before inking, coloring, and final photographing. Also known as a **rough**.

PERCEPTUAL GESTALT   The moment when disparate elements in an image are recognized to be a part of a unified whole. The mental creation of a unified image through a cognitive gathering of independent elements. For example, abstract lines and shapes close to one another in a recognizable pattern, such as a face or figure, become associated with the unified image of that figure rather than existing as separate elements.

PERF-AND-PEG   Part of the **animation table**; to ensure proper positioning of each individual drawing in the animation process (see **registration**), the animator uses paper with two holes punched on one edge. These holes line up with wooden rods, or pegs, that keep each drawing in its proper place to ensure a stable animated image.

PERFORMANCE CAPTURE   A method of digital animation in which an actor wears a bodysuit covered with sensors or small dots. The camera records not the actor but the sensors; that is, the performance is captured—movement, gestures, expressions—while the performing body remains unseen. This performance can then be grafted onto any digitally created figure. Also known as **motion capture**.

PERFORMANCE VOLUME   The "stage" on which **performance capture** is filmed. Like the actor, sets and objects are marked by sensors, and the resulting "volume" can be "clothed" in a digitally created environment of the filmmaker's choosing.

PERLIN NOISE   An algorithm that introduces elements of noise into image pixels; this prevents the "too-smooth" appearance of **computer-generated imagery** and is particularly useful for representing atmospheric elements, such as clouds, water, fire, stars, rock, and crystal.

PERSONALITY ANIMATION   An approach that emphasizes the use of movement, gesture, and, in the sound era, voice to create characters with a full range of emotion and definable traits.

PHYSICS-BASED ANIMATION   A style of digital animation that simulates how objects and environments would behave and interact in real, physical space.

PIXILATION   A form of **stop-motion animation** that uses live actors, who repeatedly pose frame by frame to create the sensation of jerky, artificial movements, or impossible movements, such as floating. In computer animation, it refers to the profusion of pixels due to low resolution also known as **aliasing**.

PLANNED ANIMATION   See **limited animation**.

PLUG AND PLAY   A computer protocol that allows peripheral devices to work with mainframe or hardware systems without any software configuration.

POSE REEL   Also known as a story reel or (in computer animation) an animatic, a pose reel combines an audio track with **layout** drawings, **storyboard** sketches, and **extremes** to give a sense of the action and timing without the time-intensive work of **full animation**. In **limited animation**, pose reels were sometimes the finished product.

POSE-TO-POSE ANIMATION   See **key framing**.

PUNCH CARDS   A tool of data processing; a piece of heavy, stiff paper contains digital information in the form of punched holes, which a computer then reads to perform computational processes.

RASTER GRAPHICS   An image file format, commonly known as **bitmap**, that produces a picture through a matrix of individual pixels. Each pixel identifies a color, and the image is created in a similar way to a photographic halftone.

RASTER SCAN DISPLAY   A **cathode-ray tube** display technology that produces images through the continual, horizontal, line-by-line sweep of the **electron gun**, moving down the screen at a specific speed or rate. All areas of the screen are swept by this technology, as opposed to selected areas or lines in a **vector scan display**.

REGISTRATION   The careful arrangement of individual drawings in drawing and photographing processes so that outlines coincide from frame to frame, giving the sensation of a stable, solid figure and/or world rather than an image that appears to jump around the screen.

REGISTRATION MARKS   Small marks placed at the edge or corner of each drawing to guide the proper placement of drawings on top of each other in the drawing (or tracing) process, or under or in front of the camera during the photographing process. Because of the shape of these marks, they are also known as "registration crosses."

RENDERING   The translation of digital inputs into visual imagery in computer animation; this requires an intermediary software that can read the inputs and generate a virtual object based on them. The rendering stage follows the modeling, animation, and lighting stages to generate the finished frame.

RENDERING TIME   The time lag between the input of computer data and the translation of that data into visual imagery.

RICE PAPER   A common material used in **drawn animation**, valuable because its semitransparency allows the animator to see the previous image in the sequence. He or she can then trace over the previous image and ensure a smoother transition from frame to frame.

ROTOSCOPE   A method of animation in which live-action footage is projected from below onto paper or **celluloid**, where the animator traces the footage frame by frame and then re-photographs the drawings as animations. The result is a closer approximation of lifelike motion than freehand drawing can produce.

ROTOSHOP   A digital descendant of the **rotoscope**; live-action footage is "painted over" by software to manipulate the image in various ways.

ROUGH   Initial pencil sketches of an animated action or scene, usually drawn by the head animator. See also **pencil test**.

RUBBER-HOSE ANIMATION   A character design style in which bodies, especially limbs, are drawn to have an elastic quality that enables them to stretch and bend with ease, without regard for joints, bones, or proper length. **Secondary action** is not common in this style of animation; body parts elongate without effect on other body parts. Often contrasted with **squash-and-stretch animation**.

RUNAWAY PRODUCTION   A domestic production for which some or all of the work is done outside the United States.

SAND ANIMATION   A form of **stop-motion animation** in which sand is placed on a **light box** and manipulated frame by frame; the sand, in greater or lesser concentrations, blocks light coming from underneath, thereby creating images. See also **under-the-camera animation**.

SCENARIO   A story outline for a cartoon, something like a script, but with minimal dialogue, especially in the silent era.

SECONDARY ACTION   The movement of related parts of a character's body when a primary part moves; for example, when a character raises her arm, her torso might move slightly in response.

Also refers to action that supports the character's personality or emotion, as when Doc polishes his glasses while thinking in *Snow White and the Seven Dwarfs*.

SECTIONAL DRAWING   A type of mechanical drawing that shows a view of the object as if it had been cut vertically by an imaginary plane. Also known as a "cutaway drawing."

SELF-FIGURATION   A common tendency of early animation in which the **"hand of the artist"** features in the animated film, as if to draw attention to the artistry involved. In most cases, this involved showing the artist drawing a figure before it comes to life, seemingly on its own.

SEQUENCE PRE-VISUALIZATION   A planning process that uses computer graphics to "test run" complex visual-effects sequences in a rough, preliminary form. This can include **wire-frame** and other unfinished versions of the final scene. In a sense, this is a digital version of **storyboarding**.

SHOOTING ON TWOS (OR THREES, FOURS)   A method of saving labor in animation; rather than creating a new image for every frame of film ("on ones"), an animator films an image for two (or three or four) frames. This creates a jerkier movement in the finished product but saves the animator the work of creating twenty-four (or sixteen, in early animation) images per second of film.

SHOT   Any continuous exposure of film between two edits. Each shot depicts a unique view.

SLASH-AND-TEAR ANIMATION   A system of animation in which an animator draws a background on one sheet of paper and then a character on a second sheet. He or she then tears away the blank part of the second sheet, leaving only the character, whose scrap of paper is superimposed upon the first (background) sheet. This second sheet is redrawn and re-torn, as needed to simulate movement, while leaving the background unchanged and stable so that it does not need to be redrawn. Also known as "rip-and-slash animation," this method was used in the silent era instead of the **cel** technique, often to avoid license fees.

SLIT-SCAN PRINTING   An **optical printing** technique that places a moveable slide with a slit in it between the camera and projector; the movements are often programmed through analog or digital motion controls.

SPOT-MARKETING   The practice of selling television shows to individual stations with built-in commercials.

SQUASH-AND-STRETCH ANIMATION   A character design style in which the body is treated as a container with a consistent volume, like a bag of water; the result is fleshy figures that "bounce" slightly in response to gravity or impacts. This style of animation implies **secondary action**; if the body stretches in one direction, it compresses elsewhere to compensate. Often contrasted with **rubber-hose animation**.

STEREOSCOPIC FILMING   A filming technique in which two cameras capture each frame from a slightly different angle to enable later exhibition in 3D venues.

STOCK ANIMATION   A labor- and time-saving practice in which creators of an animated television show would build a library of character poses and cycles (such as walking, running, and talking) to be reused from episode to episode.

STOP-AND-GO TECHNIQUE   An early style of television animation that combined still comic strip images with voice-over narration and dialogue and an occasional animated effect; often, such camera movements as pans and zooms replaced the movement of the images themselves. This saved both labor and money in the under-budgeted arena of television cartoons.

STOP-MOTION ANIMATION   An expansion of the **trick film**; a three-dimensional object is photographed for one frame and then repositioned incrementally, being photographed for another single frame after every repositioning. The result, when projected, is an object that appears to move on its own. Also known as "stop-action animation." See also **clay animation**, **object animation**.

STORY SKETCH ARTIST   An artist who draws images for a **storyboard**.

STORYBOARD A series of pencil sketches mounted in chronological order on a large board for writers and animators to review and evaluate; it functions as a rough plan for production.

STRAIGHT-AHEAD ANIMATION An improvisational style of animation in which the animator begins with the first image and draws each subsequent image in sequence, moving "straight ahead" without a concrete plan and letting the in-the-moment transformations guide the development of the film. Often contrasted to **key framing** or **pose-to-pose animation**.

SUPPORT ERASURE The use of **digital compositing** to "erase" support structures for objects, allowing them to be seen as moving on their own (for example, flying objects). Elements of a background frame are used to cover the parts of other frames where the support is visible, creating the illusion of empty space.

TEMPERA A method of painting with pigments mixed with water and egg yolks.

TEXTURE MAPPING The algorithmic interpolation of shapes and polygons over the surface of a digital object to create contrasts in depth and figure/ground dimensions.

THEATRICAL SHORT Short films that accompanied feature-length films on the program of movie theaters, especially during the studio era.

THREE-STRIP TECHNICOLOR A subtractive color process that splits the light entering the camera lens into three beams, each passing through a colored filter onto a separate filmstrip, one for each primary color. This technique layered three colors (cyan, magenta, and yellow) and produced an image that fully represented the color spectrum. Compare **two-strip Technicolor**.

TILT A cinematographic technique in which the camera remains in one place and swivels upward or downward, scanning the scene.

TIME-SHARING A method that allows a **mainframe computer** to concurrently handle programming operations for simultaneously connected terminals by intermittently processing bursts of code for each connected user.

TRAVELING MATTE A variation on the **matte** process, accomplished via **optical printing**, when one of the elements to be superimposed moves from frame to frame.

TRICK FILM Cinematographic and editing sleight of hand in which actors and camera stop in the middle of a scene in order to make a substitution, insertion, or removal of a person or object, after which the filming is resumed as normal. The result, when projected, is a magical transformation, appearance, or disappearance of that person or object. Also known as a "stop film."

TWO-STRIP TECHNICOLOR A subtractive color process that splits the light entering the camera lens into two beams, each passing through a colored filter onto a separate filmstrip. This technique layered two colors (cyan and magenta, usually) and produced an image that did not fully represent the color spectrum. Compare **three-strip Technicolor**.

UNCANNY VALLEY The term, developed in robotics, for the problematic nature of simulations that come close but fall just short of the real thing. In animation, audience willingness to accept a character's design as familiar or humanlike increases as it becomes more visually realistic, up to a point—the uncanny valley—at which acceptance turns to revulsion.

UNDER-THE-CAMERA ANIMATION A method of animation in which each frame of an animated film is created in conjunction with the filming process; this is in contrast to drawn animation, in which all the drawings are produced before they are photographed by the film camera. Under-the-camera animation often uses unconventional materials, such as sand, paint, or clay, and the materials transform frame by frame without leaving artifacts behind. See also **sand animation**.

VECTOR GRAPHICS An image file format that produces a picture by storing information about its positions in two-dimensional space through individual x,y points, as well as the lines and color spaces that exist in between them.

VECTOR SCAN DISPLAY   A **cathode-ray tube** display technology that produces images through the movements of the **electron gun** that directly follow the outlines of the shape or line displayed; in this system, the electron gun changes directions and selects specific positions on the screen instead of scanning the entire surface of the screen line by line as in a **raster scan display**.

VERTICAL INTEGRATION   A form of industrial organization in which the major Hollywood studios (see the **Big Five**) owned and controlled all three branches of the film industry: production, distribution, and exhibition. In the **Paramount Decision of 1948**, the U.S. government determined this to be oligopolistic practice and ordered the studios to sell off their theater chains.

VISUAL MUSIC   The idea that there are correspondences between sound and color, or music and image, and that therefore music can be translated into painting, drawing, or other visual media, or vice versa: that animated images can evoke music in their rhythm and tone. Animators interested in visual music often made abstract films with imagery that matched musical scores or experimented with such devices as the **oscilloscope**, which can translate sounds into electronic imagery.

WASH COLORS OR DRAWING   A pencil or pen sketch with a layer of watercolor paint, often monochrome.

WIPE   An editing technique in which one shot replaces another by means of a line passing across the screen; the new shot gradually erases the previous shot.

WIRE-FRAME GRAPHICS   A computer visualization technique used in the creation of three-dimensional figures; the wire frame is the collection of polygons that make up the rounded shape of a computer-animated figure, stripped of all but the skeletal lines that comprise its shape. This wire frame can be "clothed" in any skin.

XEROGRAPHY   A production method that eliminates the time-consuming hand-inking stage of the animation process by photocopying pencil sketches directly onto animation **cels**.

ZOOM   A cinematographic technique in which the camera remains in place while the lens increases or decreases focal length, giving the impression of moving forward or backward—though in truth the image is simply being magnified or reduced in size.

NOTES ON CONTRIBUTORS

Scott Curtis is associate professor of radio/television/film at Northwestern University in Evanston, Illinois, and associate professor in residence in the Communication Program at Northwestern University in Qatar. His research focuses on early cinema in the United States and Europe, especially the use of motion pictures in scientific and educational settings. His book, *The Shape of Spectatorship: Art, Science, and Early Cinema in Germany* (Columbia University Press, 2015), explores the relationship between expert ways of seeing—in science, medicine, education, and aesthetics—and the new medium of motion pictures. His work on animation and classical Hollywood cinema has appeared in such journals as *Film History* and *Discourse*, as well as numerous anthologies, such as *Funny Pictures* and *Sound Theory/Sound Practice*.

Alla Gadassik is assistant professor of media history and theory at Emily Carr University of Art + Design (Vancouver, Canada). Her research focuses on the history of filmmaking technology and technique, particularly cinematography and animation. She has published articles and chapters on experimental animation, scientific and studio animation, stereoscopic cinematography, and early film editing. She is currently completing a research project on the function of the frame in postwar animation and embarking on a new project on the relationship between animation and textile art.

Andrew Johnston is assistant professor in the Department of English, Film Studies Program, and Communication, Rhetoric, and Digital Media Program at North Carolina State University. His book, *Pulses of Abstraction: Episodes from a History of Animation* (University of Minnesota Press, forthcoming), examines abstract animation in cinema and computational media in the mid-twentieth century. He has also published essays on animation, avant-garde film, color aesthetics, and the history of digital technology and computer graphics in books and journals, such as *Animating Film Theory* (Duke University Press, 2014), *Color and the Moving Image* (Routledge, 2013), and *Discourse: Journal for Theoretical Studies in Media and Culture*.

Susan Ohmer is associate professor in the Department of Film, Television, and Theatre at the University of Notre Dame and the William T. and Helen Kuhn Carey Chair of Modern Communication. Her research analyzes the production cultures of media organizations, particularly during the studio era. Her book, *George Gallup in Hollywood* (Columbia University Press, 2007), examines the reactions of studios and producers in the 1940s to the emergence of market research. Her articles on animation have appeared in *The Velvet Light Trap* and *Film History*, as well as the anthologies *Funny Pictures* and *Second Star to the Right*.

Bob Rehak is associate professor of film and media studies at Swarthmore College, where his research and teaching interests include animation, special effects, video games, and media fandom. His scholarship has appeared in *Film Criticism*, *Cinema Journal*, the *Journal of Fandom Studies*, and *Science Fiction Film and Television*, as well as in the edited collections *The Video Game Theory Reader*, *Videogame/Player/Text*, *The Cybercultures Reader*, and *American Cinema 2000–2009: Themes and Variations*. He is coeditor, with Dan North and Michael S. Duffy, of *Special Effects: New Histories/Theories/Contexts* (2015) and author of *More Than Meets the Eye: Special Effects and the Fantastic Transmedia Franchise* (2018).

Kevin Sandler is associate professor in the Film and Media Studies Program at Arizona State University. He specializes in the contemporary U.S. media business, with a particular focus on censorship and animation. He is author of *The Naked Truth: Why Hollywood Doesn't Make X-Rated Movies* (2007), coeditor of *Titanic: Anatomy of a Blockbuster* (1999), and editor of *Reading the Rabbit: Explorations in Warner Bros. Animation* (1998). His upcoming book is about the history, artistry, and business of the cartoon franchise Scooby-Doo, from Duke University Press.

INDEX

Page numbers in italics refer to figures.